943.085

2/04

D1647427

The Weimar Re...

The Weimar Republic

HELMUT HEIBER

Translated by W. E. Yuill

BLACKWELL

Oxford UK & Cambridge USA

Copyright © Deutscher Taschenbuch Verlag GMBH and Co. KG, München, 1966
and 1981
English translation © Basil Blackwell Ltd, 1993

First published as *Die Republik von Weimar* by Deutscher Taschenbuch Verlag
GMBH & Co. KG, München 1966

English edition first published 1993

Blackwell Publishers
108 Cowley Road
Oxford OX4 1JF
UK

238 Main Street
Cambridge, Massachusetts 02142
USA

British Library Cataloguing in Publication Data

A CIP catalogue record for this book is available from the British Library.

Library of Congress Cataloging-in-Publication Data

Heiber, Helmut
   [Republik von Weimar. English]
   The Weimar Republic / Helmut Heiber; translated by W.E. Yuill.
      p.   cm.
   Includes bibliographical references and index.
   ISBN 0-631-18698-0 (alk. paper). – ISBN 0-631-18699-9
(p bk.: alk. paper)
      1. Germany – History – 1918–1933. 2. Germany – Politics and
government – 1918–1933. 3. Germany – Economic policy – 1918–1933.
I. Title.
DD240.H3513 1993
943.085 – dc20   93–1115
                                                                              CIP

Typeset in 10 on 12 pt Garamond
by Pure Tech Corporation, Pondicherry, India
Printed in Great Britain by T.J. Press Ltd, Padstow, Cornwall
This book is printed on acid-free paper

Contents

Contents

1

The origins of the Republic

The First German Republic was born on 29 September 1918, 26 October 1918, 28 October 1918, 9 November 1918, 6 February 1919 or, possibly, on 11 August 1919. The exact date cannot be fixed. On 29 September 1918 the high command of the army called for an armistice and the revision of the imperial constitution on parliamentary lines; on 26 October 1918 Germany's secret ruler, Ludendorff, fell from power; on 28 October 1918 parliamentary government replaced the existing constitutional form; on 9 November 1918 the Kaiser abdicated and the Majority Socialist, Scheidemann, proclaimed the Republic; on 6 February 1919 the National Assembly met in Weimar; and on 11 August 1919 the new President of the Reich, Ebert, put his signature to the new constitution.

The First German Republic expired on 27 March 1930, 30 May 1932, 30 January 1933, 28 February 1933, 14 July 1933 or, perhaps, on 2 August 1934. This date cannot be precisely fixed either. It was on 27 March 1930 that the last parliamentary government of the Reich resigned; on 30 May 1932 the last Chancellor of the Reich was dismissed, although he was not actually opposed by a majority in the Reichstag; on 30 January 1933 Hitler entered the Chancellery; on 28 February 1933 all basic democratic rights were abrogated and a reign of terror was legally sanctioned; after 14 July 1933 no political parties were permitted; and after 2 August 1934, the day that Hindenburg died, there was no authority besides Hitler, much less over him.

Simply in order to have some kind of marker, the outwardly most striking and visible breaks in continuity are normally accepted and 9 November 1918 and 30 January 1933 are defined as the boundary posts. It is between them that the Weimar Republic lies. Its birth pangs and death agonies are usually referred to as revolutions: the November revolution of 1918 and the

National Socialist revolution of 1933. Strictly speaking, they were not revolutions, for in neither case was a revolution in the strict sense of the word at all necessary; the characteristic feature of both developments was that the existing regimes had simply given up the struggle. In neither case was a revolution required, because those against whom it might have been launched could hardly wait to abdicate. Nevertheless, if the customary terminology is retained, we seem to be dealing with a specifically German brand of revolution, a variety which corresponds to the need for authority of the German people: it seems that in Germany things will never proceed along very different lines. Nowhere else in the world can established authority sleep so soundly.

The 'November Revolution', this 'touchingly naive', this 'oddest of all revolutions' (Rosenberg), in fact consisted of three very different movements. The oldest of these, and initially the most hesitant, was represented by attempts to work towards parliamentary and democratic reform of the constitutional monarchy. Long repressed by the authorities and later – in spite of the democratically levelling effect of the war – fobbed off with empty promises, these tendencies took political shape ultimately in the 'majority parties' in the Reichstag, a coalition which gradually grew to embrace the Social Democrats, the liberals (i.e. the German Democratic Party), the Catholic Centre Party, and here and there the German People's Party. The main target was in fact the notorious feudal electoral law in Prussia which dated back to 1849 and divided voters into three classes, favouring property-owners in a manner which had in the interim become intolerable.

As distinct from this widespread desire for democratic reform, extending even to the Prussian electoral law, parliamentary reform, despite the lip-service paid to the idea, was less of a grievance mainly because the majority of people felt perfectly at ease in the smoothly functioning state bureaucracy which continued to operate more or less free of corruption right into the war years. What Thomas Mann wrote as late as 1918 was typical: 'I don't want politics, I want a matter-of-fact approach, order and decency.' The working population had other worries, and, in any case, they only had to cast a glance over their western frontiers to be cured of the illusion that their social situation would automatically improve in a democratic parliamentary system. Above all, their Social Democratic leadership had long since come to terms with the constitutional authoritarian state, which after all functioned pretty well, with no more than an average degree of injustice, and they limited their efforts essentially to the elimination of individual blemishes.

Just as an impulse from below was lacking, so the transition from an authoritarian to a popular state had been inadequately prepared for in theoretical terms. Thus it came about that although parliamentary reform was the slogan which took pride of place right down to the autumn of 1918, the political parties for the most part lacked the will to assume power. Even if they were not actually afraid to assume responsibility, they nevertheless fought shy of it, lacking any clear idea of what might follow, and in the absence of any dynamic popular support from below. True, a war involving universal military service had prepared the ground for a change, and only hidebound conservative landowners of the old Prussian stamp could harbour the illusion that the clock could ultimately be turned back to the time before 1914. On the other hand, the war had also eliminated the main object against which any such reforms might be directed: if not the monarchy as such, then in practice its principal representative, an eccentric and unpredictable monarch, the Kaiser.

Wilhelm II, whose sabre-rattling and 'shining armour' had so often kept the world on tenterhooks during twenty-six years of peace, had virtually made his exit from the political stage after coining a phrase for the anthologies to the effect that, following 1 August 1914, he no longer recognized political parties but only Germans. Whether this was regarded as a belated realization of how serious the situation was, or was seen as the ultimate proof of the hollowness of this representative of the monarchy, or even of the institution as such, the voluntary withdrawal of the monarch effectively brought the monarchy to an end. When the army, yielding to public opinion, appointed Hindenburg and Ludendorff to the supreme command at the end of 1916, this signified to all intents and purposes a comprehensive, if not irrevocable, abdication. Henceforth it was not the monarch, whose power of command was purely decorative, and certainly no politician (in Germany, after all, the war was too serious a business to be left to civilians), but the new army high command which laid down the law. By the threat, now and then quite explicit, of their possible resignation, which would have had catastrophic consequences for the army and for the nation at large, this pair of generals – the legendary victor of Tannenberg and the man who was the real 'brains' – directed not only the conduct of the war, but also domestic and foreign policy, including the dismissal and appointment of the Chancellor, who was responsible solely to the Kaiser, and hence, for all practical purposes, to the army's high command. Bismarck's successors degenerated into little more than postmen bearing messages between the army leadership and the party leaders in the Reichstag, which was indispensable for voting credits. In this way the constitutional monarchy, against which the demand for parliamentary reform was bound to be directed, had turned into a military dictatorship that was virtually unassailable – at least in wartime.

Nevertheless, on 28 October parliamentary monarchy came into being through a change in the constitution, not because it had been fought for and won by the nation or the majority parties, but because it had been decreed by the high command, which had hitherto opposed any step in this direction. At the end of September, with the defection of Bulgaria, which was bound to hasten the impending capitulation of Austro-Hungary, Ludendorff had become convinced that the war was lost. In fact, this had been certain ever since the end of July or the beginning of August, when the Allied counter-attack had halted the German offensive on the western front, demonstrating that there could be no thought of a victorious conclusion to the campaign before the arrival of the Americans and the onset of a fifth wartime winter. How far the generals showed their cards to the political authorities at that stage is not exactly clear. The party leaders were probably left in the dark as to the seriousness of the situation. At any rate the government delegates to the Crown Council in Spa on 14 August appear to have been more or less well informed. However, apparently no one in a position of authority realized the need to draw instant political conclusions or the necessity – apart from various vague plans – of instantly embarking on armistice negotiations, which might still have been conducted without undue pressure of time.

On the other hand, it was to the credit of the generals, as compared with the situation in the Second World War, that in the autumn, when the Reich was on the point of being overrun from the south-east, they realized that the game was up. Not for a moment did they contemplate pointless resistance. In view of the general exhaustion of the nation and the lack of 'moral leadership' and 'solidarity', the preconditions for a 'scorched earth' policy were immeasurably less favourable than in 1944/45. Now the helm was violently jerked round: at the end of September Ludendorff demanded that an armistice should be offered forthwith, and that a government on a parliamentary basis should at once be formed. It may be that the deceitful intention to shrug off responsibility for the lost war and to let the new men 'clear up the mess' played some part here, but circumstances called for a change of course in any case. For since the entry of America into the war and the elimination of Tsarist Russia in 1917 the Allies had regarded the war as a democratic crusade. There were to be no negotiations with the old Germany.

The parties that had been 'ordered to assume power' (Eschenburg) were so ill-prepared for the triumph to which they had aspired in their rhetoric but never seriously contemplated, that they did not even have a candidate from their ranks to propose for the post of Chancellor. They had only a compromise candidate. And so it was that, a month before the constitutional changes were endorsed, the government of Prince Max of Baden was formed, backed by the parties and manned by Secretaries of State drawn from parliament. The German Reich was now a parliamentary monarchy; from the beginning of October the government was – at first *de facto*, later *de jure* – dependent on the confidence of the Reichstag. The Prussian electoral law, on the face of it the most detested bastion of the old system, also collapsed, and even the command of the army was wrested away from the Kaiser and linked to endorsement by ministers responsible to parliament.

With the benefit of hindsight it can be said that the most important step out of the past and into the future represented by Weimar had been taken. The Reich was still formally a monarchy, but the imperial crown symbolized no more than the public dignity of an hereditary president. This measure met the wishes of the democratic parliamentary movement, which were thus fulfilled, if not beyond their expectations, at least sooner than anyone had dared to hope.

However, only those in the know and with political interests noticed any difference. The parties were much too taken aback to celebrate the victory which had fallen into their lap almost against their will; reluctant to assume power, they placed too much trust in authority to be able to take over effective control of the old apparatus. From the outside everything still looked much the same. After all, who knew that Prince Max was a democrat of liberal views? And that he represented more or less the geometric point at which all the trends in the majority parties converged, including their peace resolution of 1917 which had been so fiercely attacked by the con-servatives and the Pan-Germans. A prince had taken over from a count as Chancellor; from the point of view of the mass of the population nothing had changed. Thus arose the first misunderstanding that was to lead to the November revolution and that was subsequently embodied in the idea that the Social Democratic Party had practically launched a revolution against itself.

The second misunderstanding, which to some extent founded the Repub-lic, concerned the ending of hostilities. The psychological effect of the news that an armistice was being sought was enormous. What would certainly have been a slower and more rational approach to an armistice had been blocked by undue procrastination and by military and political developments in the meantime. Now the political effects of this shock within the country constituted a fresh factor, and an even faster pace was needed if the whole business was not to fall through. The approach via the American President that was chosen was protracted, however, and took several weeks. It is debatable in any case whether the German people's confidence in a victorious peace would have survived another wartime winter. With a request for an armistice on the table a war-weariness that had hitherto been pent up suddenly erupted. Why should people go on suffering at home and dying at the front? The war must be stopped *instantly*!

At first no one had been keener to lay down their arms than the high command, but, psychology not being included as a rule in an officer's training – and certainly not in the training of Prussian officers – no account had been taken of a possible psychological reaction in the country that had not been suggested by the experience of the preceding four years. The High Command had taken a decision after receiving Wilson's third note of 23 October which made it clear that there was no intention of allowing

Germany a breathing space in which to recuperate her forces. She would not be in a position to take up arms again after the armistice, as the military leaders had imagined, and had no alternative but to submit to a dictated peace that was only loosely linked to the American President's Fourteen Points. In these circumstances General Headquarters preferred capitulation to heroic but senseless resistance to the point of total destruction.

In dispute with the Reichstag, which was not willing to take any chances on the armistice issue, Ludendorff vacated his post on 26 October, resigning as if he were just another general and not the virtual dictator of the Reich. The nation took scarcely any notice of this event. Ludendorff had been very little exposed to the glare of publicity. Although he had wielded power in Germany since 1916, the mass of the population, who were shielded from excessive knowledge by censorship, were unaware of this. It was not Ludendorff's statue into which the populace hammered their nails for victory, but the figure of 'iron Hindenburg'. Hindenburg, however, the 'secret Kaiser', stayed at his post and, following Wilson's answer, signed an order of the day defiantly urging the continuation of 'resistance with all our might'. This is what featured in the headlines. Ludendorff's fall, on the other hand, and the political capitulation of the military that it implied, passed off without the nation being aware of its significance.

A situation then arose in which a spontaneous demand for an end to the pointless struggle spread throughout the country. It was a trend that had no centre and that was not directed by anyone in particular; it was aimed against anything that seemed to stand in the way of a truce, and hence threatened institutions which, in the view of the new political leaders, were not scheduled for demolition. It was a popular movement against the militaristic and authoritarian state, or, to be more precise, against the remaining façades of that state, behind which there was no longer any real power. It started with a soldiers' strike and grew into a comprehensive 'revolt of the hungry and exhausted' (Eschenburg), a general mutiny, which, as a matter of course and by common consent, rallied to the red flag – for the simple reason that this kind of behaviour was liable to be punished under any other flag. It did not mean that more than a minority of the uniformed and civilian mutineers really were inspired by socialist sentiments.

The first action of the movement involved the High Seas Fleet, which had been instructed by the Admiralty to sail from Wilhelmshaven on 30 October and carry out a foray into the Channel. Ever since the Battle of Jutland the fleet had lain idle and useless in its harbours while the war at sea was fought by the U-boats. Now, following Wilson's demand that, as a condition of the armistice, unrestricted U-boat warfare should be discontinued, the Admiralty wished to find a substitute for this campaign and, at the eleventh hour, demonstrate the necessity of the fleet's existence. However, there were cases of sailors refusing to obey orders, the planned foray could not be carried out, and the various squadrons returned to port with the insubordinate crew members under arrest. On 4 November the Third Squadron docked in Kiel, and the sailors mutinied and took possession of the city. The revolt had not been instigated by anyone in particular, the mutineers' demands were not political, relating rather to the release of their arrested comrades, as well as to an amnesty and disciplinary changes. Neither the Independent Socialist Party, the somewhat more radical 'Independents' who had seceded from the so-called Majority Socialists in 1917 over the granting of war credits, nor the Spartacus group, its genuinely radical left wing, were behind the mutiny or in a position to influence the course of events in Kiel.

In the fertile soil of a general war-weariness the movement spread along the coast and then extended rapidly into the interior of the country. On 7 November in Munich the first German monarchy fell. It is remarkable that it was the Wittelsbachers who suffered this fate, for they were so firmly rooted among the Bavarian population that they were able to go on playing a leading part in the politics of the country for decades to come. But the ruling monarch at the time, Ludwig III, was unpopular; people had not forgotten that he had usurped the throne, taking the crown from his insane cousin Otto, instead of contenting himself with a regency, as his father had done – a mortal sin in terms of legitimacy. Besides, it had been resented that, although a keen follower of the Kaiser with territorial pretensions equal to any Prussian Pan-German, he had nevertheless been powerless to influence the policy of the Reich and had surrendered the fair land of Bavaria to the wicked Prussians. And, third, since Austria had laid down her arms on 2 November, the country had suddenly been deprived of its secure situation in the interior of the continent: it was consequently threatened by the enemy across what was now an open Austrian frontier – although only in theory to begin with. On the night of 8 November a Republic was proclaimed in Munich: the Independent Socialist, Kurt Eisner, dragging the Majority Socialists along with him, had formed a socialist 'people's government', promising a constitutive assembly. When the Bavarian monarch fled from his capital that same night, the other German crowns also began to topple.

Since that Thursday evening there had been in Munich not only Eisner's government but also a soldiers' council and a workers' council. And as successor to the Bavarian parliament there was a provisional assembly of Bavarian workers', peasants' and soldiers' councils. In Kiel, too, these councils had assumed power, and wherever the revolutionary movement appeared in Germany councils of this kind were also formed. Councils – known as 'soviets' in Russian – had first been formed in the Russian revolution of 1905, coming into existence spontaneously as revolutionary bodies with both legislative and executive powers. They were organs of a crude and radical democracy and not simply an invention or an authority instituted by the Bolsheviks. It is true that, in 1917, Lenin had promoted the

Revolution under the slogan: 'All power to the soviets!', because in this way, through the preliminary elimination of the other classes, including the bourgeoisie, the victory of the proletarian revolution and the dictatorship of the proletariat seemed to be, and in fact were, best guaranteed. As soon as Bolshevik rule had been established – and that was clearly the case by the end of 1918 – the soviets shrank into a kind of shadowy existence in comparison with the reality of party rule; they became no more than a meaningless decoration.

The German councils were, as such, autonomous institutions, the expression of a 'crude self-government' and of dissatisfaction with the traditional authoritarian bureaucratic administration and the pig-headed military hierarchy with its various privileges. They were anything but the organs of a take-over of power on the Bolshevik model. But in the light of events in Russia, they were bound to strike those who feared a parallel development as a prelude to something else. To those who were promoting such a parallel development, or who at least were seeking a socialist German Republic based on the power of the proletariat rather than a parliamentary democracy, the soviets served as a welcome vehicle for their aims. The latter tendencies – and this is where we come to the third revolutionary movement which constituted a factor during the winter of 1918/19 – were fostered by the Spartacus League, which was the only group within the socialist movement to practise open revolution, although it still belonged officially to the Majority Socialist party.

There was now an imminent danger that the revolutionary movement involving mainly adherents of the Social Democratic parties (i.e. the Majority Socialists and the Independent Socialists) who were prepared to consent to anything that would bring about a cease-fire and an end to hardship would end up in the hands of Sparticist agitators. The moderate leaders of the Social Democrats, who had already grown somewhat middle class and respectable, therefore found themselves obliged to veer sharply to the left in order to place themselves at the head of the movement. This involved retiring from Max von Baden's government and eliminating the middle-class survivors of that government (although, truth to tell, there were few left to eliminate). The Social Democratic (and the trade union) leadership thus in fact re-established that contact with their members which to a large extent had been lost in the course of the 'political truce' and the war and that collaboration with army officers, government politicians and businessmen – in short, all the representatives of the old system – which was often not understood by their rank-and-file comrades. A latent distrust of the leadership remained, however, and was to have a baleful influence on the future of the state as a whole as well as on the working-class movement in particular.

Subsequently it has been reckoned that the danger during those November days was not so great – that, strictly speaking, it had hardly existed; that the officials whom the masses chose to lead them, almost exclusively Social Democrats of one shade or another, included scarcely any Sparticists; that efforts to bring about a socialist system were bound to fail, given the attitude of the soldiers' councils, which accurately reflected the social structure of the nation as a whole, and in whose hands after all the ultimate military (and hence the only effective) power lay; that even where Sparticists had managed to become involved, they had been rapidly eliminated. But, for one thing, situations tend to look different in the heat of the moment from how they appear when they are subsequently dissected by armchair analysts. Second, the analyses may indeed be correct, but may not have allowed for the possibilities represented by determined minorities. Third, the situation in Berlin was somewhat different from that in the Reich as a whole. And given the technical standards of the news media at that time (one should bear in mind, for example, that public radio did not exist) and the chaotic disruption of communications following the revolution, almost the sole deciding factor in what might be critical hours was the situation in the administrative centre of the Reich.

The general conviction was that the Kaiser had to go. But that implied quite elementary utilitarian considerations. As a result of his swashbuckling in peacetime he was regarded in the world outside Germany as the instigator of the war, and Wilson had made it sufficiently obvious that no peace could be concluded with Wilhelm. On the other hand, large sections of even the Social Democratic leadership, with the party chairman, Friedrich Ebert, at their head, were doing their best to plan a way of saving the monarchy – even the Hohenzollern dynasty – in the form of a regency involving an under-age grandson. In this respect they shared entirely the sentiments of most working people. Nevertheless, the German Republic proclaimed by Philipp Scheidemann from a window of the Reichstag at 2 p.m. on 9 November (to the annoyance of Ebert) was not a surprise *coup* by a lone individual. The intention was to forestall the proclamation of a socialist Republic by the Spartacist leader, Liebknecht, hallowed as he was by his recent release from a royal Prussian prison. It was a matter, too, of anticipating planned action by the left wing of the Independent Socialist Party, which formed an identifiable group in Berlin, in alliance with the Sparticists and under the leadership of so-called 'revolutionary representatives'.

Could the monarchy have been saved if the parties had forced the Kaiser to abdicate in October, or at least if Wilhelm had not hesitated at the last moment before Prince Max announced the abdication on his own authority and some hours before the Kaiser's decision (Max von Baden's last official action before handing over to Friedrich Ebert)? The answer must be no. The ramshackle condition of the German dynasties was only too evident, and the dynastic idea itself, even if an armistice had been concluded immediately, had been discredited. The dynasties had been the most conspicuous element in the old order, but now they proved to be its weakest. They were also liable to impair the enemy's goodwill, in which, after all, great hopes were placed. Their hour had come.

It is obvious that the inauguration of the leader of the Majority Socialists by the last Imperial Chancellor (to be precise, the second last – Ebert himself was the last) did not furnish an adequate degree of legitimacy in this situation of radical change. For this reason, Ebert's government of the Reich, which was constitutionally still a monarchy, lasted only a single day. It is characteristic of the state of affairs at the time that the idea of confirming the Chancellor's legitimacy via the Reichstag was apparently never considered, although it was an obvious procedure that had been grounded in the constitution since the end of October. It should be borne in mind that it would not have been easy to assemble Parliament, which was dispersed all over the country. Its members had been unable to agree to remain in session even during the stirring events of the preceding days and months and thus demonstrated a degree of irresponsibility and lack of zest that is not easy at this distance to understand. Instead of declaring their willingness to act in certain circumstances as a constitutive assembly, they had calmly resolved, following every trial of strength including the constitutional amendment of 26 October, to adjourn the session. The fact that the Reichstag vanished from the scene unwept and unsung, apart from a feeble protest over the cancellation of parliamentary allowances, was a sign of the times – and of times to come.

And so in Berlin, as in Munich, there was only one authority that might endorse the legitimacy of the new government's rule: the revolutionary authority of the councils. What tipped the balance here again was the fact that the Berlin soldiers' council backed the Majority Socialists. Here as elsewhere in the country it was the soldiers who shaped the revolution and set the course it was to follow. In fact, the entire revolution and the manner in which it took place was essentially the work of war-weary sailors and home-based troops. With the support of the armed forces of the revolution the left wing of the workers' council could be eliminated. The majority of the Independents, who were in any case separated from the rest of the Social Democrats only by tactical issues which had been settled in the meantime, were prepared to enter the government. Their left wing went into opposition. In the Circus Busch on 10 November a plenary meeting of the Berlin workers' and soldiers' councils elected the new republican government of 'People's Deputies': three Majority Socialists (Ebert, Scheidemann and Otto Landsberg) and three Independents (Hugo Haase, Wilhelm Dittmann and Emil Barth). The middle-class Secretaries of State (the 'ministers' of Bismarck's constitution, which recognized no ministers as such apart from the Chancellor) were reduced to the status of experts with no say in political issues. In this way they were rendered politically impotent, but they were still there – and capable of getting up to all sorts of mischief.

The following day the armistice was signed in the forest of Compiègne and took effect at noon. This event had little to do, however, with the revolutionary events in Germany. The German delegation, led by the State Secretary Matthias Erzberger of the Centre Party, had already been given its authority and despatched by Prince Max's government and had been handed the armistice conditions by Marshal Foch on 8 November. The fact that the political parties had taken over from the defeated army leaders the task of concluding a military armistice and thus taken the odium of this act on themselves turned out to be a grave error, because it gave right-wing agitators in opposition to the Republic an additional weapon. This arrangement was not, however, simply an underhand trick on the part of the military: the reasons for it were, on the one hand, the government's fear that the generals might be too obstinate in negotiations with the Allies, and, on the other, their concern that the Entente powers would insist on negotiating only with civilians.

In the seventy-two hours they had been allowed the German delegation could achieve no more than minor alleviations of the armistice terms. Nevertheless, they signed as the new government instructed them to – as it had to in fact, if it did not want to be swept away like the old system – and as Hindenburg's telegraphed vote also demanded: 'If these points cannot be gained, the armistice must nevertheless be concluded.' For Hindenburg had remained at his post even after his Emperor had gone. The Württemberg General Groener, a man of enlightened views in keeping with the traditions of his homeland and within the limits of his profession, had replaced Luderdorff on the high command of the army, which continued to function until the signing of a peace treaty. Their tactical task was the withdrawal of the German field army from France, Belgium and the Rhineland beyond the Rhine and a 10 kilometre zone on the right bank of the Rhine, as stipulated within the time-limits laid down in the armistice agreement. Their strategic task the generals considered to be the preservation of as much as possible of the traditions of the Prussian army within the new Republic. The idea, cherished by some, of leading the front-line army against the revolution at home was a fantasy, and not feasible given the morale of the troops returning from the front. (This did not, in fact, preclude an attempt at such an intervention being made in a modified form, but it failed miserably.)

It was this policy on the part of the army command, as well as its fear that 'the cart might lurch even further to the left', that led on 10 November to the alliance with the right wing of the Social Democrats which turned out to be so significant for the further course of events. This union, which came about at the suggestion of the generals and promptly secured them confirmation of their power of command *vis-à-vis* the soldiers' councils, was certainly no romantic affair but a marriage of convenience. Each partner, especially the uniformed one, pursued his own interests with numerous reservations, including the mental reservation that given the opportunity he would get rid of his partner. It was an alliance for a specific purpose, a mutual agreement to secure the interest of the contracting parties by suppressing attempts at revolution by left-wing radicals and preserving or restoring a particular political order. At the same time, there could be no question, as far as the military was concerned, of loyalty or commitment to the new state.

Nevertheless, to label the First Republic simply the joint product of the Social Democrats and the army might be to over-simplify circumstances which were, after all, extremely complicated. It was not only the old army with which the apparently victorious Social Democrats allied themselves. It was just as much the old bureaucracy and the old justiciary, i.e. the bourgeoisie as a whole. The entire old apparatus and its incumbents were allowed to go on operating without let or hindrance, at first provisionally, but later with the republican constitution ultimately removing all their worries, guaranteeing the civil servants' 'well-earned rights' and the immunity of judges from dismissal. There was not even a temporary suspension of these privileges in the interests of a democratization of the administration and the judiciary.

Those who bemoan the bourgeois Weimar Republic in general, or its end in particular, usually see the seeds of disaster in this policy. But anyone who rejects the alternative of a socialist Republic, either on the Russian pattern or in some new German version, is bound to come to the conclusion that any solution other than collaboration with the bourgeois (in part even feudal) supporters of the old regime would have been unthinkable. There were enormous problems to be overcome in connection with the winding-up of the lost war: the demobilization of the troops and their integration into productive processes; the provision of the population with the necessities of life which were in short supply; the changeover from a war economy to a peacetime economy that would initially be on a more modest scale and involve increased unemployment. It was essential, too, not to give way to feelings of guilt and yield to the hostile powers' slightest whim. It was also necessary to preserve German unity, to hold together in all its diversity a German Reich that was barely fifty years old, and to overcome the particularistic, even separatistic, trends which had appeared in the east, west and south following defeat and which expressed a hope of more favourable treatment in the case of secession. Faced with all these factors the Social Democratic supporters of democracy, having been put into the saddle by events, were inevitably forced into a pact with yesterday's men. They believed it to be essential if the new state was not to sink quickly into disintegration and chaos, from which anything might issue, from a Bolshevik Soviet Republic to total military occupation and dismemberment by the enemy – anything, in fact, but that parliamentary democracy which the majority of

working people were striving for. And – so it appeared – not just the working people, but also the bourgeoisie. Given this strong backing from the
nation as a whole, liaison with the old institutions did not seem like a matter
of principle but more a question of re-educating the populace, at best a
problem that would resolve itself in a generation or two. It was viewed as a
transitional settlement. That the wind was soon to blow from another quarter
and that there would no longer be any question of re-education was un-
thought of.

And so, from the local level right up to the government of the Reich, the
bourgeois administration continued to function, controlled more or less
skilfully at first by the councils. The administrators had the advantage of a
fine reputation gained in the course of centuries; once they had recovered
from the initial shock they were ready with the claim that they would allow
no one, not even parliament, to interfere with their executive authority. Once
the idea of wrecking the bureaucracy had been given up, the socialist – and,
later on, other – democratic controlling organs and the administrative heads
were dependent on their loyalty, their readiness to co-operate and their
goodwill. This attitude on the part of the new rulers was based on Bebel's
view that all that mattered was the possession of political power, i.e. the
leading posts: as far as the rest was concerned, the 'machinery' could always
find 'any number of Privy Councillors' in return for 'decent treatment and a
fairly good salary'. It was only to be expected that the unbroken continuation
of an administration staffed by civil servants who were anti-democratic, as
well as anti-revolutionary, would sooner or later prove to be a hard nut to
crack for a Republic constantly shaken by internal dissension. The Social
Democrats' theory of the purely functional character of a bureaucracy
available for the use of any political system would turn out to be an illusion.

The same was true of the military hierarchy. The Social Democratic leaders
believed that they could not dispense with the Kaiser's generals: that they
needed them to supervise the bringing back of the troops and also to build
up a new defence force after the old army had been demobilized. And the
same thing applied in many other areas. Particularly important in view of the
idea of re-educating future generations in republican ways were the schools
and universities; apart from spawning a few 'rational republicans', these had
survived the transformation virtually unscathed. What subsequently emerged
from them was entirely in keeping with the spirit that prevailed there. It is
no mere chance that the first institutions to be overrun by National Socialism
were the German universities.

Similar considerations applied to the economy, which was also left
untouched. Ever since Marxism had existed nationalization had been its
principal demand. In the course of decades, however, this issue had become
more and more mere rhetoric for the parties of the Second International; it
applied at best to major firms in the primary industries, which were relatively

bureaucratic in organization and hence easy to take over; otherwise, it had mainly propaganda value. At any rate, demands for nationalization played no part whatsoever in precipitating the events of November 1918. Of course, when the revolution came about they eventually found their way on to the agenda. A socialist Republic in the sense of the radical left would have made a clean sweep here, but the government of the People's Deputies shied away from any kind of intervention.

They certainly had good reasons for doing so. It was believed that the German economy was in any case on the verge of collapse because of problems in changing over from a war footing to one of peace: a shortage of coal, transport difficulties and famine. Even to discuss possible nationalization measures, the socialist leaders feared – showing scant confidence in their socialist platform – might have catastrophic consequences, or, at the very least, in conjunction with other calamities, might impede and delay the revival of the economy. Thus, no one dared render a desperate situation even more acutely critical by economic experiments. Later on, there were also foreign policy factors to consider: it was hoped that the enemy powers would be more favourably disposed to regarding private property as sacrosanct in an economy that had remained capitalist, and that the country might thus be spared intervention and confiscations. On the other hand, the large landed estates east of the River Elbe were seen as a guarantee against Polish infiltration into eastern Germany and were safely steered through a number of critical situations because of these foreign policy considerations. To all this was added the fact that, in the days of radical change, employers had come to an understanding with the trades unions, whom they finally recognized as negotiating partners, and had conceded the eight-hour day, which had long been sought. These changes took the wind out of the sails of socialist agitators, so that such 'social achievements' seemed to have put an end to the matter. A great deal of this social and political advance, including the abrogation of legislation governing the relationship of employer and employee, occurred within the three months during which the People's Deputies were in power.

People were satisfied, then, to allow a Nationalization Commission to investigate which branches of the economy were suitable for nationalization. However, neither the mines nor the vast estates east of the Elbe, which, from this point of view, were ripe – indeed over-ripe – for nationalizing, were touched in 1919 or later. Both the 'Junkers' and the 'smokestack barons' were able to weather the revolution with their wealth and social status unimpaired. After going to ground politically for a brief period they were not only soon back where they had been but were scarcely less influential than before; indeed, given the general 'humiliation' of Germany, they had acquired the charisma of a national myth.

Certainly it can be said that things would have turned out differently if the working class and the Socialist Party had not been divided, if they had been united in their efforts to achieve a socialist Republic, and if the radicalism of one wing of the party had not forced the majority into a pact with the bourgeois camp. But why should the German working class be less internally divided than the German middle class, since the very cradle of German political life had been occupied by ideologically based parties. Since the Spartacus group led by Karl Liebknecht and Rosa Luxemburg had established itself on 30 December 1918 as the numerically negligible but politically very active 'Communist Party of Germany (the Spartacus League)', a movement of more intellectual than proletarian complexion, there had been no fewer than three Marxist Parties. Each of these in turn divided into a right wing (which provided the leadership) and a left wing, so that the neighbouring wings of the Social Democrats and the Independent Social Democrats on the one hand, and the Independent Social Democrats and the Communists on the other were closer together than the opposing wings within their own parties. There were thus in practice six trends, but only two real alternatives: a parliamentary democracy or a thoroughgoing socialist revolutionary solution. The dividing line ran through the Independent Socialist Party, which did in fact eventually split up. This further split suggested that the six weeks that had elapsed since the revolution had contributed very little to the unity of the socialist camp – which was in fact the case.

The first clashes had taken place on 6 December. A harebrained group of conspirators mounted a surprise attack on the Berlin Executive Council, the supreme permanent organ of the Berlin councils which controlled the People's Deputies at the time. The Majority Socialist commander of the city, Otto Wels, had summoned troops to protect the government. Shots were fired at the Spartacist demonstrators, and as a result sixteen people were killed. The infuriated Spartacists accused the government of the People's Deputies quite unjustly of siding with the counter-revolution so as to suppress the radical workers. The fact that the counter-revolutionaries, with an eye to the facts of life, had wanted to proclaim Friedrich Ebert President, gave such charges a semblance of justification.

Ten days later, on 16 December, the Reich Congress of Soldiers' and Workers' Councils met. This Congress marked the first occasion on which the provinces were once more involved in the development which had hitherto been dominated by bodies in Berlin. The Congress was intended to determine the future shape of Germany. This involved above all the passing or rejection of a motion calling for the convening of a National Assembly. The aims of the Majority Socialists, based on the party's long parliamentary tradition of success at the polls, were for the Congress to clear the way for a parliamentary democracy achieved in an election with the widest possible franchise. Alternatively, the policy of the Spartacists and the left wing of the Independent Socialists was to convert into a pure soviet system the authority the councils had managed to usurp. This would mean the political elimination of the bourgeoisie, at least in the short term, and would probably lead ultimately to a system which was more or less assimilated to the Bolshevik political order. The fact that both institutional arrangements were not necessarily mutually exclusive in principle had not forced its way into the political consciousness of the Congress members – apart from various more or less tactical combinations on the part of right-wing circles in the Independent Socialist Party. The argument that had been bandied to and fro within the socialist parties during the preceding weeks had offered a clear alternative in the slogan 'Councils or a National Assembly'. In Berlin, which had played the leading role up to this point, the workers' councils had declared themselves in favour of continued rule by the councils, the soldiers' councils wanted a National Assembly.

The voters, i.e. the workers and those units of the army which had not yet been demobilized, decided in favour of the government, which was in practice inclined towards the Majority Socialists. Of the 450 members of the Congress 350 backed it; the motion in favour of a National Assembly was carried with an even greater majority against the left wing of the Independent Socialists, and the Assembly was scheduled to meet on the earliest possible date, 19 January 1919. The question of the date mattered in so far as the majority of Independent Socialists who had voted for the Assembly, in fact wished to postpone it for as long as possible in the expectation that the longer the councils remained in power, exerting a controlling influence on the work of the administration, the better chance they would have of consolidating their position. The councils might represent a revolutionary counterbalance to the National Assembly and, in the long run, even constitute a kind of proletarian Upper House, thus retaining a voice in the running of the state, even if they were no longer the sole authority.

In contrast to the Sparticists, who had everywhere been voted out of power, the left-wing group of Independent Socialists comprising the Berlin 'revolutionary leaders' was represented at the Congress and, with the support of radical councillors from the country at large, they succeeded in dragging the Independent Socialist faction so far to the left that the latter had abstained in the elections to the Central Council which was to continue as a standing committee of the Congress and to act as the sovereign representative of the revolutionary German nation. The Central Council would take over control of the People's Deputies from the Berlin Executive Council. Accordingly, while the Central Council became a purely Majority Socialist institution, the three People's Deputies from the Independent Socialist Party remained on it in a personal capacity, not as party representatives: they were duly confirmed in office by the new Central Council.

Not for long, however. For, hardly had the Congress adjourned on 20 December, than a fresh incident occurred in Berlin. During the days of the revolution the so-called People's Naval Division had established itself in

Berlin Castle; the core of the division consisted of 600 'reliable' sailors despatched from Cuxhaven who regarded themselves more or less as the traditional force that had triggered off the revolution; in the meantime they had become more like a troop of mercenaries. The day before Christmas a mutiny broke out, essentially on the issue of pay. The sailors arrested the Social Democratic city commandant, Wels, and also placed under house-arrest in the Chancellery those People's Deputies who happened to be in their offices, effectively cutting them off from the outside world. But they were unaware of the secret telephone line linking the Chancellery with the supreme command of the army ever since the time of the monarchy – the same line by which Quartermaster-General Groener had offered the Chancellor the support of the former Royal Prussian Army on 10 November, support which had been gratefully accepted.

It was via this line that Ebert sent a cry for help to Groener, like a drowning man clutching at the nearest arm. The generals could scarcely wait to be asked. Although the sailors had meanwhile released the People's Deputies who had been detained, front-line troops from the surrounding area entered Berlin the following day. The street battle that ensued ended in a compromise between the government and the mutineers, because although the officers were keen the other ranks had no heart for a fight. The pathetic course of this brief action was in fact a victory for democracy: it put paid, after all, to any ideas the generals may have had of 'putting things to rights' in Berlin with the aid of troops from the front. During the preceding couple of weeks, while men were returning from the front, plans of this kind had already led to the first attempts at blackmail by the army command. Given the manifest unreliability even of the front-line troops, such plans 'to restore order' had to be abandoned, for better or for worse. On the other hand, Ebert's appeal to the generals for help, however understandable, had a bad psychological effect on the Social Democratic People's Deputies: not only had the government of the Reich been vulnerable to arbitrary action by a handful of mutineers who could not be punished for what they had done, but – even worse – the leadership of the Majority Socialists had now for the second time in a brief period (and it was not to be the last) collaborated closely with the counter-revolutionary generals in order to crush a revolutionary force.

After the Majority Socialist Central Council declared their backing for Ebert and his friends, the three leaders of the Independent Socialists resigned from the government of the 'sailors' murderers'. When the sailors had marched on the building, two of them happened not to have been present; the third, the revolutionary leader Barth (an Independent Socialist, but, like his two colleagues, without a party mandate) had sympathized with the insurgents. They were replaced by two Majority Socialists (a third substitute, Paul Löbe, was unable to take up his place because of other pressing business.) One of the new members was Gustav Noske, whose name became a symbol of the increasing alienation of the Social Democrats from the revolutionary movement. Noske took charge of the army, his colleague Wissell assumed responsibility for social policy and the economy, and the remaining ministries were distributed as follows: Ebert took over home affairs; Scheidemann foreign affairs; and Landsberg finance.

The National Assembly had not yet convened when fresh, and even more serious, unrest broke out in Berlin. The pretext was, as it often is in such turbulent times, a mere trifle: the dismissal by the government of the Berlin chief of police, who was a member of the Independent Socialist Party. On 5 January radical workers took to the streets on the summons of the Independent Socialists, the revolutionary leaders and the Spartacus League. They occupied the offices of the bourgeois newspapers and the Social Democratic paper *Vorwärts*, went on demonstrating for a further two days and then went home, because their leaders could not think what to do next. Various contingents of troops in process of demobilization in Berlin, including the People's Naval Division, had, from the outset, taken no part in the action. The Spartacists, who had formed a revolutionary committee as an opposition government, were left on their own, determined to fight the second revolution through to the bitter end, driven on by elements urging action at any price, against the sounder judgement of their leaders, Liebknecht and Luxemburg. At this stage government troops hastily assembled in the south-western suburbs intervened. They had been put under the command of Noske, the man who had managed to some degree to appease and guide the sailors in Kiel during the November troubles. He had consented to act, he said, because 'someone had to play the part of bloodhound'.

This was the first occasion on which the so-called Free Corps made their appearance, for the army which had been brought back from the front had virtually disintegrated, a process accelerated by the Christmas season. The government of People's Deputies, lacking any sort of military protection and hence at the mercy of any handful of armed radicals, had not only given its approval to the forming of such detachments, but had participated actively in forming them. Those troops who were left in the barracks and available for the purpose were for the most part men who had no homes and no jobs to go to, or who were reluctant to return to civilian life for some other reason. And the officers who made themselves available were die-hard, career soldiers of the old order. Those who had been drafted in simply to meet wartime needs had long since returned to their families and civilian life. All these Free Corps, volunteer formations, frontier guards and self-defence organizations pursued their own policies as a matter of course and very soon ceased to take any notice of the military leadership. They certainly took not the slightest notice of the despised democratic ministers. It is obvious, too, that they were reluctant to withdraw when their services were no longer required against Bolsheviks in the eastern provinces, Polish insurgents in central Germany or Communists in the Ruhr. The only reason why these private armies, which hardly justified even the term *para*military, did not seal the fate of the First Republic at the very outset was largely because the leaders of the new army, the Reichswehr, finally began to be embarrassed by their outrageous tactics.

Ebert and Noske have been accused of failing to reconstitute the army with volunteers of a democratic persuasion or to recruit a republican defence force from returning working-class soldiers. One of them was indeed prepared to act the bloodhound but neither had the makings of a Carnot or a Trotsky. Tentative efforts to form a 'Home Guard' and workers' defence force were in fact made, but they soon fizzled out. They fought against the Spartacists and, together with the remnants of the old army stationed in the Berlin barracks, if the latter had been persuaded to intervene, they might have crushed the revolt. However, the rising looked sufficiently ominous to the government. A retrospective assessment, taking into account the massive vote of confidence in the government passed by the Congress of Councils, the general mood of the Berlin workers and the comforting thought that 'after all, nothing would have happened' cannot do justice to the situation as it looked at the time. In a moment of emotional stress appearances may seem more real than the facts seen with the benefit of hindsight. Faced by pressure from the streets, confronted by crowds of workers shouting blood-curdling slogans and behaving like ferocious revolutionaries – even if they had never proved in the past to be any such thing – Ebert and Noske felt that the advice of professionals who boasted of their indispensability counted for more than any political scruples they themselves might have had. Very few of the volunteers they had managed to recruit were party members on account of the socialists' traditional objection to military action, and Ebert and Noske felt that the proven efficiency of an officer class that had apparently been stripped of its political power inspired more confidence than untried talents.

The rebellion, now backed by no more than a few thousand Spartacists, was effortlessly put down by the troops. On 15 January the Spartacist leaders, Liebknecht and Rosa Luxemburg, were arrested and then murdered by a group of officers. This deed, and the pathetic outcome of a court martial faced by the perpetrators, was attributed by many to the Majority Socialist leadership and contributed even more to the latter's alienation from relatively large sections of their supporters. The first consequence was a series of local Spartacist risings and acts of terrorism in north and central Germany, followed by renewed intervention by the military acting on behalf of the Social Democratic Party. But again this was seen only with the benefit of hindsight. The elections for a National Assembly, which were held perfectly peaceably in every part of the country only four days after the two murders, gave no hint of these events. But they also offered no evidence of the socialist dominance that had up to now marked the German scene. The two socialist parties gained 45.5 per cent of the votes cast, winning 185 of the 421 seats. The Communists had once more, against their leaders' will, called for a boycott of the election – with little effect: there was a record turn-out of 83 per cent. The bourgeois, or, to be more precise, the bourgeois and peasant parties, which had been absent from the political scene for some weeks, commanded a majority, so that the structure of the old Reichstag was essentially re-established.

There were no public opinion polls in those days, and they would in any case have found it hard to function in a time of such radical change, so that the outcome of the election had been uncertain. Besides, the People's Deputies had altered the electoral law for general elections, changing the old majority electoral law into a virtually pure system of proportional representation. In line with Social Democratic policy the franchise had also been considerably extended: not only had the age limit been lowered by five years to twenty, but women had cast their votes for the first time. This reform of the electoral law engendered all sorts of illusions, while the deceptive political scene of the first revolutionary weeks had been dominated by the working class, with the old bourgeois forces being graciously permitted to perform only subservient tasks. Given this situation, the socialist leaders might have seen in the National Assembly that was due to be elected simply another form of that authority they had originally been determined never again to relinquish. It was only after the elections that the full significance of the elimination of the councils became clear.

The Majority Socialists remained true to their principles: under the impression of this electoral result (which was repeated in local Landtag elections, where there were socialist majorities only in Saxony and Brunswick), they refrained from appealing to mob rule, but accepted the will of the national majority. They regarded the well-nigh dictatorial powers that had fallen into the lap of the socialist parties in November as purely functional, and duly handed them over to the elected representatives of the whole nation. The latter in fact did no more than fill provisionally the void created by a kind of enervation that had followed the fall of the monarchy. Was this a kind of traditionalistic paralysis? Was it a lack of new ideas, mere ineptitude or a reluctance to break new ground? At any rate, it suited the wishes of the majority of socialist supporters, who preferred compromise and reform of the *status quo* to the risks of a real revolution that might lead to chaos and anarchy. The proportion in which voters had chosen between the two socialist parties did suggest this conclusion: almost 38 of the 45.5 per cent of socialist votes, and 163 of the 185 seats, had gone to the Majority Socialist Party.

Now, however, the latter's attempt to form a new government together with the Independents failed. With armed proletarian masses at their backs it might have succeeded – even against the bourgeois majority. However, increasingly antagonized by the events of the preceding weeks, their comrades of the 'independent' left refused to commit themselves to a parliamentary democracy, i.e. to accept the sovereign will of the people and to refrain from revolutionary action in defence of the 'imperilled achievements of the revolution'. The logical conclusion was that the Social Democrats, in order to stay in power, had to turn to the right: the old coalition of the 'majority parties' in the last imperial Reichstag was thus resurrected.

At the bourgeois end of the German party spectrum, it seems, members had at first been struck dumb with fright. Then, faced with the choice between democracy and Bolshevism, they had joined in the call for a National Assembly as – generally pretty lukewarm – supporters of the Majority Socialists. A few party names had been changed, but the overall structure had remained virtually the same. The familiar image of German parliaments consisted of three sociologically defined political blocs: conservative, liberal and social democratic. Apart from minor divisions and alliances, the liberal bloc had long been split on certain issues of principle. The division went back to the beginnings of the movement, when liberalism had been coupled with nascent German nationalism. Bismarck's realization of the conservative dream of German unity, which made little sense in the political landscape of 1848, had confronted the liberals with a crucial dilemma: those for whom the national issue was predominant had come to terms with Bismarck's Reich as National Liberals and had united in a party (succeeded by the German People's Party) which, along with the conservatives, ensured majority backing for the government, and which in the eyes of the Wilhelmine era 'was just about acceptable'. Those, on the other hand, for whom liberalism (which had once more succumbed to Bismarck's 'blood and iron') was more important than the achievement of German unity, had joined the Social Democrats in opposition as Progressives, or Democrats.

Along with the Social Democrats and the Democrats, the Centre Party was the third 'enemy of Bismarck's Reich' into whose hands the defeated regime confidently placed that same Reich. The Centre Party, the party of political Catholicism, did not fit particularly well into the pattern of the other parties. This fourth bloc had in fact been constituted rather later, not as a social or purely political grouping, but as a religious movement originally concerned with cultural policy and to some extent cutting across the boundaries of other parties. As a religious party, it is true, it could not very well act as if it were liberal; on the other hand it was able, by changing its inner centre of gravity, to be both monarchistic and republican (since the alliance of throne and altar had applied only to Protestant altars), conservative as well as democratic, even socialist, if necessary.

Thus, of all the bourgeois parties, the Centre Party had managed to take the step into the republican and democratic future with the greatest ease.

Under its old name it had retained its old membership: about 20 per cent of German voters had sent ninety-one Centre Party members to the National Assembly. With the Catholic clergy as its reliable election agents and with no designs on the rest of the Christian population (attempts to found a Christian People's Party had faded out in a matter of weeks), the Centre Party had remained the most stable party in the First Republic. Because of its central position there was never a government without the Centre Party, because even after the National Assembly it was never possible to form a majority to the right or left of the Centre. But during the meeting of the National Assembly, and, formally, even before it met, the Centre Party did suffer a loss: the secession of the Bavarian party organization, which was more strongly federalistic, legitimistic and more right wing. Not only did this branch of the party become independent, as the Bavarian People's Party (which it has remained to this day in the form of the Christian Social Union), it was often to criticize the mother party in the future, both on matters of principle and in terms of personalities.

In the liberal camp the dawn of a new era was a chance to bury ancient differences, which had by now largely been overcome, and to proceed to the founding of a common collective which would embrace bourgeois and democratic elements. Current events ensured, however, that the centre of gravity was on the left, with the old liberal trend. The effect was that the arch intended to span the new party was altogether too wide. Besides, the reluctance of the founders of the party to compromise themselves by association with the proponents of annexation and a victorious peace in the National Liberal leadership, although understandable, had political disadvantages. Prominent in this leadership was Dr Gustav Stresemann, the former leader of the National Liberals in the Reichstag, who had clung stubbornly to the supreme command of the army and who was regarded as 'Ludendorff's young man'. His attempts during the last weeks of the war to forge bonds with the majority parties had consequently been rejected as the time-serving ploys of a 'political chameleon'. Stresemann, who had been excluded from the new German Democratic Party (DDP), succeeded, with the help of the right wing of the National Liberals, in having a motion rejecting the union passed by a majority. The result was a rump party under the name of the German People's Party (DVP). The People's Party did not expressly adopt commitment to the monarchy as part of its programme, but its leaders never missed an opportunity of stating what they thought of 'the undignified retreat from the high ideals of the German Empire and the Prussian monarchy'. It was distinctly middle class, with an important wing in heavy industry, and was correspondingly anti-Social-Democratic.

Attempts by this industrial wing to link the People's Party to the party on their right failed, just as a previous alliance with the left had fallen through. The party on the right were the Conservatives, now calling themselves the

German National People's Party (the further removed a party was from the people, the more it felt obliged by current circumstances to offer at least verbal evidence of solidarity with the people). The nationalists, i.e. the rural landowners and their followers, together with what was at first a fairly limited section of the upper class and of industry, had indeed reluctantly consented to recognize the parliamentary form of government as the only possible form in present circumstances, but they still continued to stand by the monarchy. This had been stated in highly qualified terms when the party was founded in November 1918, but was later quite openly declared. The monarchy, it is true, had been rejected, as emerged clearly from the elections to the National Assembly: the National People's Party had received 10.3 per cent of the vote and forty-four seats, while Stresemann's People's Party had gained no more than 4.4 per cent of the vote and nineteen seats. Even in conjunction, these two parties were weaker than the German Democratic Party alone, which, with its 18.5 per cent of the vote, sent seventy-five delegates to the Assembly.

Thus, apart from splinter groups, a right-wing opposition of sixty-three and a left-wing (Independent Socialist) opposition of twenty-two delegates were faced by a bourgeois democratic centre of 166 members, and a further 163 Social Democrats.

This was the structure of the constitutive body that met on 6 February – not in Berlin, but in Weimar. The fact that it met in Weimar had symbolic significance: the cradle of German humanism was to serve at the birth of the new state. In addition these were sound practical reasons for not holding the Assembly in Berlin: after its experience with the Congress of Councils, the government of the People's Deputies wished to secure the National Assembly against the pressure of the mob and the campaigns of their hostile socialist comrades, the Independent Socialists and the Spartacists, who were still relatively powerful in Berlin. For it was by no means obvious at that stage that the January battles, which were later to be termed the 'Battle of the Marne of the German Revolution' (nowadays we would say the 'Stalingrad') had exhausted the revolutionary impulse, at least in Berlin. And even a hopeless assault, such as was launched no more than two months later, might have assumed dangerous proportions, had the constitutive body been within its grasp.

2

The constitution and the peace treaty

The National Assembly faced two major tasks: the drafting of a new constitution for the Reich, and the conclusion of a peace treaty. But first of all it was necessary to put a roof over the head of the young state. The premises had already been provided: the People's Deputies had prepared a draft and the Central Council, in line with its previous actions and its Social Democratic membership, had placed its plenary powers in the lap of the National Assembly. The job was done in an astonishingly short time: on 10 February, four days after the opening of the Assembly, a 'law on the provisional authority of the Reich' consisting of ten articles was passed. It stipulated the election by the Assembly of a president who would hold office pending the election of a new president on the basis of the future constitution of the Reich. This provisional president would appoint a Reich ministry and his orders and decrees would require endorsement by a minister.

The following day Friedrich Ebert was elected President of the Reich by 277 out of 379 votes. A day later he appointed the first cabinet, a coalition government of Social Democrats and members of the Centre Party. They had declared their readiness to join the government after accepting three conditions laid down by the Social Democrats: unqualified acknowledgement of the republican state, stringent taxation of property and wealth, drastic social policies, including the nationalization of suitable concerns. The former People's Deputy, Scheidemann, became Prime Minister of the Reich, six Majority Socialists were members of the cabinet, including the People's Deputies Landsberg, Noske and Wissell as Minister of Justice, Defence Minister and Minister of Economics respectively. The Centre Party and the Democrats provided three ministers each, including the leader of the Centre Party, Matthias Erzberger, as Minister without Portfolio who also had responsibility for armistice matters, and the Democrat Hugo Preuss, whom the People's Deputies had appointed to look after home affairs, as Minister of the Interior. Count Brockdorff-Rantzau became Foreign Minister, or, in fact, remained in this function, to which he had been appointed by the People's Deputies. The new government was in fact a continuation of the People's Deputies government under another name, and with political equality granted to the bourgeois ministers in their own departments. In theory three other combinations would have been possible, apart from this 'Weimar coalition' of the three parties committed to a democratic republic: a combined socialist minority government with support from the streets and the councils; a Majority Socialist minority government tolerated by the other democratic parties; and a bourgeois cabinet ranging from the Democrats to the German Nationalists. The first of these possibilities would have meant the continuation of the revolution, which the Majority Social Democrats could not be persuaded to support. The third would have led at that time to grave unrest and would have been at odds with the representation of the parties in the last Reichstag. The second might indeed have been feasible, but the two bourgeois parties were not in the least interested in a voluntary prolongation of the exclusion from power which had so far been forced on them.

Along with the President of the Reich and the government, the law of 10 February had referred to a further institution. This did not have to be created, however, for it already existed. In the interests of those who had appointed it, the constitutive assembly of the sovereign nation had anticipated the provisions of the constitution and had renounced a basic right. The future 'territorial substance of the free states', it was stated, might only be changed with their consent. The 'free states', however, were represented *vis-à-vis* the state as a whole by a Committee of States, with which the government had to agree draft proposals for submission to the National Assembly, and the consent of which was necessary for the enacting of legislation for the Reich. If this consent was not forthcoming, the issue had to be decided by a national referendum.

The fact was that during the preceding three months illusions nourished by Berlin's isolation during the early days of the revolution and held by socialist as well as bourgeois politicians, to the effect that there was only one single and unified Germany, clashed dramatically with the real situation in the rest of the country. For there secessionist traditions had survived the November revolution intact. After all, every regional capital had had its own revolution – Munich, for instance, even before Berlin. There was also the old federative argument that more individuals can play an active part in a federative system than would be be possible in a single, unitary state constructed on rational principles. Hence, an astonishing phenomenon could be observed: Prussian or Bavarian socialists were often more – or at least just as – ardently Prussian or Bavarian as their most conservative or feudal predecessors. A party might be as centralistic and unitarian at the top as it liked, its newly fledged functionaries in the regional authorities from Berlin to Karlsruhe thought differently. They had crawled into the vacant federal- istic cocoons and felt cosily at home there. And so a battle began, with the federalists attacking the threat of 'Prussianization', and the unitarians de- nouncing the persistence of the 'sovereignty fraud inherited from the former princes'.

The liberals, like the Social Democrats, were in principle unitarians. And it was into the hands of a unitarian liberal, the Berlin constitutional lawyer Hugo Preuss, that the People's Deputies placed the task of drafting an official constitution when they put him in charge of the Ministry of the Interior on 14 November 1918. Only two weeks after the revolution, however, on 25 November, the representatives of the individual states, the revolutionary new ministers with their retinue of former Royal, Grand Ducal, etc., civil servants, had turned up in Berlin for the first Reich Conference of German States with the aim of pouring their federalistic water into the centralistic wine of the Reich authorities. In this way, then, one of the fundamental features of Preuss's draft constitution had already been under- mined when the National Assembly met: the reform of the Reich into a 'corporate people's state rising by stages through a series of self-governing districts' on the model of English self-government, i.e. a decentralized unitary state with regions (*Länder*) that would be restructured without regard to their old form, as the latter simply reflected the fortuitous policies of various dynastic houses. These regions would no longer be founding partners of the Reich and semi-autonomous constituent states, but simply the bearers of a kind of expanded self-government.

This Utopian plan for a state constructed solely on rational and functional lines and incorporating idealized features from foreign constitutions was wrecked on hard political facts: inertia, the instinct for self-preservation of the regional bureaucracies, and the historically rooted federalistic mentality of large sections of the population. However much the objective factors suggested the need for a new, centralized structure in view of impending crises and threats from abroad, the power of tradition was greater. The rapid revival of autonomy in the most important areas of Germany, the actual constellation of power and material interests, represented a massive obstacle to any such development. This was not only true for Bavaria, where Kurt Eisner, a Berliner and a Jew into the bargain, who had come to Bavaria in 1907 and to Munich in 1910, behaved more like a Bavarian federalist than any Wittelsbacher could have done. He no doubt hoped to gain in this way the special favour of the Allies, who were united in their hostility to Prussia. It applied *mutatis mutandis* to the other south German states, which hesitated, however, to make common cause with him on account of his recklessness.

In particular, he had published documents on the question of German war guilt that were as indiscreet as they were controversial. His aim was to attack the prime authority of the Reich in foreign policy but the documents were of course eagerly seized upon by the hostile powers.

And it applied above all to Prussia, that odd federal state, which constituted in population and area two-thirds of the Reich as a whole. The division of Prussia – whether administratively by constitutional act or in terms of secessionist demands fostered and supported in large areas of the country – was the cardinal problem of any reform of the Reich. Its solution was doomed to failure through the attitude of the People's Deputies, and that of the Social Democrats in general (not only the Prussian Social Democrats), who wished to create as much of a unitarian state as they could, but were not willing, on the other hand, to surrender Prussia where they had gained a base that they maintained until 1932. The Social Democrats found themselves here in alliance with the old Prussian bureaucracy, and of course with the military, all of whom recommended Prussia as the only clamp capable of holding the Reich together and counterbalancing powerful centrifugal forces. They were also supported by the ambition of adjacent hostile states which, with one exception, were aimed at Prussian parts of the state. These made the existence of Prussia a political issue and, given the precarious situation, a factor in foreign policy, which hence took precedence over domestic quarrels.

Such secessionist threats continued to be the card that trumped all the arguments of the pure as opposed to the Greater Prussian unitarians. And they were not by any means as trivial as they may seem in hindsight. After all, it was a great temptation to gain better treatment by the enemy powers and not to have to tighten one's belt quite so much in future, if this could be done by deserting the compromised ship of the Reich, perhaps only temporarily and for purely tactical reasons. At any rate, Prussia's territory remained as unimpaired as that of the other regions, although Prussia no longer had its former overwhelming influence on the policy of the Reich. Apart from the consolidation of the Thuringian states, nothing was done in practice in terms of a reform of the Reich throughout the entire Weimar period. The joining of Coburg to Bavaria in 1920 and the absorption of Waldeck into Prussia in 1922 or 1929 were carried out for different reasons, and in fact their effect ran counter to such endeavours.

The government of the People's Deputies had tried to pin down the individual states to a provisional decision. When Eisner in particular threatened to call a conference of prime ministers, the government had invited the representatives of the provincial administrations to a second conference in Berlin on 25 January 1919, in order to salvage by negotiation as much as possible of the unitarian draft. The result was practically nil, indeed Eisner went so far as to question the sovereignty of the impending National

Assembly. What came of it in the end was a Committee of States and further negotiations which led to the compromise of a second, and this time considerably more federalistic, draft constitution; this was made possible only by a great deal in the way of concessions on the part of the Reich authorities. There was actually a reason for this conciliatory attitude: the hope of a final revision of the constitution in the National Assembly, where the temptations of federal sinecures did not play a part, and where a further impulse might be imparted to the unitarian cause.

And this hope was not a vain one. The constitutional committee of the Assembly even wanted to give the President and the government more than the latter thought feasible in the light of protests from the provinces. Ebert in particular proved to be a man of compromise who, at least in form, made rather more palatable what the National Assembly expected the provinces to swallow. In fact, the government of the Reich did not relinquish in negotiation very much of what the representatives of the people had granted it. This must be seen as at least a partial victory for the unitarian lobby when compared with the wildly proliferating federalistic ambitions of the weeks preceding the National Assembly. Those who nourished these ambitions would have liked to see the Reich re-established as a mere association of free states. The victory was made easier by the virtual elimination of Bavaria on account of disturbances following Eisner's murder on 21 February 1919. The unrest culminated in a seizure of power by the councils and the imposition of a form of direct rule by the Reich. The constitution turned out as it did, in fact, only because Bavaria was not involved. This, to be sure, had the disadvantage that the second largest of the states, which tended to veer politically from the extreme left to the extreme right, never felt itself bound by a constitution that had been arrived at without its collaboration.

It was no mere chance, then, that this crucial issue featured in the very first section of the constitution: 'The Reich and the states'. The constitution was accepted on 31 July by the 262 votes of the coalition parties against the seventy-five votes of the Nationalists, the People's Party, the Independent Social Democrats and a number of Bavarian members. In its basic features it copied the model set by Bismarck, with some few, albeit vital, modifications to the advantage of the Reich. The states (not, as they wished, the 'free states') did retain their territorial integrity unimpaired, but Article 18 on the reform of the Reich deleted the blocking clause in the law on the provisional authority of the Reich: henceforth structural changes supported by a majority in the Reichstag would be possible, even against the will of the state concerned (in practice this turned out to be a meaningless provision). The old Federal Council (Bundesrat) was retained as a 'Reichsrat', but the dominating position of Prussia was abolished and half of its votes (now still, as was previously the case, limited to two-fifths of the Reichstag total) were transferred to the provinces and hence could no longer be mandated by the

Prussian government. More significantly, however, subject to certain conditions, a vote in the Reichsrat might be overruled by a majority in the
Reichstag. Thus, the 'assembly of states', which had been planned at one
point as a genuine second chamber, vanished from the scene. The same fate
befell the reserved rights of the south German states, while the Reich also
assumed powers for a large number of particular areas, including powers to
extend its competence still further.

Above all, the Reich had ceased to be a poor relation of the states in regard
to liabilities arising from the war, especially the anticipated reparations
payments: it now had the authority to administer purchase taxes and customs
duties in place of statutory contributions from the states. This was just the
beginning of a process that culminated during the next few months in
Erzberger's financial reforms. These secured for the Reich absolute financial
autonomy as regards direct taxes, and in particular the authority to raise a
uniform income tax throughout the country, with a share earmarked for its
own use. They also created a complete fiscal administration, a separate inland
revenue service for the Reich. The tables were turned: the states became
hangers-on of the Reich, uniform taxation was guaranteed, and various
tax-havens for certain categories of income and property disappeared.

All this indeed represented a distinct advance in a unitarian direction, but
in contrast to the original intentions of the unitarians around Preuss, the
old motley territotorial pattern with its functional inefficiency had been
preserved. But the failure of the father of the constitution was even more
evident in the numerous marks it bore of the authoritarian mentality of the
ministerial civil servants who had drafted it: very little was left in the end of
the grand idea of self-management. This is where we may detect more
affinity with the constitution of Bismarck's Reich than can be deduced from
particular parallels in structure and institutional bodies, where such simil-
arities are normally sought.

The form taken by the political organs of the Reich had to some extent
been anticipated by the provisional authority granted to the Reich. In its
essentials the Weimar constitution corresponded to the arrangements made
then and during the final phase of the old constitution of October 1918.
Under the influence of the bureaucracy and a reinvigorated middle class
allied with the secret wishes of the Social Democratic leadership, which had
been only temporarily pushed aside for tactical reasons, the forces of inertia
represented by the traditional institutions triumphed all along the line over
the revolutionary impulses of the autumn. A Reichstag within the framework
of the Reich was once more envisaged as the sole representative of the
people, with a franchise identical to that for the National Assembly. In the
thirty-five huge constituencies this system of proportional representation
with the widest possible franchise had no more than organizational significance. Only candidates on lists drawn up by the party hierarchies stood for

election, not individuals. The scheme did in fact reflect an over-scrupulous sense of fairness and it ensured that large numbers of votes were not cast in vain, but in its impersonality it was scarcely suitable for a period of parliamentary indoctrination. Apart from the gulf it created between voter and candidate, it encouraged mediocrity in the political parties and obstructed the emergence of leaders with minds of their own or of independent young politicians who were not backed or financed by some lobby or other. The constitution itself made no mention of political parties, and by fostering the fiction of the member of parliament who was responsible solely to his conscience and the nation at large, an unduly large share of the blame for future problems tended to be placed on 'party bungling' or 'party swindles'.

Everything that had been decided in advance by the convening of the National Assembly was definitively confirmed in those articles of the constitution that referred to the Reichstag. Any notion of councils or soviets, even in the form of a second-tier authority representing the sovereign will of the nation, was finally laid to rest during the first six months of 1919. Events in the country at large played some part here, but no longer a major part.

After Noske's Free Corps had restored order in Berlin during January, further intervention by government troops ensued in various areas of the Reich where unrest, strikes and demonstrations had resulted as a matter of course from disputes with bureaucratic and middle-class elements who were now regaining their confidence. Intervention by the executive took place for the most part in central Germany, in the Ruhr and the North Sea ports. The troops gained the upper hand everywhere: following the demobilization of the old army and the defection of the soldiers' councils, the workers' councils were isolated and no longer had an effective executive. In March there was a general strike in Berlin and a rebellion staged by the People's Naval Division who feared for their survival. The rising was put down with brutality and bloodshed. Liberal use was made of Noske's 'order to fire', or, to be precise, 'order to kill'. During the first days of May the occupation of Munich by government troops marked the end of this phase and also the final suppression of the soviet movement.

The murder of Eisner by Count Arco-Valley, a 21-year-old lieutenant from an old aristocratic family, had taken place when the Bavarian Prime Minister was on his way to the inauguration of the newly elected Landtag with his resignation in his pocket. The elections on 12 January had inflicted a crushing defeat on his party, the Independents: they had gained no more than three of the 180 seats. Even in combination with the socialists they were in a minority with sixty-four seats, and together with the Farmers' Union (*Bauernbund*) they could muster only eighty seats. On the same day as Arco's assassination of Eisner there had been another assault, this time by a workers' councillor in the Bavarian Landtag, which eliminated Erhard Auer, leader of the Majority Socialists. It also led to a whole new wave of revolutions in Bavaria. The two socialist parties together with the Farmers' Union formed a minority government under the Majority Socialist Hoffmann, which relied on the support of the councils. The majority in the Landtag, intimidated by this fresh outbreak of violence, passed a vote of confidence giving the government plenary powers, and then went home.

Soon afterwards, however, at the beginning of April, a fresh wave of revolution, starting in the new Soviet Republic of Hungary and passing through Austria, which was in a similar state of political ferment, ultimately affected Bavaria. A number of literary figures from the Schwabing district played a leading part, and the Munich Central Council succeeded in formally proclaiming and establishing a Soviet Republic in Munich and Southern Bavaria. The Bavarian parliament was thus not only *de facto* eliminated but totally abolished. Since 7 April a Council of People's Deputies consisting for the most part of Independents and Anarchists had been in power in Munich. Their chairman, it is true, had to be admitted to a mental hospital within a matter of days.

Hoffmann's government fled to Bamberg and began to plan a march on Munich from Franconia. They were too weak, however, and Berlin had to send a number of Free Corps, who were joined by volunteer detachments from the government of Bamberg. The leaders of the soviet capitulated before the advancing troops, but now the Munich Communists, led by the Russian revolutionary, Eugen Leviné, and Max Leviens seized power on 13 April. Leviens had also come originally from Russia, but he was a German citizen and had served in the German army during the war. They began to confiscate and 'nationalize' – amongst other things residential property – with radical zeal, and organized a 'Red Army' under the command of a sailor by the name of Egelhofer. The forces of Hoffmann and Noske were obliged to fight a number of actions against this Red Army before they were able to occupy the Bavarian uplands and, between 1 and 3 May, the capital, Munich. The Soviet Republic made its exit with the murder of ten hostages and the army took its revenge with hundreds of summary executions. Following these events Bavaria was ruled, in a formal sense, by a new middle-class government on a somewhat broader basis under Hoffmann. In fact power lay with monarchistic and radical – or, at any rate anti-republican – right-wing elements who were continuously reinforced from all parts of the Reich. These elements had their roots in the mood of the middle class, who had swung wildly to the right following the stirring, indeed hair-raising, events of the councils' rule. They were also backed by the tradition of particularism, which henceforth was aimed not from the left but from the right at Berlin and the 'Marxist' rule of the Reich.

All these events, however, had finally put paid to the idea of soviets or councils. The Majority Socialists – not to mention the bourgeois parties – were unwilling to allow the councils to wield any influence on political life, so they dwindled away and became institutions of a purely social complexion in an economic and industrial context; they ceased to be a political problem and became of mere economic and social significance. The council movement was indeed incorporated in Article 165 of the constitution. Apart from workers' councils in places of employment, district councils and a Reich workers' council, this provided for worker participation together with representatives of the employers in proposed Regional Economic Councils and a Reich Economic Council which would be charged with the drafting of nationalization laws. Except for the workers' councils, however, which were solidly based in law, all these institutions, together with nationalization itself, failed to materialize on account of the continuing drift of political power to the right. They never got beyond the stage of discussion papers, or, as in the case of the Provisional Reich Economic Council which emerged from the old Central Council, a tentative beginning.

If everything had thus settled back into the well-worn tracks of October 1918, one thing remained problematic in establishing the allocation of political power: the position of the President of the Reich, who had replaced the Kaiser. With the benefit of hindsight it has been suggested that there were two choices: a weak president on the lines of the French Third Republic of the time, elected by parliament and in practice dependent on parliament, with his role reduced to that of a symbolic head of state; or a strong president on the American model, elected by the people and supreme head of the whole executive. It has been further suggested that the construction of the Weimar constitution decided in favour of a strong president popularly elected for a term of seven years and invested with command of the armed forces, although he would not normally exercise executive power. He was also provided into the bargain with a weak president's power to dissolve parliament. In France, it is true, no president who had risen from the ranks of parliament had ever dared to exercise this power since Marshal MacMahon's attempted *coup d'état*. It was nevertheless incorporated into the Weimar constitution, together with Article 48, which gave the President sole authority to rule for a limited period without recourse to parliament – and even up to a point without regard to the basic rights embodied in the constitution – in the event of 'major' disruption or threat to safety and public order. This power turned out to be a dangerous anti-democratic weapon: 'major' disruption or a threat to public order proved to be highly flexible concepts. Parliament had the right to cancel such 'emergency decrees' by the President following their implementation. Presidental decrees also had to be endorsed by the Chancellor, who was formally appointed by the President and could be replaced if necessary, or by one of his ministers. These provisions were, however, inadequate safeguards.

It has since been pointed out, quite rightly, that the President of the Reich was modelled less on a French or American pattern than on his predecessor, the German Emperor, in the final phase of the latter's competence. Moreover, arguments about the constitutional design of this office could hardly remain on a theoretical level, considering that there was an actual and very active incumbent in the post that was to be created. No wonder then that the whole debate was conducted with an eye to that incumbent, and that, consciously or unconsciously, the office was designed to fit that honest soul, Ebert. After all, by his untiring and successful efforts as a mediator in the course of the discussions on the constitution he had built up such a fund of confidence that ultimately even the federalists regarded a strong president as a desirable counter-balance to the unitarian influence of the other organs of the Reich, the central bureaucracy, say, or the parliament. There was also the fact that Ebert himself, in contrast to his comrades, argued the case for a strong president as a substitute for the monarch whom he had relinquished only under duress: personally, and against the advice of his friends, he had set his sights on this office rather than that of Chancellor – but his aim was certainly not simply to have a 'red pennant' fluttering over the ship of state.

There was at least a theoretical possibility that the President might possess wide-ranging powers, since given the centralization that had taken place, he had even more sweeping powers of command over the armed forces than his monarchical predecessor had possessed. In view of this, the competence of the Chancellor to determine the guidelines of policy, as laid down in Article 56, could only be valid as long and in as far as the Reichstag, on the confidence of which he depended, actually continued to be an effective political factor. How far the marked plebiscitarian element in the presidency was altogether consistent with a parliamentary democracy without giving rise to severe functional defects has been the subject of lively debate among constitutional experts in the political sciences. This element of the plebiscite was reinforced by the instrument of the referendum which might be invoked not only against decisions of the Reichstag and the Reichsrat but also in the form of a political initiative following a popular petition, i.e. after registration of one-tenth of the electorate in public lists. In fact this provision was never of much significance in practice. The President represented an authority on an equal footing with parliament; he was directly appointed by the 'sovereign people', as parliament was, and able to appeal to the people unilaterally and in opposition to the parliamentary authority by means of a dissolution and a referendum. His authority to run the country did not obtain in a normal situation, for normally that authority lay with parliament and the government, and as long as these factors were able to act there was no danger: indeed, the President's influence could serve as a beneficial restraint. In an emergency, however, a great deal, if not everything, would inevitably depend on the personality of the President. As the authority of parliament increasingly crumbled away, however, a situation eventually arose where a state of emergency became the norm. Nevertheless, it can hardly be disputed that the powerful presidency, and even the aristocratic Field-Marshal and President who subsequently held the office, tended to delay rather than hasten the end of the Republic.

This is not the place to enter into a detailed discussion of the constitution and its history, and it would in any case be of no more than theoretical interest. Only the catalogue of basic rights contained in Article 57 calls for special mention. It had not been drafted by Preuss in all its comprehensive detail; its guiding principles had been copied at the request of the Social Democratic People's Deputies 'from the 1848 Constitution, as far as they were still applicable'. The final result was a hotchpotch of heterogeneous ideas, interests and wishes which was certainly still predominantly liberal in tendency, but which began with a piece of political folly: the abolition of the titles Privy Councillor (*Geheimrat*) and Commercial Councillor (*Kommerzienrat*) and a ban on the award of decorations and honours. The Republic thus deprived itself of a highly effective – and uniquely inexpensive – mode of rewarding services and securing the citizens' loyalty to the new state by means of their vanity. The puritanism revealed in this gesture, which gave the whole Republic an inexpressibly dull, even dingy character, was no doubt worthy and sensible: it underlined the principle that all Germans were equal before the law (which in fact they were not, because 'the law', after all, was personified in those who administered it). In this way, however, the yearning for a little glamour that could not be legislated out of existence was shifted to relics of the past and to those who trafficked in them.

And, finally, the new black, red and gold ensign of the Reich should be mentioned. The old colours from 1848, expressing the liberal aspiration to a united Reich, were by no means inappropriate for a fresh start. They were also the colours of Greater Germany, and hopes of a union with what was left of Austria still persisted: both the National Assemblies in Vienna and in Weimar had voted unanimously in favour of such a union. A change of the national colours, however, presupposes a genuine revolution such as that in which the tricolour had blotted out the Bourbon lilies. Here, however, the rift had not gone deep enough. Even the Democrats were split over the vote on the ensign of the Reich, and an absurd compromise, thinly disguised as a version for use abroad, had retained the old black, white and red in the mercantile ensign, with the new colours of the Reich superimposed in one corner. After the initial democratic wave had subsided it became even clearer that far too many people were still attached to the old colours of Bismarck's Empire and that they considered the change as disrespectful, as truckling to the enemy, or even as having been imposed by the enemy. The overwhelming majority of those employed in the bureaucracy, the legal system and, of course, the army, the real pillars of the state, remained 'black, white and red' and hence had reservations at least about the new state. But the declared right-wing also adopted black, white and red as the standard to which they initially rallied, just as the left had rallied to the red flag. Between these rival banners the colours of the Reich had become the target of derision and contempt and they did not even enjoy the protection of the courts in this Republic.

So much for the Weimar constitution. It was, of course, a compromise between various interests, but this was not in itself a mistake. As a whole it was thoroughly serviceable and, given a more favourable political development, it would doubtless have served its purpose. However, circumstances did not take a propitious turn. That is why criticism of the constitution has detected more structural flaws in it than is probably justified. Explicitly or implicitly this criticism is based on the belief that the disaster of Hitler could have been prevented, or at least limited, with a better constitution: with reduced or increased effectiveness of the party system; either without states at all or with more weight accorded to the states; with a President elected by parliament and not by the people; with a first-past-the-post electoral system; and, above all, without that ominous Article 48.

Perhaps it was indeed the excessive cosmetic appeal and the would-be perfection of the Weimar constitution that hastened the end of the First Republic, but the Republic did not perish because of the constitution, which was in no way to blame for the failure of certain things to work. However attractive the constitution and the Republic might have been, and however far they might have matured without any sort of improvisation or 'structural compromises', Hitler would still have subverted them, given the yearning and the distress of the masses. The Basic Law of the Second Republic was understandably keen to avoid repeating old errors, although things which turned out to be errors in yesterday's circumstances need not necessarily be errors today. The approach was not sufficiently radical, however, to go beyond mere structural problems and to apply the axe at the point at which lay more causes of the failure of the Weimar political structure than in all the structural flaws of the constitution taken together: the stubborn and almost unimpaired intellectual traditions, and the social and political power structures of the old authoritarian state, which have persisted in large measure up to the present day.

The Weimar constitutional discussions were subject not only to the pressure of internal conflicts: they were held also under the shadow of the peace treaty. On 7 May 1919 Count Brockdorff-Rantzau had been handed the fat volume containing the draft of the treaty in the Versailles Hall of Mirrors, where the coronation of the German Emperor had taken place in 1871. The Allies had declined 'negotiations', from the outset, fearing a second Congress of Vienna and a German Talleyrand who might drive a wedge into the far from monolithic block of their alliance. For this reason the indignant government of the Reich had originally intended to despatch only a Privy Councillor to Versailles. The German delegation was only

permitted to submit 'observations' within a three-week period. They had
scribbled diligently, but had been unable to make many changes. The note
of 16 June which they received in reply set a deadline of five days – ultimately
extended by forty-eight hours – for them to accept a version of the treaty that
had been only slightly modified. If no agreement was forthcoming at that
point, then the armistice would end; in other words, the Allies would begin
their march into the territory of the Reich on the right bank of the Rhine.

After the terms of the treaty became known in Germany a wave of
indignation swept the country, for they interpreted Wilson's Fourteen Points
in an extremely broad sense. In the National Assembly which met in the
Assembly Hall of Berlin University on 12 May only the speaker of the Independent Social Democrats had spoken in favour of accepting the Versailles
terms, suggesting that the Assembly be content to await the world revolution,
which was already on the march. All the other parties, however, had agreed
with the 'unacceptable' verdict of the Prime Minister, Scheidemann, who had
cried out with great feeling that he hoped the hand might wither that so
fettered Germany – in other words, the hand that signed this treaty. Reading
today the various assessments of what was imposed on Germany in the
Versailles compendium of 440 Articles, we can see that there is a considerable difference of opinion depending on whether the assessor was writing
before or *after* the Second World War: the immediate effects of renewed defeat
have redefined to a considerable extent the criteria by which Versailles was
previously judged.

The conditions were indeed hard beyond any doubt. But the war also had
been hard and long. Hard, too, had been the conditions which initially almost
the entire German public and latterly a number of stalwart proponents of a
victorious peace had meant to impose on their defeated foes. And, finally,
what had been imposed on a defeated Russia only a year before in the Treaty
of Brest-Litovsk, and on a defeated Rumania in the Peace of Bucharest, was
also hard. The hostile states, especially France, which had suffered severe
destruction, saw no reason to arrange matters to suit German wishes and
needs. It is true that the spectre of Bolshevism, which threatened the entire
capitalist world, had just raised its head, but it was still regarded as a transient
phenomenon. Unlike in the years following 1945, the threat of Bolshevism
was still too weak to secure mitigating concessions for Germany in return
for serving as a bulwark against it. The danger of part of Germany becoming
Bolshevist was for a time acute, and the risk of a consequent Allied invasion
followed by a dissolution of the Reich added to the risk of the country's
disintegration and restricted still further Germany's freedom to act at home
and abroad. After 1918 the existence of the Soviet regime tended to have
almost exclusively negative effects on Germany.

The measures imposed in the following areas were drastic. First, the Allies
demanded almost total disarmament and reduction of the army and navy: the

army to 100,000 men, the navy to 15,000. Their equipment was specified down to the last round of small-arms ammunition and reduced to the arsenal of an army involved in a civil war, without aircraft, submarines, tanks and so on. Second, the Rhineland was to be demilitarized and occupied for a five-year period. Third, besides a long list of payments in kind, Germany had to agree to sign a 'blank cheque' in recognition of the obligation to make good war damage suffered by Germany's enemies, to a total amount that would not be fixed by an inter-allied Commission until May 1921 (because the Allied statesmen had been unable to agree on a compromise between French demands and American reservations). Finally, there were to be major territorial losses.

That Alsace-Lorraine was lost to Germany had already been laid down in the Fourteen Points and the armistice. That colonies would also be lost was to be expected. But that *all* of Germany's colonial possessions would be demanded could not have been deduced from the fifth of Wilson's Points. Given the colonial practices of other foreign powers, it was rendered hardly more plausible by the flimsy justification given in the accompanying note to the effect that Germany could no longer be 'entrusted with responsibility for training and educating the population' because of the way it had run its colonies. Moreover, further concessions, justified by the right of nations to self-determination, were proposed, which affected Germany's vital interests in the east.

The provinces of Posen and West Prussia, apart from minor remnants, were to be ceded to the new Poland created by the Germans as a defence against Russia; thus, Poland gained the access to the sea promised in Wilson's Fourteen Points. This dismemberment of a state's territory, unprecedented in the world at that time, was calculated to demonstrate to any German who cared to glance at a map showing the 'Polish corridor' separating East Prussia from the remainder of the Reich the scandalous nature of this *Diktat*. Moreover, plebiscites were proposed for parts of West Prussia, for southern East Prussia and (the only mitigation of the original conditions which had been achieved in Versailles) for Upper Silesia, of which a small strip of territory, the so-called *Hultschiner Ländchen*, was to be immediately ceded to Czechoslovakia. The East Prussian territory north of the Memel was also lost without a plebiscite. Following a period of Allied administration this 'Memel territory' was annexed by Lithuania via a military *coup* in 1923. Finally, plebiscites were to be held in North Schleswig in Denmark's favour (conceded in 1864 to Austria, the victorious ally at that time, but later redeemed), and in the districts of Eupen and Malmédy in favour of Belgium.

If the right of nations to self-determination was taken into account right down to county (*Landkreis*) level at the expense of Germany, this principle was non-existent wherever it would have ruled in favour of Germany. A union with the German territories of Austria, which was unanimously desired by both parties, was expressly prohibited. After all, Germany's enemies had not fought a war and made sacrifices only to end up by turning Little Germany into Greater Germany. Politically, it was all too understandable. In the era of absolutism the blatant struggle for power and possession was tricked out, at best, with legalistic arguments. But an age of national wars required that certain moral principles be assumed, and these principles tended to collide violently when it came to the actual facts of politics and the psychology of the nations concerned. In the matter of self-determination, as elsewhere, the party which came off worst in any given case was bound to see these principles as pure hypocrisy and a source of grievance: this was a price that had to be paid.

The widespread indignation over the 'unacceptable' treaty had in the meantime given way to calmer considerations. Of course, the *Diktat* could be turned down. But what would happen then? The total occupation and presumably even the dismemberment of the Reich – quite apart from the fact that the wartime blockade, which had merely been eased during the armistice, would once again strike the starving nation with its full force. Was this not simply to play into the hands of Clemenceau, Germany's bitterest enemy in the victors' ranks? There was no unanimity, however, amongst those who were to take the decision, the parties of the Weimar coalition. Differences of opinion cut clean across all the parliamentary groups. The Social Democrat Scheidemann, the Democrat Preuss and the leader of the German delegation, Brockdorff-Rantzau, who belonged to no party – i.e. the Prime Minister, the Minister of the Interior and the Foreign Minister – were all against signing. So was the President of the Reich, Ebert, although not as decisively so as his colleagues.

The cabinet and the coalition split on this issue. Scheidemann, who had taken up a position unambiguously opposed to signing, resigned on 20 June after majorities in the Centre and Social Democratic parliamentary parties had voted to accept the treaty with only two reservations. Ebert, who would likewise have liked to resign, was persuaded to stay at his post. He appointed Gustav Bauer from his own party, hitherto Minister of Labour, as Chancellor. The cabinet included only representatives of the Social Democrats and the Centre Party. The Democratic Party, who feared the rivalry of the People's Party on their right as much as the Social Democrats feared the Independents on their left, refused to join the cabinet or to sanction the peace treaty. In October, once the danger had passed, they rejoined the government. The Foreign Minister, Count Brockdorff-Rantzau, who was close to the Democrats, resigned and was replaced by the Social Democrat Hermann Müller. The most powerful force in Bauer's cabinet was the Finance Minister, Erzberger, of the Centre Party. This party's role as the leading party of government began at this point and was to end only with Brüning in 1932.

The National Assembly had to take a decision on 22 June. Remarkably enough, in Weimar as in Germany generally, most of the indignation was directed not against the really drastic terms of the treaty but against two points of honour. This well-nigh Gallic reaction was based partly on the fact that in 1919 Germany still cherished the illusion that the peace treaty was not meant seriously, that things are never as bad as they seem, that the whole thing was nothing but rhetoric and threats. It was also based on the fact that two eminently practical issues were linked to these points of honour: on the one hand, relations with the Republic's allies in officer's uniform; on the other, the question of reparations. Two articles in particular provoked vehement protests: the first was Article 228, which called for the extradition for trial by Allied courts martial of all Germans identified by the Allies as having been charged with 'acts in contravention of the laws and usages of war'. The preceding article demanded the extradition of Wilhelm II, who was to be tried by an inter-Allied court. Since this demand was addressed to the neutral Dutch government, it was of a purely Platonic nature. The second article was Article 231, the famous 'war-guilt' paragraph.

The very fact that this paragraph was not embodied in the preamble or immediately following it, but was given such an astronomical serial number and almost hidden in the undergrowth of the treaty, suggests that it originally had no programmatic significance. It was merely the introduction to Part 8, 'Reparations', and was meant to justify the latter. This, too, was part of what was required by modern, democratic, international etiquette. Ever since there had been wars, the defeated party had always had to pay some tribute to the victor. This was regarded as a matter of course and no one had thought it necessary to offer or to seek a particular moral justification. Now things were different. There were to be no more tributes. In his programmatic speech of 11 February 1918 Wilson had expressly proclaimed peace without annexations (apart from Alsace-Lorraine, the injustice of 1871), but also without forced levies. 'Reparations' were quite a different matter, however: they presumed an element of guilt. Of course, the Allies were perfectly free to suggest that Germany alone was responsible for the war, and the rest could have been left to the historians of both camps, who have pounced on this problem with unflagging zeal, right up to the present day. It was absurd, however, and quite unnecessary to demand a written confession from the German people that they had started a war which had been forced on the Allies – even if the demand might not have been all that ill-intentioned to start with.

The German peace delegation had protested vigorously against Article 231. A memorandum by a team of legal experts was followed by a reply in the form of an Allied note. This dispute inflated the Article into an issue of principle, which it was to remain throughout the fourteen Weimar years in the form of the 'war-guilt lie' so bitterly contested by the conservative and

nationalist factions. The paragraphs referring to war criminals did not have
the same long-term effect, but in 1919 their implications were, if anything,
even more explosive. The government had to take particularly careful account
of the sensitivities of the generals, and of the entire officer corps, on whom
the Republic depended for support. Besides, the government would need
them and the 400,000 or so other ranks who remained, as long as repudiation
of the treaty and a resumption of hostilities was a matter of debate.

The high command – still represented by Hindenburg – was questioned
by the government about the possibility of military resistance to invading
Entente troops and replied in the negative. The conditions of the armistice
had made absolutely sure that the Reich could not resort to armed force
again. Hindenburg's additional remark that honourable defeat was nevertheless preferable to such a shameful peace certainly embodied the heroic note
that well became a military commander with no political responsibilities, but
it could scarcely serve as an appropriate guideline for the authorities in
whose hands the responsibility for the decision actually lay. At that point
most of the other generals favoured rejection of the treaty and a resumption
of hostilities in the east. They dreamed of reconquering the province of
Posen, which had already been handed over to Poland, and of pursuing even
more ambitious goals, while in the west there were utterly Utopian hopes of
a disintegration of the Entente, mutinies and revolutions. All this had
prompted the Quartermaster-General, Groener, to cast his influence into the
scale in favour of accepting the peace treaty. Thus military circles were finally
prepared to accept the Versailles conditions – albeit minus the 'shameful
paragraphs'.

On 22 June the National Assembly authorized the government to sign the
peace treaty by 237 to 138 votes – with the reservation that the two
contentious issues be omitted. Apart from a few delegates, most of them
absentees, the two socialist parties, the Centre and six Democrats voted in
favour, the majority of the Democrats and the entire right wing voted
against. If there had been tentative signs that the Allies were not prepared
to let the treaty fall through on account of a couple of reservations on the
German side, they were not exactly encouraged by two events that became
known at the very moment that Germany had declared she was ready to
accept the treaty. These were the scuttling in Scapa Flow of the German fleet
that had been interned after the armistice and was to be surrendered under
the terms of the the treaty, and the burning in front of the Berlin Arsenal of
captured French ensigns, which were also due to be returned under the peace
treaty. At any rate, the Allies presented an ultimatum demanding signature
within the originally stipulated period, of which – as they were careful to
point out – a mere twenty-four hours remained.

The ultimatum caused considerable consternation in Weimar. The attitude
of the military was especially critical. It was only after long hesitation, with

grave misgivings and on condition that the paragraphs relating to war guilt and extradition should not be accepted, that they had abandoned their plan of heroic resistance to the end under the slogan 'Death rather than slavery'. Now they threatened openly to quit the service if the treaty was signed without being amended. Indeed, they put it even more plainly: the commander of the troops stationed around Weimar stated bluntly that in the event of the treaty being signed unamended it would not be possible for the troops to protect the National Assembly and the government. Ebert turned to the high command. 'As a German, and not as Quartermaster-General', Groener advised the President to sign. During this critical telephone conversation Hindenburg 'quietly left the room', as he had done in Spa on 10 November in the preceding year. He thus left his leading colleague to act the part of the 'black sheep' and retained his mythical heroism.

This meant nevertheless that the military leaders at least consented to the signing of the treaty without launching some kind of putsch against the Republic. They had thought mainly of setting up a military dictatorship with Noske, the generals' Social Democrat intermediary, as a sign of respectability. An address unanimously approved by the National Assembly appealed to the army's professional honour. The gamble came off: only one East Prussian general who shared the ambitions of Field-Marshal Yorck had to be placed on the retired list as a precaution.

Thus, on that 23 June, when the decision had to be taken, in the places where it mattered the view prevailed that the nation's existence and the unity of the Reich should not be put at risk for the sake of a couple of 'points of honour': after all, much weightier matters had had to be accepted. But even the parties which had been in favour of acceptance did not dare to vote expressly for the 'shameful paragraphs' in a new division. Instead, recourse was had to a trick by which the previous day's vote was deemed to authorize unconditional signing of the treaty without a further vote. The parties who had voted to reject the treaty made specific statements in which they credited the majority with acting from purely patriotic motives. For, in fact, no one was able and willing to accept responsibility for refusing to accept the peace treaty and the consequences that might then be expected. The fact that those who accepted it (and, after all, someone had to accept it) had reason to fear even then that it would be held against them, gave rise to dire forebodings. Five days later in Versailles the Foreign Minister, Müller, and the Transport Minister, Bell, on behalf of the other partner in the coalition, put their signatures to the treaty, which was to come into force after ratification by Germany and the three major Allied powers.

Of the 'shameful paragraphs', the 'war-guilt lie' became a dangerous explosive charge in the new structure of the Reich, while the extradition issue petered out shortly afterwards, in the winter of 1919/20, with a plain statement on the part of the Reich government that it was 'impossible' and an offer, accepted by the Allies, to have war criminals who had been identified by name, tried by a court of the Reich. A dozen cases in all were dealt with in a suitably desultory manner after May 1921 – the severest sentence passed being four years imprisonment in two cases – and the matter was then considered closed. The Allies were even prepared to turn a blind eye when the two men who had been sentenced to prison terms 'escaped' in a matter of weeks and were never recaptured.

In spite of sincere attempts to paint as black a picture as possible, Germany survived losing the war surprisingly well in *economic* terms, although the consequences included the amputation of 13 per cent of her territory, including valuable areas of good agricultural land as well as industrial complexes. In *psychological* terms this was less true. The peace treaties imposed in 1918 on her defeated foes, Russia and Rumania, in Brest-Litovsk and Bucharest, were now forgotten by the Germans. Forgotten, too, was the wartime assumption that at some point Germany's defeated enemies would have to pay the costs of the war. That had been obvious to everyone at the time; many people had said so and the entire financing of the war had been very largely based on that assumption. (The former financial autonomy of the individual states may have had something to do with this.) For instance, Wilhelm II had drawn up accounts in 1917, according to which England and the United States would each have had to contribute 30,000 million dollars, France 40,000 million francs and Italy 10,000 million lire.

But that would have been a totally different matter. In that way the whole world would have shared Germany's expenditure on the war. Now, however, Germany was being asked to pay the bill for the rest of the world. This, at least, was how it seemed to the average German. His adversaries' generously charitable estimate of the damage inflicted on their civilian populations (which included amongst other things the maintenance claims of military victims of the war and their dependants) did little to make him think otherwise. The reparations issue thus turned out to be not only the most awkward in a technical sense, but also the most dangerous problem for the stability of the Weimar constitutional order that was inherited as a legacy of Versailles. When the colonial losses and the territorial wounds had ceased to smart and had more or less healed, when the occupation of the Rhineland was coming to an end, when the nation had somehow come to terms with disarmament, had in part evaded it or was still negotiating on the issue, although all these topics still served as subjects for agitation; it was clear that no major progress was likely to be achieved on any of them. It was reparations, however, the German 'colony', the 'enslavement of generations to come', that offered the anti-democratic right their unfailingly effective lever against the state. In the final analysis, as it happens, Germany did not pay all that much by way of reparations – at any rate in proportion to the demands made by her enemies.

3

Via the Kapp putsch to the first Reichstag elections

In the second half of 1919 the burden of reparations was only one of two major financial worries facing the Reich, but it was obvious that it was bound to aggravate considerably an urgent topical problem: the payment of Germany's own war debt. As already mentioned, the first half of the war had been entirely, and the second half (when at least war gains had been realized) very largely, financed by loans and treasury bonds at the expense of the country's future. Consequently, at the end of the war the Reich had debts of 153,000 million marks, i.e. thirty times the pre-war figure and three times the nation's gross national product before the war. There were no vanquished enemies on to whom this burden might be shifted. An attempt had been made to do this in Brest-Litovsk, where Russia had been required to pay 8,000 million roubles, but this could no longer be enforced. As a result, the Republic had to set about raising funds from its own people. The new Finance Minister, Matthias Erzberger, therefore aimed not only to balance the budget, but also to produce a surplus that would pay off these debts and provide for reparations. His stringent taxation policy did have a relatively powerful impact on lower-income groups, but it was mainly aimed at the property-owning classes and those who had grown rich during the war. He introduced, for instance, as a revolutionary and enduring innovation, a uniform and progressive income tax, as well as death duties. But Erzberger failed – mainly for two reasons.

In the first place, his measures were based on the assumption that high moral standards would apply in matters of taxation, but there were no such standards in a nation which had been shocked by defeat and which believed its last reserves were threatened by a sudden and drastic flood of taxation. In the face of Erzberger's rigorous legislation and in spite of strict controls on the export of capital, money fled abroad or else looked for other ways to evade the state's grasp.

The second main assumption on which Erzberger's policy was based – and also its main aim – was stability of the currency. Already during the war inflation had set in. The printing presses, working at top speed, had increased the circulation of paper money from 2,000 to 22,000 million marks, but this increase was not matched by anything like an adequate supply of goods. By the end of the war the mark was worth little more than half its peacetime value, and the process had continued at an increased rate in 1919. The abolition of wartime economic controls caused the purchasing power of the mark to fall still further in relation to the true situation, while the peacetime economy called for more and more credit, since the general depression and insecurity led to an alarming decline in productivity. Major imports were required to stimulate the economy and to feed the population. Since reserves of gold and foreign currency were inadequate, these had to be paid for with an increasing volume of paper marks, which were looked on with suspicion and accepted with reluctance. Thus, the country's debt had steadily increased and money circulation had risen correspondingly to 45,000 million marks. The real purchasing power of the mark had fallen to one-third by the middle of the year; by the end of 1919 it was down to one-eighth.

It was believed that this process could not only be halted, but – remarkable illusion – actually reversed. These ideas about the financial consequences of a lost war, clearly seen nowadays to be Utopian, turned out to be erroneous, although the first Social Democratic Minister of Finance, Wissell, subscribed to them. This was the second factor that ruined Erzberger's tax reform. Indeed, his measures, which were intended to stabilize the currency without driving the state into bankruptcy, served to encourage inflation and make it more palatable to the wealthy classes who were now being so heavily taxed, for it lightened the burden of all debts, including those which were owed to the state. Not only was the yield of Erzberger's taxation reduced by inflation, its direction, the proposed equitable distribution of liabilities, was also fundamentally changed. The capital levy known as the *Reichsnotopfer*, for instance, the most controversial of Erzberger's taxes, turned out, thanks to inflation, to be a mere bagatelle in the case of large private fortunes which were intricate and took a considerable time to assess; the smaller property-owners, however, could be dealt with rapidly and were consequently bled white.

The stability of the currency also presupposed that the hostile powers would collect reparations on a scale which matched Germany's ability to pay. It is true that the actual payments played only a small part in the collapse of the German currency. Nevertheless, the payments schedule for 1921 had an equivalent psychological effect and, along with other factors, helped to foster the impression that any attempt to stabilize the currency and manage the budget was illusory. People preferred to follow a policy of *laissez-faire*, taking the primrose path to the printing press that had eased the burden of public debt hitherto and was to do so again in the future. There was still another factor. The surrender of the mercantile fleet, the loss of overseas investments, the continuing stagnation in foreign trade, problems in converting the economy together with reduced productivity and a number of other factors created an economic emergency and paralysis that suggested the tempting solution of inflation. The consequent money surplus not only led to a false economic boom in the private sector at home; thanks to the international undervaluation of a depreciating mark combined with the exploitation of a vast pool of available, and hence cheap, labour following demobilization, it led also to a resumption of exports at dumping prices.

In the end inflation seemed the lesser of two evils to the government and to almost all the other institutions which had a voice in deciding monetary policy – the Reichsbank in particular. Apart from providing a convenient method of financing the expenditure of the Reich by means of the printing press, inflation obviously guaranteed a high rate of employment and equally obviously dampened the revolutionary mood of the working population. A consistent policy of stability would have brought about a marked rise in unemployment, at least for a certain time, and consequently would have led in all probability to further attempts at revolution on the part of the left. For these reasons the government refrained from pursuing a vigorous anti-inflationary policy and Erzberger's promising initiatives were watered down. Far from controlling inflation, the Finance Minister's budgetary and taxation policies merely helped, as did the inflation itself, to discredit the Republic, especially in middle-class circles. They also served to render even more obnoxious a name which was in any case incriminated by the signature at Compiègne. To make matters worse, the republican government did not dare to open the nation's eyes to the full extent of the catastrophic financial and economic situation. Instead, even in republican quarters, the pretext of reparations was often seized upon in order to shift abroad the blame for the financial disaster of the war that the old regime had lost. This kind of cover-up was in part motivated by considerations of foreign policy, but there were also reasons for adopting it at home.

On 23 June advocates and opponents of the Versailles Treaty had credited each other with seeking the best interests of the Fatherland. However, this day was not to exert much influence on the style in which domestic politics were to be conducted in future. Quite the contrary: from then on the democratic Republic was exposed not only to assaults by its opponents on the left but had to contend with the even more embittered hostility of the right. Those who hitherto had taken cover behind the lesser evil of a parliamentary democracy for fear of a further advance of the revolution ventured forth once again, now that the middle-class Republic had been consolidated – although it rested on the goodwill of generals and officers who were at best reserved and uncommitted. They proceeded to pour scorn and contempt on the new state and, in its dismal situation, they found an increasing number of adherents who did not bother their heads with intricate reflections on why and wherefore. And so, from the summer of 1919, the political scene in Germany was dominated by incipient erosion of the parties who had put democracy into power and who had been given such a convincing mandate in the elections to the National Assembly only a few months previously.

Reasons for this have been given above. However, it was not only the receding revolutionary wave that was at work, washing back to the right – once the danger had passed – all those who had landed up with the democratic parties for fear of something worse. And neither was it only the effects of the calamities affecting money, the economy and employment. The third factor was the price the Republic now had to pay following Versailles for the widespread illusion of the past winter: that a lenient peace would be gained in exchange for the deposition of the old regime and the introduction of democracy *à la mode*. For the honest German the case was clear as day: the German people had been tempted into a trap by the carrot and now they were to feel the stick. But who had acted as the enemy's agent in this confidence trick? Who was to blame for the nation being duped in this way? Those Germans who had laboured to introduce democracy, of course. Weren't they the people who had worked to that end since halfway through the war? Had not the German people been systematically incited to violence? Had not the armies held their positions in enemy territory until the very end – 'undefeated in the field'? Had not even Russia finally been forced into submission and the stranglehold of a war on two fronts thus broken at last? Who, then, had the surrender of this army on his conscience – an army that had been victorious for four whole years?

It was on 18 November 1919 that Hindenburg launched the legend of the 'stab in the back'. In August the National Assembly had appointed a parliamentary committee of investigation to look into past events from the outbreak of war until its end, paying particular attention to the question of war guilt and the causes of Germany's defeat. Good Germans, of course, at once detected the odour of 'nest-fouling' in such questions. And Hindenburg was a very good German. He had been summoned before the committee in a roundabout way. The committee had wished to hear Ludendorff as a witness regarding the opening of unrestricted U-boat warfare. The 'Commander', as his followers called him, was determined to be questioned only in the company of his erstwhile chief, whose national prestige had not been in the least shaken. For, with a kind of peasant cunning, Hindenburg had contrived to let others risk their skins when unpleasant decisions had to be taken, especially at the end when things had turned particularly nasty.

Both generals were by now private individuals, for, in accordance with Article 160 of the Versailles Treaty, which required the disbanding of the General Staff, the supreme command of the army had resigned immediately the treaty was accepted. And so Hindenburg duly turned up – not to perform his civic duty, however, but to teach this riff-raff of a parliamentary committee a lesson. The committee included an Independent Socialist by the name of Cohn who had allegedly been given funds by the Soviet Embassy to foment a revolution and who had already been insulted more or less with impunity and to frantic applause from the right, by the former State Secretary Helfferich, now a rabid German Nationalist, when the latter gave evidence to the committee. Instead of answering questions, Hindenburg read out a written declaration culminating in a statement by an English general who was supposed to have said that the German army 'had been stabbed in the back'. Where the blame for that lay, the legendary hero of Tannenberg went on, was plain enough.

We still do not know who wrote the declaration that found its way into the Field-Marshal's pocket – presumably it was Helfferich or Ludendorff. The reference to the English general was also dubious: Sir Frederick Maurice, to whose interview with the *Neue Zürcher Zeitung* in December 1918 Hindenburg was alluding, had not used the phrase 'stab in the back' himself; it came from the general's interviewer. But what difference did that make? Cohn had wanted to sit in judgement on Hindenburg, and Hindenburg had given him the answer he deserved. The phrase, 'undefeated in the field', which Hindenburg had peddled surreptitiously ever since the end of October 1918, following Wilson's third note, and which Ebert also somewhat clumsily promoted in an address to troops returning to Berlin, had now been cast into a striking and rousing slogan. Hindenburg, as Groener saw him, 'although phlegmatic and indolent, was eager for glory', and he had now added a new page to his legend. As it turned out five years later he had also qualified himself as a presidential candidate for all those people who were 'sick of floppy hats' and wanted a president 'in a helmet'.

But the 'stab in the back' legend that was so soothing to an injured national self-esteem persisted. It was itself to stab in the back the state that had been forced on the German people, or that they had been persuaded to accept by democrats who had themselves been duped, or even by democratic traitors in league with the enemy following a contrived military defeat. If we wish to make a fair judgement of this endeavour simply to ignore the defeat, we have to bear in mind the situation in 1918. The dangerous stranglehold of a war on two fronts had just been broken with the overthrow of Germany's enemies in the east, so that she had both hands free to deal with her adversaries in the west, where her armies were stationed still 'deep in enemy territory', without a single foe on German soil or anywhere near it. Compare this with the total and undeniable military defeat of 1945.

At the end of the year the anti-republican right was considerably reinforced. Following the armistice in the east, German troops had remained in
areas hitherto occupied by the Russians. The conditions of the armistice had
indeed annulled the Treaty of Brest-Litovsk but had only foreseen a
temporary function for the German troops in the east as a bulwark against
Bolshevism. In the Polish sector of the new 'marginal states' the Poles
thought that, with Allied support, they could look after themselves, and on
the opposite side, towards the west, they immediately laid their hands on
what had formerly been Prussian territory. In the Baltic states, however, the
situation was different. There, German assistance was needed to foil the
intention of the Tsar's Bolshevist successors to reintegrate these states into
Russia. The troops of the old German army could not be retained for the
most part – being just as keen to return home as their colleagues elsewhere
– but they were replaced by volunteers recruited in the Reich who were
prepared to protect the eastern German provinces from a Bolshevik invasion
and to find new homes on the Baltic. Thousands poured into the 'Iron
Division' and the other volunteer corps and the influx could not be stemmed
even when the Baltic annexations turned out to be a mirage. For this was by
no means what the Allies had in mind. At their instigation the government
of the Reich forbade more – official – recruitment in May, and during the
summer ordered that the territories be evacuated.

In the Baltic states, however, this had no effect. Insisting that the promises
of land and settlement made by the new Estonian and Latvian administrations be kept, the volunteers stayed put and continued their private war, still
financed for some time by the German government and steadily reinforced
by recruits from the Reich. They hoped to slip through somehow between
the Entente and the Bolsheviks and to be rewarded by the grant of
settlement land. Perhaps they even hoped to restore the monarchies in Russia
as well as Germany from bases on the Baltic. For a long time the German
government could not make up its mind what to do. A number of government authorities in eastern Germany – even some which were under Social
Democratic control – openly backed the volunteer corps. Middle-class circles
even cherished the illusion that they could form a common front with the
English against Bolshevism and outflank the Allies, thus instantly improving
Germany's wretched situation abroad. Before the end of the year, however,
the Baltic illusions had faded. Following the defeat of the Bolsheviks and
intervention on a massive scale by the Allies in November, the nationalist
governments who had been protected by the volunteer corps no longer
needed the latter's services and they were forced to return to the Republic,
whether they liked it or not. They returned with the impression they had
been abandoned and betrayed – and with feelings that were far from friendly.

In the Reich the situation was still strained. On 13 January 1920, forty-two
left-socialist and Communist workers lay dead in front of the Reichstag,

where the National Assembly was still in session and dealing with the law on workers' councils in factories. The Prussian police had gone into action against a mass demonstration demanding powers for the councils that went beyond merely social legislation. The sole result of these attempts by the radical left to salvage what remained of the revolution in their sense was that the Majority Socialists – once more branded as 'murderers of the working class' – lost even more of their adherents. On the other hand, what seemed like never-ending campaigns by the mob drove the middle classes, who were anxious to maintain a newly restored social stability, into the arms of an increasingly mettlesome right.

The right and the left, who both gained through this political see-saw, were equally keen to put an end to the National Assembly and replace it with a newly elected Reichstag. The view on the right was that the Social Democrats would then finally vanish from the government and the situation would instantly improve. On the left they had the same idea, *mutatis mutandis*. The wishes of the coalition parties naturally tended in the opposite direction: they wanted to delay the elections until the autumn, after the harvest, when they might expect to profit from an improved supply situation. On 9 March they voted down a motion put by the Independent Socialists and backed by the Nationalists and the People's Party, calling for the dissolution of the Assembly by 1 May, elections to a Reichstag, and a presidential election by the whole nation as prescribed in the constitution, rather than by the National Assembly, as hitherto. A few days later, however, a series of events ensued which altered the situation: radical circles on the right reckoned that the Republic was ripe for violent overthrow.

What triggered it all off was largely the personal moral defeat of one of the most prominent representatives of the Republic. Matthias Erzberger, now Minister of Finance, had not been sparing in his criticism of the taxation policy of his imperial predecessors. In this connection his chief antagonist was Karl Helfferich, formerly head of the Treasury Department in Bethmann Hollweg's government and subsequently Home Secretary and Vice-Chancellor. Helfferich struck back: he felt in any case that his career as a statesman had been frustrated by the Republic in general and Erzberger in particular (at whose instigation he had been forced to surrender the Vice-Chancellorship to an elected member of parliament). In newspaper articles and in brochures he hurled a whole sheaf of accusations at the Minister. They ranged from the pernicious features of Erzberger's policies since the peace resolution, which had allegedly linked his name with Germany's shame, to accusations of personal enrichment. His aim was to force Erzberger to bring an action for slander which would give Helfferich the chance to reveal his opponent's past and his policies to the public gaze in every detail.

And Erzberger did sue him. The trial began in Berlin on 19 January. The Public Prosecutor had declared the public interest in the case and had undertaken the prosecution. From the outset Erzberger was at a disadvantage in the proceedings, which revolved around three of Helfferich's accusations: offences against propriety, habitual mendacity and the mingling of personal financial interests and political activities. The court, like almost all the Weimar courts, was against the Republic and the bench was prejudiced. The Protestant middle-class public were predominantly hostile to the Roman Catholic plaintiff – who had, moreover, put his name to the treaty signed in Compiègne. During the latter stages of the trial Erzberger was suffering from the effects of an attempted assassination: following a court session a discharged ensign had wounded him with two pistol shots in chest and lungs – the first consequence of Helfferich's rabble-rousing slogan: 'Get rid of Erzberger!' The defendant succeeded in proving certain trivial irregularities on Erzberger's part – little wonder, given the painstaking scrutiny of the man's whole life. The Minister had indeed been somewhat lax and lacked sound judgement in money matters. Besides, his adversaries carried on the fight with every conceivable means. With the aid of various civil servants they had even contrived to steal Erzberger's tax return from the Revenue Office and then published it. At first sight it appeared to prove tax evasion by a public advocate of rigorous morality in taxation matters and the author of draconic tax legislation. The fact that the accusation later turned out to be unfounded made less impression politically than the sensation originally caused by the suspicion.

During the course of the trial the Public Prosecutor practically went over to the defendant's side. This move made a profound impact on the public, because – although formally correct – it would have been unthinkable in the case of a minister under the old regime. On 12 March Helfferich was fined 300 marks. The paltriness of this penalty was justified in the court's view by the fact that the defendant 'had managed in essence to prove the truth of his allegations'. 'In essence' was, admittedly, an exaggeration, but under the three heads stated by the prosecution the court had found Helfferich's allegations justified in sixteen out of a host of instances. Erzberger's political career was finished. He had taken leave from his ministerial post when his tax return was published; after the verdict he resigned, in order to devote himself to clearing his name – which, up to point, he was able to do.

Of far more significance than his personal fiasco was the setback the Republic suffered in the Moabit court on that 12 March. Here, after all, it was not simply two hostile individuals who were crossing swords, but – and this was the general understanding – the *ancien régime* and the new state. These two entities had never confronted each other in an election, because the National Assembly had been elected as a choice between a democratic and a socialist Republic. This was the first public encounter between 'yesterday' and 'today' – and 'today' had not emerged entirely unsullied. The Republic's adversaries on the right believed that their hour had come.

On the day after the verdict was announced the naval brigade of Captain Ehrhardt marched through the Brandenburg Gate and occupied the administrative quarter of Berlin. As these things happen, by sheer chance – at least so he stated later in court – General Ludendorff happened to be strolling past the Brandenburg Gate just before seven o'clock that morning. Colonel Bauer, once the Quartermaster-General's right-hand man, had also played a leading part in the enterprise. Throughout Germany all those of a like mind sniffed the coming dawn. Shortly afterwards, the renowned nationalist poet Dietrich Eckart flew in from Munich, having been provided with facilities by the army authorities there. In his company was the publicity agent of a local nationalist splinter group, already calling itself a party, which had just held its first meeting: Corporal Adolf Hitler.

Of course, this action was not just a consequence of the Erzberger verdict; it had been prepared long in advance. Besides hostility to the Republic and indignation over extradition, which was still a burning issue, it was above all an expression of the dissatisfaction of the officer corps and concern for their jobs: some 15,000 officers had already been forced to retire, and the same fate awaited another 5,000 during the next stage stipulated by the Versailles Treaty, which in the meantime had reduced the armed forces to 200,000 men. The return and disbanding of the Baltic volunteer corps had contributed further to their anger. The Ehrhardt brigade was among the units affected by the demobilization order. The men had refused to obey and had been backed by the army commander responsible for the Berlin area. On 9 March they had called on Ebert and Noske to dismiss the army's Chief of Staff, now the highest ranking military leader established in the Ministry of War, and a man who had remained loyal to the constitution. This demand had long been on the cards, so it came as no surprise when it was reported during the night of 13 March that the brigade had left the Döberitz training area and started to march on Berlin. An admiral had already been sent to pacify the rebels, and now a couple of generals were despatched – to no effect. The situation became increasingly dramatic in the course of the night.

Noske, the Minister responsible for the army, summoned the leading officers of his Ministry in order to discuss defensive measures, for it was now clear that there would be an armed clash. This, however, was the occasion on which the famous words were spoken: 'The troops will not fire on one another.' The man who said them was General von Seeckt, head of the *Truppenamt*, the successor to the disbanded General Staff. With the exception of the Chief of Staff, General Reinhardt, all the officers agreed with Seeckt. Thus, the units of the Reichswehr, which the government had formed to meet the threat from the left, refused to act against a threat from the right. During that same night the government fled to Dresden before the advancing naval brigade, and then, since the local commander of the Reichswehr, Maercker, was not entirely reliable, moved on to Stuttgart.

In the meantime the new 'Chancellor' Kapp ruled in Berlin. For a new political leader had also been found. Dr Wolfgang Kapp, a rabid Pan-German, together with Admiral Tirpitz, had founded the fanatically patriotic and annexionist Fatherland Party; he was now a member of the People's Party (DVP). In East Prussia, where he had been regional director in the provincial administration in 1906, he had played a major role. The leading part he played in the putsch was an expression of the special demands of East Prussia which went as far as regional autonomy. These demands had been put forward in Berlin in the weeks just past, with reference to the geographical separation of East Prussia from the Reich, but they had not been accepted.

There was also a new cabinet and, as the Commander-in-Chief of the army, the former commander of the Reichswehr Command Group I, General Baron von Lüttwitz. The Kapp government was recognized east of the Elbe, in Silesia, in Pomerania and East Prussia. In the north, local Reichswehr generals seized power, and in Mecklenburg they even forced the legitimate authorities to resign. In a number of other places too there were troops and authorities who favoured Kapp. The naval staff, for instance, also put themselves under the new government – albeit with the result that the ratings placed their officers under arrest. In spite of this kind of patchy support, Kapp and his friends failed: the amateurish enterprise, which had not been politically prepared for, lasted just four days.

There were two reasons for its failure. One of them was a general strike by workers throughout the country. It was called by various organizations ranging from the Independent Socialist Party through the Trades Union Congress to the Democratic Party in response to the fugitive legal government's appeal to resist and disobey orders issued and measures taken by the leaders of the putsch. That the workers heeded the government and resisted the forces of reaction is not surprising. What *is* astonishing is that the government's appeal was also heeded by a large section of the middle-classes, who did not take Kapp's undertaking seriously. Most damaging was that the civil servants in Berlin went on strike, an unprecedented event in Germany. The Kapp government was left hanging in mid-air; it did not have the hands to carry out its orders and decrees, nor did it have the money, for the Reichsbank refused to issue cash without a constitutionally warranted signature. Kapp had been able to gain the support of individual military units, but he was not backed by the leadership of the Reichswehr. The men gathered around Seeckt may have refused to help the democratic government, but that did not mean they were prepared to support Kapp's crazy escapade. They smiled indulgently and watched all the fuss about Kapp with a kind of benevolent neutrality.

This wait-and-see attitude revealed the shaky footing on which the democratic Republic stood; on the other hand, it is what saved it. This was the first occasion on which Seeckt's ideal of an ostensibly 'apolitical' Reichswehr was manifested, together with that claim to undisputed leadership which the General was to express three years later in the words, 'Nobody can carry out a putsch in Germany but me.' But he never did carry out his putsch, not even on that occasion, and certainly not such a bungled affair as Kapp's putsch. Of the two black, white and red parties even, only the German Nationalists raised their hands to swear allegiance to Kapp. The government in Stuttgart could even afford to turn down offers of mediation – from No-man's-land as it were – from General Maercker and from the Vice-Chancellor and Minister of Justice, Schiffer, the only member of the legitimate government to remain in Berlin. On 17 March Kapp realized the game was up, and Ehrhardt's men retreated to Döberitz.

The failure of the Kapp putsch did not help, however, to stabilize the Republic. This was because of the consequences that followed. The general strike had been so startlingly effective that its elated instigators still believed, even in 1932, that they were holding up their sleeve a trump card which would protect them from any danger from the right. But it was easier to call a general strike than to call it off again. After all, the Independents and the Communists had not joined in simply in order to put the Weimar coalition government back in power once more and have everything the same as it had been. In the Ruhr a Red Army several divisions strong arose and occupied several towns. The Social Democrat Carl Severing, appointed Reich Commissioner, tried in vain to persuade them to lay down their arms by promises of an amnesty. The ambiguous attitude of local army commanders and the advent of various Free Corps leaders during the days of the Kapp putsch hardly made these offers palatable to the working class.

There were outrages of the sort common in civil war, especially against recalcitrant officials. Starting on 2 April Reichswehr units under the command of General Watter began to move into the Ruhr. They included Kapp formations who had only a few days previously rebelled against the state and who had returned to 'the ground of the constitution' only after the failure of the *coup*. The workers' forces were suppressed with considerable bloodshed. The campaign had a sequel, for the entry of Reichswehr troops into the demilitarized zone gave France an initial pretext to impose sanctions: French troops marched into the Frankfurt and Darmstadt area and occupied it temporarily. Although it did not have the same kind of repercussions abroad, the Communist domination of the border areas of Saxony and Thuringia which followed the Kapp era was no less replete with acts of terrorism committed by both sides. It was here that Max Hölz for the last time declared a Soviet Republic on German soil: it, too, was suppressed by the Reichswehr and Free Corps but only after prolonged and bloody fighting.

The political upshot of all these actions was that further sections of the nation were alienated from the democratic centre and driven to the right or the left for fear of the other extreme. In the Social Democratic camp an attempt was made to stop this drift away from the centre: in a sharply critical speech attacking the Reichswehr Scheidemann brought about the downfall of his party colleague Noske, who had to pay the price for the unreliability of the pampered officer corps. Opposition within the party had long attacked his policy towards the Free Corps and the Reichswehr in a series of votes of no confidence. Under the pressure of agitation from the socialist left Noske's party stopped his parliamentary career. The result was that the Social Democratic Party – apart from states such as Prussia – was not in a position to train competent leaders and, following the resignation of the People's Deputies, was led by mediocre personalities. In Noske it lost one of its remaining major political talents and was obliged to leave the vital Reichswehr Ministry to the bourgeois parties for lack of a successor to this demanding post. There was a further consequence. The beginnings of co-operation between the workers and the army, although not viewed with much cordiality by either side, had been achieved in the alliance between Ebert and Groener on 10 November 1918. The process had been continued through Noske's policy, but it had been too indulgent to the army for his party comrades to stomach. This now turned out to be a political dead-end, with long-term consequences.

The integration of the armed forces, initially from March 1919 as the 'provisional' and under the Defence Law of spring 1921 as the established Reichswehr, was a central issue in the stabilization of the new order. It was essentially a matter for the Majority Social Democrats as the major political factor in the first years of the Republic. Reluctance to launch a revolution had prevented the formation of a revolutionary workers' army, while pressure from the left had stopped the gradual reconstruction of armed forces imbued with the republican spirit and had either left or returned control to the old officer corps of the imperial era. This being so, it was an essential precondition for the success of this republican experiment that the newly formed army, and in particular its leaders, should be prepared to change their views and their entire way of thinking in a democratic and republican sense.

That this would not be easy for them was obvious from the very beginning. In the Empire the officer had belonged to a class that was privileged – not materially, but in terms of social prestige. The actual or imagined values and precepts of this class had also in large measure set the standards of civilian life. It was less the actual military might of Germany that had earned her the reputation of militarism throughout the world than this domination of civilian life by serving and reserve officers and, on a lower level, the associated image of the Prussian non-commissioned officer in factory and family. In return for the unprecedented esteem accorded to military uniforms an especially distinctive relationship of mutual dependence with the monarchical head of state had been developed. The king's authority was based on the army, but the authority of the army was equally dependent on the monarchy and guided by it. This whole system had now collapsed. Would it now prove possible to substitute the colourless and impersonal middle-class, Social Democratic Republic for the colourful personality of the monarch as one of the partners in this bond of loyalty?

It is true that the army and the officer corps had been so inflated by the demands of the war that it ought to have been possible to find and filter out new cadres who were at least not resistant to the new order, eliminating those elements who were unacceptable in a republican sense, now that the forces were being brought back to a peacetime footing (and, indeed, to the considerably reduced peacetime footing demanded by the victorious powers). However, the personnel available to the new armed forces after the ending of wartime mobilization were recruited from the same social classes as the old army. On the other hand, the workers and the Social Democrats now had to pay the price for having left defence policy entirely to those in power during the imperial era. They suddenly found themselves faced with a new task without any cogent notion of how to tackle it.

The idea that it might have been better to do without this army altogether is appealing in its logic. Numerically weak and practically disarmed, surrounded by heavily armed neighbours, the army made no military sense in any case: it was of no use in foreign policy and at home it was a liability. It might have been better to make do with a politically reliable police force designed to meet internal needs which would not have been dependent on the military experts of the old army. But on closer examination this turns out to be merely a bloodless theory, divorced from what was feasible at the time. It would simply not have been possible for any party or any politician to renounce voluntarily the remnant of an army that Germany was permitted. And if the army was to be retained then that army must be as effective as possible, in spite of – or precisely because of – its weakness. The best, and moreover the most readily available soldiers, however, came from the social class from which they had always come. And the best and most expert officers, who could be recruited most rapidly and needed no training, were in fact the old officers.

If the old leaders were thus put back in the saddle on the army side, while the other side retained its traditional distrust, their co-operation could be no more than a temporary alliance for purely practical purposes. The fact that the Allies, fearing a repetition of Scharnhorst's so-called *Krümpersystem* of short-term conscripts, had imposed on the defeated Reich a professional army of long-service soldiers, served only to block any development in the direction of a people's army. As things had turned out, any attempt to bridge the gap between the working masses and an aristocratic and middle-class army was bound to be so difficult that it would succeed only in the course of a calm and untroubled process of development and under the auspices of a confident Social Democratic regime.

The Social Democrats were pulled hither and thither, however, between the effort to develop the coalition they had formed with bourgeois forces to the right of them and the fear of being overrun by the radicals on their left. They were consequently virtually incapable of acting, too unsure of themselves and too weak to act as an integrating factor *vis-à-vis* an officer class whose self-confidence had been signally restored. With the benefit of hindsight it can be seen that the one attempt that had some chance of success was doomed to failure. Because Noske had to lean across a gulf that was as broad as it had ever been, he lost his footing on the Social Democratic ground, slipped and fell. It was not Noske who integrated the generals into the Republic, but the generals who integrated Noske into the Reichswehr, until he figured against his will as a potential military dictator in various plans for a putsch. In fact, he would have been no more than a proletarian screen.

The Kapp putsch – an anti-Noske putsch – did at least bring the Republic the advantage that it sealed the fate of those military circles who believed they could simply turn the clock back and restore the monarchy together with their bouquet of social privileges. On the other hand, the new Reichswehr, which had failed to serve as the Republic's shield, was discredited in the eyes of those classes of the population who were committed to democracy, especially the workers who were loyal to the constitution. Moreover, when Noske fell, the Chief of Staff, the one general who had been prepared to oppose Kapp and his men, gave up and resigned. His successor was appointed by the Minister of Justice, Schiffer, the only minister to stay in Berlin, who had got on quite well with Kapp; for that reason he lost his post a few days later in a government reshuffle. His nominee was that other general, Hans von Seeckt, who had suggested that the troops would not fire on each other – or, to be more precise; government troops would not fire on their comrades, the mutineers.

This change had a deeper significance: Reinhardt's advice had indeed been true to the constitution, but it was very probably unrealistic. Seeckt's chilly refusal presumably was more in keeping with the true state of affairs. Nor was it the case that Seeckt had collaborated with Kapp's people. He had handed in his resignation, had granted himself leave and had gone home. For he did not care in the least for Kapp's operation, believing it to be, at the least, ill-timed, and he was personally on bad terms with a number of those involved, including Ludendorff. He had no wish to overthrow the Republic, but on the other hand a civil war, a 'pitched battle in front of the Brandenburg Gate' between troops who had only recently been fighting side by side against a common foe, did not seem worthwhile to him either – and it was not to seem worthwhile to him at any time in the future.

With Seeckt, whose appointment was confirmed by Ebert only after prolonged hesitation, the watchword in the Reichswehr was 'wait and see'. Those concerned were too realistic to believe in a return to the old order, but they were also too aristocratic to commit themselves to a Republic of the *petite bourgeoisie* and the proletariat. What mattered was to build up the Reichswehr on the old Prussian lines but, for the foreseeable future at any rate, to renounce political ambitions and to steer clear of the Free Corps and their predilection for the putsch. Thus, the Republic would be recognized as a fact of life, but the Reichswehr would not be implicated in its 'dirty' politics. The upshot was a political vacuum inwardly dedicated to old traditions and the old authoritarian state, a more or less autonomous 'state within a state'. While not exactly hostile to the actual state, the Republic, it had no liking for it; it was formally incorporated in it certainly, but *de facto* on a voluntary basis only, as a kind of provisional coalition partner, committed in the final analysis solely to a vague idea of a Reich beyond the Republic.

The Reichswehr thus practised a kind of contemptuous loyalty. It was reliable, as far as its weakness permitted, against an external enemy, even more reliable against the inner enemy from the left – but against those from the right: well, that remained to be seen. The intention was to be 'apolitical', but this applied absolutely only to the individual soldier and officer and was confined, as far as the leadership was concerned, to minor everyday issues. As far as major matters were concerned, in foreign as well as domestic policy, the army command certainly wished to have a finger in the pie. Moreover, an 'apolitical' stance of that kind, a sort of neutrality towards one's own state, by no means excluded manifold bonds of cordial sympathy with the black, white and red opponents of the Republic. One would have to wait and see. It was a matter of concentrating on the military tasks in hand and training core units for a new trial of strength which would be bound to lead sooner or later to a revival of Germany's greatness. It was a question, too, of making good the army's deplorable weakness – by efficient training, but also, of course, by secret infringement of the Versailles Treaty, in so far as this was at all possible. To achieve this higher patriotic goal the army leadership was even prepared to work hand in glove with the Bolsheviks. For the German generals had nothing against *Russian* Communists; after all, had not Lenin been transported to the scene of his deeds by Ludendorff – and why should people have become politically more astute since then?

The future policy of the Reichswehr thus included an illegal element. Measures which contravened both the letter and the spirit of the Versailles Treaty could naturally only be implemented in secret, veiled in patriotic obscurity. There thus arose the paradoxical situation that Versailles shielded the anti-, or at least, undemocratic autonomous development of the Reichswehr from the prying eyes of the democratic authorities. Any attempt to draw public attention to the practices of the Reichswehr General Staff either had the appearance of high treason in the eyes of the average patriot, or else could be nipped in the bud on that pretext. (Just as in Germany the question of whether the old regime was at least partly to blame for the war was a political taboo which has had its effect in fossilized forms up to the present day. Here, too, there was the danger of playing into the enemy's hands.) Even high treason, Eschenburg writes, called for the protection of the relevant paragraphs on treason – and it did in effect enjoy this protection, at least indirectly. But for this to be effective the powers of control of democratic, and especially of parliamentary, authorities had to be reduced to a minimum. This Seeckt succeeded in doing by concocting a new constitutional situation from the constitution of the Reich and the Defence Law which was passed in March 1923.

According to the constitution, the President of the Reich was Commander-in-Chief of the armed forces as a whole and the power of command was exercised on his behalf by the Reichswehr Minister, so that the latter had a double responsibility: on the one hand, like every other minister, he was responsible to parliament, while on the other hand, he was responsible in his special function to the President, who was independent of parliament. Seeckt managed to undermine the position of the Reichswehr Minister, which had been filled by the Swabian Democrat Otto Gessler following Noske's fall. Nothing much was left of the Minister's 'power of command' once the Chief of Staff, instead of being merely a technical advisor to his Minister, blossomed out into a general at the head of the army with executive command (*Kommandogewalt*). The main function of the Minister was now merely to act as a parliamentary shield behind which the Chief of Staff could take shelter.

The General was much less self-effacing in another direction, however: he contrived to have access not only to cabinet meetings but also directly to the President. How direct this access was and how much at odds with the arrangement intended by the fathers of the parliament may be seen from the fact that they had envisaged a third civil authority, apart from the President and the Reichswehr Ministry, who would be set over the military chief. This was to be a parliamentary State Secretary, but in fact the post was never filled. Thus fenced in, the responsible Minister was reduced to a not particularly influential civil servant who might be eliminated at any time, and even replaced if necessary, by the 'general at the top' provided the latter was able to arrive at a good understanding with the President as Commander-in-Chief. (Here again we may observe how the pendulum in Bonn has swung in the opposite direction in the case of every constitutional arrangement in the First Republic which turned out to be inept.)

Gessler's elimination was made easier by his personality. Since none of the Social Democrats had been willing to get his fingers burnt, the appointment of the former Minister of Reconstruction was in response to Ebert's wish.

Now that Noske, whom he had been reluctant to let go, had placed a powerful weapon against mob violence in the government's hands, the President was looking for someone capable of striking a balance and training the new Reichswehr to become a highly efficient and yet loyal political force. Gessler, who described himself merely as a 'rational republican', did in fact strike a balance, but as the son of a non-commissioned officer and unable to claim any military qualification other than a year's conscript service, he was no match for the intriguing generals, Seeckt in particular.

Noske's fall after the government's return to the capital had also brought down Bauer's cabinet. The trade union leader Legien, who had triumphed after Kapp's defeat and who had also been involved in the dismissal of Noske, did his best to set up a pure workers' government. This plan would of course have been tantamount to a resumption of the revolutionary movement, and that would not have been to the liking of the Majority Socialist leaders. It failed in fact (the Noske wing had suffered an annihilating defeat) but less for this reason than because of the doctrinaire attitude of the left wing of the Independent Socialists, who refused to take part in any government of the present democracy. Thus the Weimar coalition continued, and under Hermann Müller (Social Democrat and former Foreign Minister) as Chancellor many of Bauer's old ministers returned to their posts. At the same time the Prussian government, having stumbled through the Kapp putsch, emerged from the crisis considerably strengthened in its membership. Here, too, it was a Weimar coalition, with two energetic Social Democrats as its most prominent members: Otto Braun as Prime Minister and Carl Severing, who had proved his mettle in the Ruhr during the Kapp putsch, as Minister of the Interior.

Kapp's *coup* had a third and final series of consequences in Bavaria, but these pointed in the opposite direction to those that had shaped political events on the River Isar following the shock the middle-classes had suffered during the local 'soviet' episode. When news of Kapp's putsch reached Munich it seemed to the bourgeois forces that their hour had come. In Bavaria this meant, to an increasing extent, the right-wing forces, including the Bavarian People's Party, that offshoot of the Centre Party that set the political tone here. After all, fear of Eisner and the soviets was no longer acute, so that the restraint practised hitherto, which did not reflect the results of elections to the Landtag, no longer seemed called for. Hoffmann's government, originally socialist, had been transformed into a coalition following its return from Bamberg at the end of May 1919, but it had not entirely forfeited its Social Democratic complexion. This was because the middle-class partners, still shocked by the soviet regime that had only just been overthrown with the help of the Reich, did not venture on to the scene.

In the meantime, however, a number of active volunteer corps had sprung up and were steadily being reinforced from the north. In addition there were, as almost everywhere in the country, local self-defence militias (defence against the left, of course), the so-called Home Guards (*Einwohnerwehren*). In Bavaria they had founded a formidable umbrella organization under the command of a forestry official called Escherich. The Bavarian People's Party, under the influence of the 'peasant doctor' Georg Heim, had swung over to a federalistic policy with the aim of restoring the monarch, but it had not been joined by the Social Democrats. This was the response to a new campaign for a unitary state, proceeding this time from Prussia. Erzberger's financial reforms were seen by their author as merely the first step in a series of measures intended to integrate the Reich, beginning with the judicial system. Such developments provided sufficient grounds for local agitation. In the National Assembly the delegates of the Bavarian People's Party, with the exception of Heim, had voted for the constitution and were already being openly accused of treason. The Party Conference on 8 January 1920 had cancelled the working arrangement it had hitherto had with the Centre Party in the National Assembly. It had also withdrawn the Bavarian Party ministers from the national government and thus cut the last links with the mother party. From that moment on the fate of the Hoffmann government was sealed.

It was the news of the Kapp putsch in Berlin that set things in motion in Munich. Using a minimum of force the leaders of the Home Guard and other middle-class activists, in alliance with the commander of the Reichswehr in Munich, brought down the Hoffmann administration on 13 and 14 March. (It could have been done in a parliamentary fashion, but an ultimatum delivered by a general obviously seemed more punctilious.) One of the leaders of the movement, Dr von Kahr, the former head of the administration of Upper Bavaria, became the Prime Minister of what was now a purely middle-class coalition government. Less than a year after the end of the Soviet Republic the last Social Democrats thus vacated their ministerial posts in Bavaria, and their party was unable to stage a come-back for the next quarter of a century. Bavarian politics over the following years, the beginning of a People's Party era that lasted until 1933, were governed by a curious alliance of the blue and white opposition to the Reich as such, and the black, white and red opposition to this particular Reich. Their aims were totally different, but they had in common a detestation of the black, red and gold Republic.

It was not only in Bavaria that the Social Democrats made a mass exit from government, barely two years after the November revolution that had been launched under socialist auspices; it happened in the Reich as well. The Kapp putsch had no judicial consequences to speak of – a total of three insurgents landed up in the dock and only one was found guilty! It did have political consequences, however, and one of these was that the coalition stopped trying to delay the elections to the Reichstag that were now due. They changed their tactics, partly in order to counter dissatisfaction on the right with the National Assembly's tenacious hold on life (one of the Kapp faction's grievances), but partly also in the expectation that the effect of the putsch – the obvious political and administrative incompetence of its leaders and its inglorious end – would be to reverse the middle-class swing to the right. In March the Müller government announced that elections for the Reichstag would be held and the poll took place on 6 June. The result was a heavy defeat for the republican and democratic forces, and a corresponding success for the parties on both wings.

In the elections for the National Assembly in 1919 the middle-class public had barely recovered from its fright, and the fear of violent revolution was still deeply ingrained. Now, however, their self-confidence had been restored. The Republic, one might say, had disappointed them. Recovery had been slow; it had not made peace any the less expensive. In fact, things had simply been a great deal better before. The working classes, on the other hand, responded by pointing to the 'Noskes': they had launched a revolution the sole result of which, if you looked at things in their true light, was that their own Social Democratic leaders had boarded the gravy-train and were hob-nobbing with the 'scroungers' of the old regime. So the dissatisfied middle-classes had drifted off to the right, and the disgruntled workers to the left. Others were to follow; the trend away from the Republic and democracy in general had not yet reached its peak in either direction.

The Democratic Party lost 3.3 million out of 5.6 million voters,* retaining only thirty-nine of their previously held seventy-five seats. The Social Democrats declined from 11.5 to 6.1 million votes and from 163 to 102 seats – their sacrifice of Noske had not paid off. The Centre Party also suffered losses, which in part, however, went to the benefit of their subsidiary, the Bavarian People's Party: instead of the 6 million who had voted for the Centre in 1919, the party now had only 3.6 million, and the Bavarian People's Party 1.2 million votes, with sixty-one plus twenty-one seats, compared with ninety-one seats in the National Assembly. Thus, the Republic was borne essentially on the backs of three parties, for this function could be ascribed to the Bavarian People's Party and the German People's Party only with considerable reservations. And those three parties could rely on the support of no more than 43.6 per cent of the voters compared with 76.1 per cent at the National Assembly. To put it another way: they had not only lost a solid three-quarters' majority (329 out of 421 seats), they had no majority at all, for the coalition now controlled no more than 202 out of 454 seats. This was when the catchphrase 'a Republic without republicans' was coined. At

*The figures quoted here do not include the constituency of Oppeln, where the election was postponed until 20 February 1921 on account of an impending referendum. The Centre Party won seven seats here, the Social Democrats six, the Democrats and the Nationalists one apiece.

any rate, the coalition represented a shrinking and fairly ineffectual minority. The Democrats' fear of pressure from their right wing and – even more – the Social Democrats' fear of pressure from the left increasingly paralysed the political life of the Republic. A grand coalition extending from the Social Democrats to Stresemann's People's Party (who would take over the flank, with the concomitant fear of being 'overtaken on the right') was still feasible at the outset. However, it could be realized only rarely and even then at the cost of strained relations between its opposing wings – and corresponding political instability. Only the religious party, the Centre, had no rivals to fear once the locally limited split with the Bavarian People's Party had taken place. It was to prove a stabilizing factor in the democracy during the years that followed.

The winners in the election were the inner fringes of the two wings. This was the interim result of a centrifugal process, but the process did not stop there. On the right of the Reichstag there now sat sixty-five members of the People's Party instead of nineteen. That meant that virtually all of the People's Party voters who had defected the previous year had now found their way back to the successor of their old party, once the fear of revolution had subsided and dissatisfaction with the Versailles Treaty had increased. The attempt to found a grand, consolidated Liberal Democratic Party had thus finally failed. The Nationalists had also added twenty-six seats to the forty-four they had held hitherto and were now the strongest middle-class party in the Reichstag. Overall, 8.2 million Germans, instead of 4.7 million, had now voted for parties inclining to the right. There was a corresponding drift to the left from the centre parties who supported the state: in this case 2.3 million votes had become 5.5 million. The Independent Socialists, who had been a hopelessly small minority in the National Assembly with their twenty-two deputies, compared with the 163 Majority Socialists, now entered the Reichstag with a parliamentary representation of eighty-three members, not that far behind the 102 Social Democrats. And the Communists, who had taken part in a national election for the first time, had won four seats.

This impressive performance by the Independent Socialists was, however, an illusory success and did not bridge the gulf between the two wings of the party that had existed ever since the revolution. In the very year of its triumph the party fell apart. Two preconditions for its disintegration had been realized. On the one hand, the Communist Party of Germany, backed by Lenin, had shed its left wing at the Heidelberg Party Conference in 1919: the extremists on the left had been discredited by their mindless policy of insurrection and were denounced as 'adventurers' and 'Utopians'. (As the Communist Workers' Party of Germany, the expelled members were never anything more than an insignificant splinter group.) The Communist Party had then resolved to concentrate on political activity in parliament and the trade unions. On the other hand the Bolshevik leadership had stipulated such conditions for the Independent Socialists' association with the Third International then being founded that the party's right wing was to all intents and purposes excluded. The right wing, for its part, was prepared to accept political responsibility in the prevailing circumstances and regarded as hopeless the second revolution that was being propagated by international Communism. In October 1920 the major left wing of the Independent Socialist Party, led by the old revolutionary representatives from Berlin, was amalgamated with the Communist Party of Germany, which was currently following a rightish course, to form the United Communist Party of Germany (VKPD), which very soon dropped the word 'United' from its title. The Communist Party thus became for the first time a mass party with almost 400,000 members. Only now did it acquire an efficient party machine, a respectable press with more than thirty daily newspapers and, for the first time, influential posts in the trade unions. The right-wing minority of the Independent Socialist Party under the old leadership first tried to survive as a rump, but, in the nature of things, drifted more and more into the arms of the Social Democratic Party, until a merger came about in Nuremberg in September 1922, with only a small splinter group staying out. From then on there were two viable mass parties in the socialist camp, which differed basically in policy, tactics and the views of their voters.

The last politically significant act of the old Independent Socialist Party had been to refuse to join the government of the Reich in the summer of 1920 following its election success. The leaders of the Majority Socialists, however, shocked by the shattering election results, regarded the participation of the Independents as a condition for staying in government, for this was the only way they thought they could forestall the continuing flight of their voters to their left-wing rivals. Understandably, the Independent Socialist leadership had even more acute worries of a similar kind (vis-à-vis the Communist Party), given the internal weakness of their party; they consequently had no desire to participate in government. If the Social Democrats were unwilling to form a government without the Independent Socialists, they thought it even less likely that their voters would stomach an extension of the Weimar coalition to the right to include the People's Party (DVP), the party of big business.

Thus, on 26 June, the first purely middle-class government of the Reich was formed. What had been impossible a year earlier as putting the very existence of the state and the social system at risk, passed off as a matter of course. Fehrenbach, a politician of the Centre Party from Baden, the last President of the imperial Reichstag, formed a government which the People's Party entered for the first time. The party did indeed issue a declaration on this occasion, in which it took its stand on the ground of the existing Republic. All the same, it still had a kind of 'black, white and red' sheen and had only recently called for a restoration of the monarchy under the Crown

Prince, who was even more detested on the left than his father had been. This bourgeois coalition commanded 168 out of 459 seats and was thus the first minority government of the Republic; but it was to be succeeded by others with similarly slender support – a somewhat dangerous development for such a young and unstable parliamentary democratic system.

A transfer of responsibility to the opposition was not feasible, however, because the Anglo-Saxon system of two alternating parties with pragmatic policies had never been established in Germany, or anywhere else on the Continent for that matter. Here, a number of much less flexible and often stubbornly doctrinaire ideological parties faced each other. Even the party blocs capable of forming coalitions amongst themselves were only three in number and none of them was in a position to form a government by itself. The Republic's enemies on the left, as seen from the republican centre, were out of the question, and in any case not capable of forming an alliance. It was possible at least to talk to those on the right, they had not been shot at, one could exchange greetings with them in the street, albeit somewhat frostily hitherto. And so, in June 1920 (and from then on) what mattered was to clamber out of the political trenches of 1918 and somehow or other arrive at a compromise arrangement to co-operate, first with one and then with both of the black, white and red adversaries, or at least to tolerate them. The fact that this was possible enabled the 'Republic without republicans' to survive for a time. Very soon, however, a further enemy loomed up on the right of the parliamentary stage who no longer wanted to return to the Empire, but looked forward towards new and distinctly questionable shores. As this enemy grew stronger and stronger, there was no question of an arrangement with any other camp: by then the end was in sight.

Fehrenbach's cabinet was thus dependent on the goodwill of the Social Democrats and this was granted to them in view of the international situation and also because it was the only alternative at home. It is easy to brand this attitude on the part of the Social Democrats – having their cake and eating it – as an evasion of responsibility, a lack of a sense of political responsibility and an attachment to the tradition of opposition in the imperial era. It was what made a number of other minority cabinets necessary, but with things as they were, the Social Democrats hardly had a choice. Unconditional collaboration with the revived forces of the middle-classes and agricultural interests would have needed such major cuts in even the most moderate socialist policy that their supporters would hardly have accepted them. It is highly possible that a Social Democratic Party that had stayed on to share the responsibilities of government at that stage would have been ground down into insignificance. A democracy certainly calls for compromise and a balance of interests, but a grasp of this piece of political wisdom was hardly to be expected from a section of the nation which until recently had held undivided power in its hands.

4

Reparations, inflation, terrorism

In every state foreign and domestic policy constantly interact. Nevertheless, certain periods can be identified in which one or the other predominates, attracting the attention of rulers and ruled alike. If we consider the history of the First Republic from that aspect, then it appears that the second of its three phases was clearly dominated by foreign policy, while home affairs bulked large in the third phase. The first phase, however, constitutes a mixture, although it does not lack a certain inner coherence. From the summer of 1920 foreign policy was in the forefront for a period of two-and-a-half years. The Treaty of Versailles had come into force in the spring, and it was only now that its severity was fully realized. The fact that all its terms were actually seriously meant, and that France especially was determined that her former enemy would swallow the pill, however bitter, helped to advance still further the process which had already begun to decimate the republican forces. Public interest was now focused on the start of negotiations with the Allies on the conditions for implementing the Treaty and on possible side-effects.

In the meantime, however, the Allies had lost one of their partners. Wilson's treaty, which incorporated the statutes of the League of Nations, the American President's favourite child, had not commanded the necessary majority in Congress, and in the autumn isolationism had triumphed overall with the election success of the Republican Harding. Germany gained no advantage from this, the separate peace treaty with the United States in August 1921 expressly reserved to the Americans all the rights they had enjoyed under the Versailles Treaty. Nevertheless, there was understandable elation at this evident softening of the Allied front, for this turn of events seemed to favour the Anglo-Saxon trump card which the German Foreign

Office hoped to play against their principal antagonist – France. If we look back at the situation, there seem to be no grounds for elation. America's elimination from the ranks of the negotiators had the same effect as her subsequent withdrawal from the Rhineland: it strengthened France, i.e. the intransigent hostile wing of the Entente. What was more, France had now lost the guarantee of her territorial integrity promised her by Wilson. Her fear of her Teutonic neighbour with the larger population (those '10 million Germans too many') which was in an uneasy state of political ferment had hardly been allayed by a victory won only with the aid of almost the entire world. That was why France, like Shylock, was to insist all the more on her pound of flesh under the Versailles Treaty, trying to hold Germany down as best she could and for as long as possible.

This is not the place for a detailed discussion of the meetings between Germany and the victorious powers at the conference table, of which the first took place in Spa in July 1920 – although events in Germany had a bearing on the conference. On the one hand, the leading German negotiators were constantly under pressure from the Reich, and on the other, the talks did not merely revolve around delivery and payment dates (which were usually enforced in the end by ultimatum). The participants in the conference were concerned also with affairs in Germany and did not hesitate to intervene. An issue of this kind, for instance, was the reduction of the German army to a strength of 100,000 men, as stipulated in the Versailles Treaty. German efforts to have the figure doubled failed, and an extension of the deadline beyond the end of the year could not be negotiated.

In this connection the various paramilitary organizations very soon began to loom large: they comprised nearly one hundred volunteer corps, numbering in all about 150,000 men, plus the Home Guards formed in various parts of Germany with the support of the Reich to counter insurrection, or the threat of insurrection on the part of the left. The grand total of all these organizations was tantamount to having the entire nation under arms. After all, there were ample stocks of weapons available from the armouries of the old army. All this was kept secret from patriotic motives, and the government turned a blind eye, in spite of the obvious military ineffectiveness of such forces and the political perils they entailed. Such activities naturally incurred the displeasure of the hostile powers, who repeatedly demanded that the Free Corps and the Home Guards be disbanded. The government of the Reich, which still lacked its own executive machinery, shrugged off responsibility for the Home Guards to the individual states, suggesting that they should be disbanded, or at least reorganized and their armaments limited. Most states complied with this suggestion, but some did not.

The most vociferous protests came from Bavaria – on the point of becoming the Eldorado of the right, which had been homeless since the war. The local Home Guards had in fact had combined to form the so-called

Organisation Escherich (*Orgesch*) and had begun to engage actively in politics. The new Kahr government, of course, was not keen to dispense with its retainers and most powerful supporters. In the course of the succeeding years the Allies undertook various steps and there were fierce arguments between Berlin and Munich, which opposed disarmament legislation introduced under Allied pressure just as it had opposed earlier summonses. Instead of disbanding the Home Guards, it responded with a provocative parade, the regional Home Guard marksmanship display. It was not until June 1921, following an Allied ultimatum, that the Bavarian Home Guards capitulated, allowing themselves to be disarmed and disbanded. Kahr's attempts to make these organizations acceptable in Allied capitals as an instrument of federalism had failed, in spite of some initial support by the French in the case of Bavaria. This was largely because of the nationalistic course they pursued, which in the end even led to their alienation from the Bavarian People's Party. Kahr had also hoped that this problem might disappear in the fuss about reparations, with which it had been linked on the agenda of the international conferences, but this hope, too, had been disappointed.

The retrospective specification of Germany's reparation payments which now had to be agreed upon did in fact form the cardinal issue in those months and years. And as the inability of the powers to agree on this point had suggested, it turned out to be such a thorny and heated question that all manner of other issues might have been accommodated in its shadow. In Versailles fears had already been expressed that the assessment of the damage for which Germany would be required to pay compensation mattered only in relation to the *scheduling* of her contributions. The actual *level* of the payments would depend, for better or for worse, on what could be extracted from Germany in the thirty years of a single generation, which the treaty had stipulated as the redemption term of the debt that was now to be assessed. Reasonable people could foresee that even if Germany were charged 'only' with the generously assessed damage and loss to civilian populations, and not with the full cost of the war to her enemies (reckoned to amount to 400,000 million gold marks), then the first factor was bound to outweigh the second. Haggling started about the ability and willingness of the Reich to pay and was backed up by reports from various experts whose opinions differed wildly.

The German delegation in Versailles had striven to prevent a sword of Damocles being suspended over the nation and to have the amount of the reparations debt actually written into the treaty. Her adversaries had been offered 100,000 million gold marks, payable in annual instalments free of interest over fifty or sixty years. Whereas the right in Germany had raised a howl of protest over this 'insane' offer, the Allies had responded merely with a tired smile: the offer was equivalent to no more than 30,000 million with interest, or paid in cash on the spot, and they wanted rather more than that (without, admittedly, ever obtaining as much as that in the end).

And so the situation had remained until the qualifying date, 1 May 1921, by which time the Reparations Commission was supposed to fix the amount of Germany's debt, and Germany was to make a down payment of 20,000 million marks. The deadline came closer and closer without the issue becoming any clearer or less controversial, given the turbulent economic developments in Germany and the progressive collapse of the currency. At an Allied conference in Paris during January 1921 the first concrete, albeit provisional, decisions were taken. The idea was to ask for 226,000 million gold marks, payable, in contravention of the Versailles Treaty, in forty-two (instead of thirty) annual instalments rising from 2,000 to 6,000 million – plus 12 per cent of the value of German exports, also for a period of forty-two years. (This was an index-linked factor which made it possible for the creditors to profit from a possible boom in the German economy.) At the beginning of March this proposal was discussed with the Germans at a conference in London. The latter pointed to their catastrophic situation and offered a total of 30,000 million gold marks – on condition that Germany retained Upper Silesia. The discrepancy seems puzzling but it was in part due, as in the case of the Versailles calculations, to different methods of assessment that were dictated by domestic political factors on either side.

On the forty-two annual instalments 'proposed' by the Allies, totalling 226,000 million gold marks, advance payments might be made which would be discounted up to May 1921 at 8 per cent. If the total sum were discounted at 8 per cent at current values, then only 53,000 million would be left. The German side had rounded this down to 50,000 million and also deducted what had been paid hitherto: 21,000 million by German reckoning. This was where the main difference lay: in the first place the Allies were not prepared to have anything at all deducted and, second, they reckoned that payments so far had amounted to no more than 8,000 million marks. In fact, the German estimates had been falsified to an absurd degree, as was later admitted. The balance of 30,000 million in the German account was to be financed as far as possible by an international loan, for which concessions abroad – like tax exemption, say – were expected. The remainder – 22,000 million, it was estimated – was to be paid in easy instalments following a pause; these instalments would be subject to interest, but at 5 per cent rather than 8 per cent. It was believed that the guarantee of improvement represented by the export levy could be dispensed with in view of this generous offer, which in any case assumed an improvement in Germany's economic situation.

The subsequent course of the dispute at the conference culminated, as was customary at that time, in an ultimatum and the threat of sanctions – with Germany at first refusing to give way – then the actual introduction of sanctions, in this case an occupation of the Rhineland ports in Düsseldorf,

Duisburg and Ruhrort and confiscation of the Reich's customs and harbour dues there. This meant that the conference had failed, and the German delegates departed, to be suitably acclaimed at home. In that same month, on 27 April, in the absence of the German negotiators the Reparations Commission fixed the amount of Germany's debt definitively at 132,000 million gold marks. On 5 May the Allies handed over a new written ultimatum with a time-limit of six days, coupled with a threat to occupy the Ruhr if it was not complied with. Germany must undertake to accept the schedule of payments – 2,000 million marks annually plus 26 per cent of the value of her exports. There was also the matter of a 12,000 million advance that was still outstanding according to the Allied reckoning – as well as the final disarming of the Home Guards, and the trial of Germans identified as war criminals, which had not even begun.

The fixing of the reparations burden meant that the second part of the peace treaty had now been implemented. For the third time, following Compiègne and Versailles, a cheque drawn on the past had to be cashed. Once more the question was: who was going to do it? It was at this precise time that Germany suffered a further blow. On 20 March a plebiscite had been held in Upper Silesia, which was occupied by Allied troops: 717,000 votes (60 per cent of the total) had been cast for Germany and 433,000 for Poland. In Germany it was hoped this result meant that the territory would remain in the Reich. But the Versailles Treaty had laid down that it was the Allies who would define the frontier in Upper Silesia, taking into account 'the geographical and economic situation' as well as the wishes of the local population, as expressed in a plebiscite. And so an Allied plebiscite commission set about fixing a definitive frontier, to the great disappointment of Germany. In order to ensure a *fait accompli*, however, Polish volunteer corps, emboldened by the passivity of the French occupation contingent, invaded Upper Silesia on 2 May. Fehrenbach's government resigned the following day.

Now that it was once again a case of pulling chestnuts out of the fire, the time was ripe for another cabinet on the Weimar coalition model. The People's Party resigned from the government: in accordance with their established patriotic practice, they did not care to be burdened with Germany's shame. The Social Democrats had breathed a sigh of relief following the split in the Independent Socialist Party on their immediate left: they had regained a measure of political mobility, for the gulf separating them from the Communists was still too deep for major defections. They thus felt able to rejoin the government. The post of Chancellor remained with the Centre Party, although this time it went to a man of the left wing, Joseph Wirth, who had hitherto been Finance Minister. The other prominent figure in his cabinet, initially as Minister for Reconstruction, was the industrialist and writer Walther Rathenau, son of the founder of AEG (General Electric Company). Rathenau had made a name for himself during the war by organizing the supply of raw materials. He was now a member of the Democratic Party, although he had not had any particular political function hitherto. His appointment by Wirth caused a sensation, for Rathenau was Jewish – and an unbaptized Jew at that, whose pride had prevented him from purchasing that ticket to European culture. Nevertheless he virtually worshipped the Nordic and Germanic races and their prototypes.

Wirth and Rathenau became the exponents of a course in foreign policy that came to be known as the 'policy of fulfilment' and was attacked with hysterical hatred by their opponents. Their policy was aimed at convincing their former enemies as best they could of Germany's goodwill and her eagerness to comply with their demands. In this way they hoped not only to improve their relationship with the victorious powers but to convince them that a large part of those demands simply could not be met by Germany, even with the best will in the world. It was a policy which was wrecked, if we may anticipate the outcome, on the intransigence of the French. Admittedly, given the unbridled behaviour of the opposition in Germany, France could hardly be expected to welcome a policy of fulfilment which might well turn out to be ephemeral. France in fact chose the opposite alternative, responding to the goodwill shown by the German politicians by turning the screw even tighter and making the position of the latter even more insecure. The German statesmen's futile appeals to the conscience of the world did nothing but provoke anew the scorn of their enemies at home. It was a vicious circle from which there was no obvious escape, and in which the proponents of the policy of fulfilment – along with the democratic Republic – were hopelessly trapped. At home, therefore, the policy of meeting the enemy's demands achieved nothing but the continuing decimation of those democratic forces that were once more made to answer to the German public for the bankruptcy of the former authoritarian state. As far as foreign policy went, there was no alternative apart from bluster and threats which would have put the very existence of the Reich at risk, had they been put into practice.

Wirth's policy began by accepting the London ultimatum, and hence also the debt of 132,000 million marks. It became clear only later that it was not just a matter of raising the cash; the much greater problem – affecting the entire international financial economy – lay in actually transferring the sums that were due. In practice, and shorn of all the trimmings connected with compensation, the plan required Germany in the first place to pay the 40,000 million mark war debts of the Entente, and of the United States in particular. That was one reason why the principal creditor, France, who was to receive the lion's share (50 per cent) of German reparations payments, was so insistent on her promissory note being met. (Britain was to receive 22 per cent, Italy 10 per cent, Belgium 8 per cent and all the other countries together 8 per cent.)

This meant, then, that for so many years to come a considerable capital sum would flow across the Atlantic in a westerly direction, without any equivalent in cash or goods moving in the opposite direction. During that period the German people would have to take over, as it were, a part of America's output, while the American people would have to accept these payments as a kind of pension, with a corresponding reduction in their own output. Quite apart from the question of how that might be organized, such a 'pension' ran counter to the elementary interests of the American economy. Moreover, a blood-letting of this kind, if it exceeded the permissible economic and financial limits, was bound to ruin the German currency. This in turn could not fail to have an effect on the international financial system and on other currencies.

During the reparations negotiations in London the German side had suggested that the reconstruction of war-damaged areas (for which Germany really did have to pay, together with other civilian costs) should be carried out, not simply by deliveries in kind, which had in any case been sought on a copious scale, but by German firms and German labour. This would have removed a major burden from the cash account of the German debt. True, it would not have been in the interests of France, where the transformation of the economy had thrown up problems of unemployment and the provision of jobs similar to those in Germany. In principle, however (apart from merely passing the 'transfer' problem to France), this solution might indeed have suggested a way out of the reparations calamity. Towards the end of the Second World War plans to employ German forced labour in the victorious states flourished, but ended up merely as hordes of prisoners-of-war on a scale reminiscent of the ancient world. These plans owed much to the grim experiences with reparations payments following the First World War.

In the given circumstances there remained only two other solutions; both were tried and both helped to bring about first economic and then political catastrophes. Until 1923 Germany purchased the foreign currency it needed for its reparations payments. The purchases were financed by stepping up the operation of the currency presses, a factor contributing even further to the feverish condition of the German currency, which had been badly shaken by the expense of the war. From 1924 the reparations debts were *de facto* redesignated, with the annual payments which flowed via the Allied creditors to the USA returning as loans. This led to another foreign obligation which was to have dire consequences when the worldwide economic crisis set in – especially in view of the irresponsible use to which the borrowed money was put.

The internal indebtedness of the Reich, the 150,000 million marks the war had cost, was eliminated by inflation. Inflation, in fact, wiped out the liabilities of all debtors and offered crafty profiteers an opportunity to acquire major assets cheaply. It also helped German industry, especially the export industries, to experience a vast, albeit unnatural and unhealthy, boom.

Inflation is usually associated with the year 1923, when the numerical delirium of hundreds of thousands, millions and, ultimately, billions achieved its most dramatic climax. However, if we look further than just at the influence inflation had on everyday life and its tragicomic features – like the wages that had to be spent the day they were received because they would have no more than a fraction of their purchasing power the following day, the queues in front of the grocery stores and all the other distresses of the day – and consider instead the effects of inflation which, as social and political factors, governed the Republic's fate in the succeeding period, then we can see that the inflation was virtüally over by the beginning of 1923.

The most momentous result of the inflation in every respect was the destruction of financial reserves, and hence of the sense of social security of a large section of the traditional German middle-classes. Innumerable members of those classes had been deprived of considerable capital assets by the loss of the war, since the Reich was no longer in a position to underwrite the capital that had been invested in war loans. Many now lost the remainder of their capital as a result of the devaluation of the currency. Even those who owned property or land – assets which were not only secured against inflation but, as in the case of agriculture, actually benefiting from inflation – did not always escape scot-free. Infected by a general speculative fever which fostered illusions of immense profits, many people of private means or owners of small or medium-sized businesses found themselves ruined following what had seemed like extremely profitable sales. The middle-classes were not annihilated as a section of society by the war and inflation. But the loss of their sense of security, which vanished along with their material reserves, meant that considerable sections of the middle-class, especially the old pre-industrial bourgeoisie, lost their political bearings. Apart from the fact that the inflation and its consequences were unhesitatingly blamed on the Republic, there was an increasing readiness to listen to doctrines of political salvation of the most lunatic kind – especially if they offered conspiracy theories and, for instance, explained this otherwise inexplicable disaster by reference to the intrigues of 'world Jewry'. There was an increasing readiness, too, to entrust the fate of the Reich to a 'strong man' who, it was hoped, would prevent the threatened reduction of the nation to a proletarian level, which was seen to some extent to have already come about.

The economy and economic policy were also to feel the effects of inflation for a long time to come. Investment activity, even in the good years of Weimar – following the stabilization of the mark – remained too slight to support a lasting economic boom; those investments that were made had to be financed to a fair extent by foreign loans, because inflation had brought about a shrinking of the German capital market. Moreover, potential growth industries, such as the car industry, hardly counted as pillars of the economy, essentially because the domestic market had been reduced by inflation. In this sense the inflation contributed powerfully to the great economic crisis of the years between 1929 and 1935. The fact that no effective counter-measures were taken during the great crisis was largely due to a fear of inflation.

But all this did not follow simply from 1923. Already at the beginning of 1920 the mark had fallen to one-tenth of its pre-war value; in the summer of 1922 it was worth only one-hundredth, and by the beginning of 1923 the value and the purchasing power of one old gold mark was equal to 2,500 paper marks. In other words: someone who had had a personal fortune of, say, 50,000 marks (a respectable sum for the circumstances of the time and an adequate nest-egg for old age) and who had invested it in gilt-edged securities, would have possessed only 5,000 marks at the beginning of 1920. By the middle of 1922 this would have shrunk to 500, and by the beginning of 1923 it would have been worth no more than 20 gold marks. At the end of the giddy numbers game of 1923, the investment would have been worth 0.0005 pfennigs; but this, after all, was simply juggling with figures and was like losing a 20-mark note after the loss of an entire fortune.

In spite of this perfectly simple calculation, we can still find almost everywhere in the relevant literature, remarks to the effect that things were not all that bad until 1922, or even 1923. So we read, for instance, that it was not until the middle of 1922 that inflation began 'to assume threatening proportions' (Conze); until then it had been merely 'creeping' and 'scarcely noticed' (Schwarz). It was – allegedly – the occupation of the Ruhr that had led to the 'collapse' of the German currency, it was passive resistance that had 'ultimately caused the catastrophe of German inflation' (A. Thimme), and it was only now (1923) that 'German savers had lost all they had' (Rosenberg). In fact, these savers were not in a position to lose anything at all, because they had nothing left to lose. Even in the early summer of 1921, before the foreign currency for the first 1,000 million gold marks due – and paid – under the London plan by the end of August had been raised by means of the currency presses, our saver's 50,000 marks would have been worth little more than 5,000 marks.

There is no doubt that the inflationary development caused by the loss of the war was spurred on by reparations payments. Indeed, it is conceivable that the relatively stable exchange rate of the mark in 1920/21 might have been held at something between one-tenth and one-fifteenth of its pre-war value. But reparations were neither the cause of the devaluation of the mark nor did they bring about its catastrophic scale. Nor was it reparations alone that prevented a stabilization of the currency, although they were used by the German side as an argument to explain their inability to pay.

On the other side, however – especially in France – German inflation was seen as a device used by the government of the Reich to disguise Germany's financial situation and to evade reparations as far as possible. Indeed, the German government had been unable to resist the temptation to seek refuge from the French appetite for reparations behind their chaotic currency situation. They were not averse to making it impossible for the Entente powers to assess Germany's ability to pay and were eager to demonstrate to their creditors their inability to meet the demands made on them. For these reasons the government of the Reich was tempted time and time again to let things simply take their course. The fact that the German authorities for the most part accepted inflation without doing anything about it has little to do with helplessness in the face of a novel and bewildering phenomenon. Even the President of the Reichsbank, Havenstein, long regarded as a sorry figure, was fully aware that the causes of the inflation were to be found in German financial policy. He believed, however, that it was necessary to put up with this calamity for patriotic reasons, and, as already mentioned, in order to forestall new internal crises.

Above all, people were afraid of what was bound to follow the inflation. At the time Germany's economic situation seemed to be splendid. Although a great many people had lost everything they had – lost much more indeed than the war had cost overall – there were, of course, others who had gained by these losses: productive industry, operating virtually tax-free and with relatively cheap labour, was in a position to export at dumping prices, while the workers, in spite of wage increases, were being cheated of part of their earnings. The continued devaluation of the mark, which could be counted on with absolute certainty, also acted as a further attraction for foreign buyers. The expansion of foreign trade naturally had an effect even on industries that were not directly involved in the export business, so that there was a general expansion of the economy which rapidly solved the immediate post-war problems of industrial conversion. The problem of unemployment no longer existed: the labour market was characterized by full employment. If the inflation were to be followed by deflation, however, drastic setbacks might be expected everywhere. This gave the government and the industrial circles involved an interest in continued inflation.

In their areas of responsibility they had certainly taken various positive steps to prevent the inflation – and hence the economy – from grinding to a halt. The aim was rather to spur it on and to drive the economic temperature even higher. Hugo Stinnes built up a West German industrial empire in a fabulously short time through speculation during these years and believed that he was also destined to play a major political role. He became a symbol of all those who rose to the surface on the tide of the inflation, who floated there at their ease and did all they could to maintain their gratifying situation for as long as possible. Economic life flourished splendidly, inspired by a never-ending, breathtaking boom on the Stock Exchanges. Speculation had ceased to be speculative and had become a matter of rapacious grabbing by those in the know, so that a Marxist historian like Arthur Rosenberg has described the recession as the revenge taken by big business for the fright it had experienced on and after 9 November.

Of course, this inflation could have been stopped sooner. By ruthless restriction of credit regardless of the economic disadvantages, by rigorously applying Erzberger's taxation legislation and by reducing the value of money to one-tenth by 1921, the currency might have been stabilized, even allowing for the 30 gold marks *per capita* in reparations payments *per annum*. And it was actually stabilized at last in 1923 in much less favourable technical and psychological circumstances. The social consequences, it is true, could only be slightly alleviated, for medium and small ownership had already in practice paid the price. But perhaps the nation might have been spared the consequences of the weird monetary juggling act of 1923. Neither the old regime nor the lurking enemy can be blamed for what incompetence, an obsession with the afflictions of reparations policy, fear of revolution and sheer greed brought about. Democratic freedom turned out to mean, amongst other things, licence, freedom for Stock Exchange jobbers and mediocre political talents.

In the meantime there was no respite for the Republic; how could there have been in these circumstances, under unremitting pressure both from abroad and from adversaries at home? Admittedly, the danger from the left had receded, at least for the moment. Apart from minor incidents in Hamburg and the Ruhr, the power of the Communists had been temporarily exhausted in 1921 with a final rising of radical workers in central Germany. This had begun with local incidents in the Mansfeld coalfield and had involved a professional revolutionary, Max Hölz, who had made his name in the Vogtland the previous year. Neither the general strike that was hoped for, nor a mass insurrection of the German working classes took place, and the rising, which had spread to Leuna and Halle and looked at first quite dangerous, was put down in a matter of days by the Minister of the Interior, Severing, with the support of the police and the Reichswehr. Bolshevik hopes of achieving world revolution at one fell swoop had faded, while Lenin, anxious to pass as a suitable negotiating partner in the world at large, had been obliged to back-track in Russia with his 'New Economic Policy'. The era of left-wing revolt was over, then, as far as incitement to international revolution was concerned. World Communism in general had moved away from revolutionary campaigns, which were now deemed to be hopeless, and had begun to join the parties of the Second International in fighting everyday political and social issues by legitimate means – a development which was to culminate later, after several lapses, in the policy of a Popular Front.

In the months that now followed contacts were made between Seeckt's Reichswehr and the Red Army. These helped the Soviets to build up their armed forces, while they also provided the Germans with facilities, free from Allied supervision, where the Reichswehr might construct, test and operate weapons that were prohibited under the Versailles Treaty. In the minds and political vision of the Reichswehr leadership it seemed that a renewed partition of Poland was an objective within their grasp, and that they need take no account of the Allies. They were thus following the Russophile Prussian tradition and the notion that their hereditary enemy was in the west. The Bolsheviks, for their part, encountered a situation for the first time that was to be repeated frequently in the following decades: they discovered that it was much easier to get along with German Junkers, industrial magnates and other reactionaries than with Social Democratic workers and their leaders, who were somewhat sceptical about Bolshevik achievements.

The fact was that those Germans from whom the Bolsheviks hoped to gain at least financial support discovered in the latter their conservative Russian friends of yesteryear. True, in the meantime they had taken up some crazy political notion, but this posed no immediate threat, as events in Germany had shown. As far as the Bolsheviks were concerned, the chief enemy was the Jewish, democratic, capitalist system and the philistine civilization of the west, with its lawyers and men of letters. On the other hand, large sections of the social class who were to be freed from their capitalistic fetters – i.e. the Social Democratic workers – profoundly disliked the dictatorship of the proletariat in its Russian form. Contrary to Marx, this form of government had emerged virtually straight from serfdom and was unable to conceal its origins. These workers, if not all that well disposed to the essential spirit of the west, were at least less prejudiced against it than the mass of the middle-classes – not to mention the Prussian aristocracy, who still dominated the Foreign Office and the army in spite of all the upheavals that had taken place.

Contacts between the Soviets on the one hand and the Reichswehr and the German Foreign Office on the other reached right back to the revolution. Following the withdrawal of German troops and the volunteer corps from the Baltic, relations between the two states had become less strained. In the summer of 1920, when the Red Army had stood for a time at the gates of Warsaw before being repulsed by a Polish army that had been reorganized by the Entente, the gaze of the German army and diplomatic corps was firmly fixed on the east. Following the unsatisfactory outcome of their Polish campaign, the Soviet government had appealed to the government of the Reich for help in reforming the Red Army. In 1921 a thinly disguised trade agreement was concluded and there was also collaboration in military matters and in the armaments industry. On the German side the collaboration was arranged and carried out by the General Staff of the Reichswehr with the knowledge, approval and financial support of the government. The practical results of this co-operation with their Bolshevik brothers-in-arms, which continued until 1933, were in fact of no greater consequence than the political counterpart to the rapprochement, the famous Treaty of Rapallo. Taken together, however, they helped to reduce pressure from the left within the Republic: after all, when relations were so cordial in the field of foreign policy, it would hardly have been good form to create more than conventional internal difficulties for one's new-found friends.

Rapallo was signed by a man into whose overall political plan this demonstration of anti-western sentiment did not fit. This was Walther Rathenau, who had in the meantime become Foreign Minister. Wirth's government had resigned in October 1921 as a protest against the Allied decision concerning Upper Silesia. Korfanty's Polish volunteers had been repulsed and the self-defence forces of the German population had been supported once more by volunteers from other parts of the Reich. Once again defensive actions had been fought by Free Corps similar to those which had crushed Polish risings in the summers of 1919 and 1920. In the eyes of their leaders the remobilization of the Free Corps, who had long since been disbanded and vanished from the political scene, was a triumph of organization. The democratic government, however, looked on it with mixed feelings – but what other course was open to them? The Reichswehr could not be sent into action in a plebiscite area. The Polish surprise attack was frustrated by the volunteer corps in military actions culminating in the storming of the Annaberg. The troops assigned to the Allied plebiscite commission who favoured the Polish side (that applied particularly to the French) found themselves obliged to restore order in the area.

The German and Polish forces were held apart by Allied troops, mainly a British division, and were later forced to withdraw and disband – although this was done only partially on both sides. It was mainly Britain and France who could not agree on the demarcation of the new frontier. The problem was passed to the League of Nations, and they appointed a four-man commission. Only the Spanish member represented a neutral power, the Belgian, Brazilian and Chinese members having all been numbered among Germany's wartime enemies. The new frontier, announced on 20 October 1921, reflected the composition of the commission. It assigned to Poland three-quarters of the industrial part of the region, the Upper Silesian coalfield with its mineral resources, irrespective of the fact that towns like Königshütte, which had registered a German majority in the plebiscite, were left on the far side of the new frontier.

In Germany there was great indignation over this ruling, which was regarded, with some justification, as an act of sheer coercion. Apart from the Saar, the status of which was to be settled in the more distant future (fifteen years after the implementation of the Versailles Treaty), Upper Silesia was the last of the plebiscite areas – and economically the most important. The other plebiscites had already been conducted between February and July

1920. In Schleswig, as expected, the northern zone had opted 75 per cent
for Denmark, while almost 95 per cent of the population in the southern
zone had voted in favour of Germany. Apart from the division into zones
that tended to favour Denmark, this was a fair result, which not even Hitler
changed in 1940. In Eupen-Malmédy the Belgian occupation authorities
turned the plebiscite into a farce: anyone who wanted the territory reinteg-
rated into the Reich had to enter his name in a public list. Massive Belgian
intimidation ensured that no more than 271 of the 33,700 electors dared do
this. In spite of German protests, the Council of the League of Nations
acknowledged this electoral travesty. On the other hand, the plebiscite area
in southern East Prussia and in the adjoining West Prussian counties beyond
the Vistula had fallen to Germany, with almost 97 per cent of the predominantly Polish-speaking population opting for the Reich.

All this had taken place more than a year earlier. In the meantime Germany
had once more become a partner in negotiations, so that a crude ruling on
frontier issues now seemed something of an anachronism. What is more,
Upper Silesia was not just a prosperous industrial region: through the
thrice-repeated battle with Polish insurgents the very name had acquired a
well-nigh legendary ring. The decision by the League of Nations consequently unleashed a storm of protest, which Wirth's cabinet resolved to join by
formally resigning. Wirth, in fact, formed a new cabinet at once, although
without broadening its basis, as might have been desirable in a time of crisis
– in this case by the inclusion of the People's Party to form a grand coalition,
such as was formed for the first time in Prussia in November. Instead, there
was a narrowing of the basis, at least in a formal sense, because the
Democrats once more dropped out, for fear of competition from the right
wing, who had remained in opposition. On this occasion Wirth himself took
over the Foreign Office, but three months later, at the end of January 1922,
he passed the post over to Rathenau. Walther Rathenau, Wirth's political
protégé, had proved himself in the previous cabinet. Recently, he had also
won his spurs in the field of foreign policy as leader of the German
delegation at the meeting of the Allied Supreme Council in Cannes.

In Cannes the topic had once more been German reparations, and, in
contrast to the generally clumsy manoeuvres of his predecessors, Rathenau
had been able for the first time to establish a certain personal rapport with
the Allied statesmen. He was eager to obtain a postponement of payment
and a reduction in the amount. His attempts proved fruitless in the long run,
however, because the French Prime Minister, Briand, fell from office during
the Cannes conference. He had been at least personally conciliatory, but
he was naturally at the mercy of French public opinion, which demanded,
for one thing, 'sécurité' against France's Teutonic neighbour. For the Reich,
although momentarily defeated, was if anything even more menacing now,
in terms of population and vitality, than it had been before. And with her

growing economic and financial problems, France clung with almost hysterical stubbornness to the promise 'L'Allemagne payera tout' – all the more so as she felt that she had been let down by her British allies on both counts.

This was because, on the other side of the Channel – although nowhere else, in fact – a process had begun which the German signatories of the Versailles peace had been banking on: a conviction had grown up that, in many respects, the treaty could not be implemented as signed. The process had started at the beginning of 1920 with the publication of a book on the economic consequences of the peace treaty by the English economist John Maynard Keynes, who was a member of the British delegation. He had sharply condemned this 'Carthaginian peace' and the reparations in particular. The book was greeted in Germany with understandable enthusiasm, but it was also grist to the mills of the Republic's enemies. There were additional conflicts of interest which had led to an estrangement of the two powers in the Entente Cordiale. German policy placed exaggerated hopes on this alienation and foolishly tried to exploit it. Following the withdrawal of the USA from European politics, the British attitude was calculated to drive France even further into inflexible and embittered defiance. In Briand's successor, Poincaré, the wartime President Clemenceau's implacable Versailles policy was once more institutionally secured. Before this happened, however, Cannes had produced one result: an invitation to a European world economic conference, with Germany and Russia both taking part. The conference was to be held in Genoa in April.

Up to a point, Rapallo was a by-product of Genoa. In view of the importance of this conference, where Germany was to reappear for the first time as an equal partner on the international scene, Chancellor Wirth himself had travelled to Genoa, along with Rathenau. The more muddled the situation in the west seemed to become, the greater became the temptation of an active policy in the east, but both politicians had so far resisted this temptation. By the end of 1921, however, a treaty with the Soviet government had been worked out and was due to be signed at Rapallo. The Russians had wished to conclude the treaty in Berlin on their way to Genoa, but Rathenau still hesitated for he had only just committed Germany to a pro-western policy. The victorious powers had been irritated by the threat of world revolution, which they were unable to suppress, and it was obvious that any understanding between the defeated power and the authors of that threat was bound to seem like a provocation to them and their associates.

In Genoa, however, matters took a fresh turn when – thanks to Russian indiscretions – an agreement between the victorious powers and the Soviets seemed to be on the cards. This would have given the Russians access to German reparations under the terms of the Versailles Treaty in return for the Soviets acknowledging the pre-war and wartime debts of the Tsarist regime. Whether this was in fact the case or whether it was an astute move on the part of the Soviets is open to question. It was argued that Germany's bankrupt estate, so to speak, was actually a fixed amount, measured by the country's productivity, so that any new creditor would merely reduce quotas at the expense of the existing creditors, without in any way increasing Germany's payments. This argument certainly had a lot to be said for it. In Germany, it would have been claimed, however, that Russia's accession to the Versailles Treaty would once again have closed the ring of Germany's adversaries that had been split open by the Bolshevik revolution. Besides, every additional hungry guest at the table would have prolonged the meal. On the other hand, it was hoped that, sooner or later, Germany's adversaries would be satisfied with a final settlement that would no longer be assessed on Germany's ability to pay but, presumably, on rather more sober expectations. This final payment, it is true, would have to be considerably larger if a further war-damaged country was added.

In this dilemma the German delegation had made an Easter excursion to Rapallo and had come to an agreement there with the Russians that they would mutually renounce the costs of the war and of civilian damage. Germany also agreed that she would renounce for herself and on behalf of her citizens all claim to assets that had been nationalized in Soviet Russia. Moreover, it was agreed that the two countries would accord each other 'most favoured nation' trading terms and establish diplomatic relations. If Germany had ever had any real chance in Genoa that concessions would be made in regard to reparations (which is in any case more than doubtful), this agreement effectively put paid to it. The Allies, who were annoyed by the Soviets' emergence from the diplomatic ghetto, also suspected that there were secret clauses in the Rapallo Treaty, in particular military clauses. There were in fact no such clauses; there was simply no need for them.

The German action, which was regarded as deceitful, provoked universal indignation in Genoa. The Allied front, which had begun to crumble, was once more welded together. That the economic conference did not end in spectacular failure was thanks only to the prudent moderating influence of the British Premier, Lloyd George. But that was all that was achieved, and Poincaré could scarcely have imagined a better start to his period of office. In June he torpedoed German attempts to obtain a moratorium and a reduction of reparations payments by publicly refusing his consent. Any hope of an international loan thus vanished, and the German currency plummetted once more within three months to one-seventh of its former value. The chance of regulating the financial situation in Germany and of obtaining reparations payments in the foreseeable future was correspondingly reduced – which did not seem to bother the French in the least. Poincaré's wishes were aimed elsewhere: at the 'productive pledge' of the Ruhr, on which he meant to lay his hands should Germany turn out to be insolvent. This would be tantamount to a belated fulfilment of certain French demands which had not been met at Versailles. If the Reich were to collapse as a result, so much the better: after all, the disintegration of Germany was the ultimate aim to which all French nationalists aspired. That point was soon to be reached.

The signatures at Rapallo did indeed mean that there was no longer a threat of Russian demands for reparations, but for a long time to come they were no more than an empty gesture as far as the German partner was concerned. It is true that they helped to restore Germany's battered self-confidence, but there was precious little substance to them otherwise. Actually to play the Russian trump card, which was in itself of little value, was naturally not possible at that stage, when Germany was in the grip of the Allies and at their mercy. And it was grotesque that it was actually the 'politicians of fulfilment' with their western leanings who had allowed themselves to be drawn into the Rapallo affair – Rathenau with grave misgivings, Wirth with rather less reluctance. The treaty also met with a mixed reception in Germany, being both welcomed and rejected on the left as well as the right. On the left, for instance, the President of the Reich, who was distinctly inclined to the west, was appalled, and the chief of the Reichswehr staff, who stood in the tradition of Bismarck, was delighted. Some thought that the treaty was a needless provocation of Germany's enemies, others took it to be the first step in an independent policy, a desperately needed boost to Germany's standing in the world. It was even taken as the first sign of a German and Russian encirclement of Poland and the start of an active policy aimed at revising the Versailles Treaty.

But although right-wing official circles in Germany had paved the way to Rapallo and welcomed an agreement with that other pariah of world politics, Soviet Russia, the hatred of large sections of the right for the 'politicians of fulfilment' could not be diminished by the Easter event of 1922, nor their malicious propaganda curbed. On 24 June, while Rathenau was on his way to the Foreign Office in an open car, he was murdered by a hand-grenade thrown by two former naval officers, members of Ehrhardt's brigade. It was on Rathenau that the hatred of the 'national' circles was focused. He represented the national humiliation of the traitorous 'policy of fulfilment'; he wanted to deliver Germany up to the Bolsheviks (no one seemed to notice that this accusation was at odds with the first charge). And, what was more, he was racially an alien, a representative of 'world Jewry', one of the 'Elders of Zion', as the members of the murder squad ranted in their staggering political simplicity after their arrest. The floodtide of anti-Semitic disapproval that had swelled when Rathenau entered the government, and surged even higher when he took over the prestigious Foreign Office, had now engulfed him.

Rathenau had been aware of this danger from the outset, of the 'enemy behind his back' who would stop at nothing. He could hardly have failed to see it in view of the rabble-rousing propaganda campaign from the right, which extended from furious parliamentary attacks by the nationalist opposition at the top, as it were, to plain incitement to murder 'the goddamned Jewish swine' at the bottom. Political murder had reached epidemic proportions in Germany among the politically and socially neglected young people on the right, the 'front generation'. Liebknecht, Luxemburg and Eisner had been the first of many victims. Even after the turmoil of the revolution had subsided, such heroic deeds remained the fashion in certain circles, whose members were blind to political realities and thought that Germany could be freed from the yoke of her enemies if only their alleged henchmen could be done away with.

Getting rid of political enemies by means of a revolver or some other relic of the war years – in other words, 'sentencing' the 'traitors' – was for these people a legitimate and, in the eyes of like-minded associates, an entirely honourable political tactic. This was particularly so for the large number of former volunteers who been 'left out' when the Reichswehr was recruited and thus did not even have the feeble loyalty to the state of their salaried former comrades. After their old units had been disbanded they had remained organized in a network of all kinds of illegal paramilitary formations which defended themselves from 'traitors' liable to denounce them. They were financed by wealthy landowners and big business, and although they were not exactly respected by the General Staff of the Reichswehr, they were nevertheless shielded and used as reserves and, to some extent, as operational units. They stood by in case of occasional 'mob incidents', as for instance in Upper Silesia, while they waited for some more momentous hour to strike.

Kapp's heroes from the Ehrhardt brigade found it especially hard to change back into mufti and they continued to serve their Fatherland in the thinly disguised 'Organisation Consul'. They thought it useful to enliven the humdrum daily life of the bourgeoisie by attacks on various 'traitors' in the system. In the previous year, 1921, the leader of the parliamentary group of the Bavarian Independent Socialists, Gareis, had been shot dead. And – to mention only the 'successful' assassination attempts – just three months later, on 26 August, two Ehrhardt officers had murdered Matthias Erzberger while he was out walking during a summer vacation in the Black Forest. Erzberger had only just announced his return to political life. Even this shoddy act of revenge for Compiègne, directed as it was at the wrong target, was widely greeted with enthusiasm in right-wing circles of the middle class. At that time the President of the Reich had issued a decree based on Article 48 of the constitution that provided an instrument designed to deal with the unbridled propaganda of the press and of party meetings hostile to the constitution. The parties of the right mounted an attack on the decree, and in Bavaria, which still retained – in spite of protests from Berlin – the state of emergency declared against the left in the days of soviet rule, Kahr actually refused to implement it. The official attitude to right-wing delinquents was quite plain: the head of the Munich police force personally assisted Erzberger's murderers to make good their escape abroad!

Kahr, backed by increasingly powerful right-wing groups outside parliament, was keen to avoid a second capitulation such as he had experienced in the matter of the Home Guards. He meant to use this infringement of the police authority of the individual states as the starting-point for a renewed federalistic protest movement. (The implementation of the emergency decree was solely a matter for the Minister of the Interior of the Reich.) His ultimate aim was to break away from the 'Marxist' Berlin system (to these people anything at all in which Social Democrats were involved was 'Marxist', no matter how remotely or indirectly). For this reason he was utterly opposed to any compromise. It was only when more reasonable circles in the Bavarian People's Party refused to be involved in such an act of open defiance and induced Kahr to resign that a compromise was negotiated under his successor, Count Lerchenfeld. This put an end to the state of emergency in Bavaria and ensured that the Berlin measures for the protection of the Republic were valid within the white and blue-striped frontier posts of Bavaria, albeit in a modified form. For a second time an open conflict with Bavaria had been avoided, without any effective stop being put to Bavaria's development into an anti-Marxist 'cell', i.e. an anti-democratic happy hunting ground for all sorts of forces and trends hostile to the Republic.

The outcry over Rathenau's murder was no less vehement. It had taken place, incidentally, only three weeks after an unsuccessful attempt on Scheidemann's life. Now, for the first time, a minister in office had fallen victim to right-wing terrorists – an individual, moreover, with impeccable credentials. None of the common clichés applied in his case: Rathenau was unquestionably neither a crank like Eisner, nor a Communist agitator like Liebknecht, nor a possible profiteer like Erzberger. The bourgeois conscience could not be squared with the argument 'It served him right'. The workers protested with a twenty-four-hour strike, and there was some bloodshed. In the Reichstag the nationalist Helfferich was shouted down and virtually forced to leave the chamber. It was he who had, previously with Erzberger and now with Rathenau, manifestly sown the seed that had borne bloody fruit in the grenade thrown by the assassins, once again members of the Organisation Consul. On the eve of the murder the Foreign Minister had been attacked in the most intemperate terms by Helfferich: Rathenau had been accused of being indifferent to national interests and, by his policy of fulfilment, was blamed in part for the 'frightening devaluation of the German currency' and the 'crushing' of Germany's middle classes.

Once more, and even more drastically than after the murder of Erzberger, the democratic Republic had recourse to countermeasures. In the Reichstag the Chancellor delivered a speech culminating in an appeal to eliminate the atmosphere of murder and poison that prevailed in the country, and warning against the enemy 'who stood on the right'. The President signed a new decree under Article 48 'for the protection of the Republic', which renewed and rendered more precise the bans and penalties imposed in the preceding year. This original decree had been rescinded in December by a majority made up of parties from both left and right: Social Democrats, Independent Social Democrats, Communists and Nationalists. The new legislation provided for a tribunal composed in part of lay justices to deal with offences against the constitution. It even proved possible in the following month to replace the emergency decree by an amendment to the constitution designed to protect the Republic. This was achieved only because, under Stresemann's influence, almost all the People's Party representatives in the Reichstag voted together with the coalition parties and the Indepenedent Social Democrats, thus ensuring the necessary two-thirds majority.

Apart from the Nationalists and individual members of the People's Party, the Bavarian People's Party had also voted against the amendment. There was thus renewed resistance in Bavaria on the part of federalistic and nationalistic elements to any measures designed to protect the integrity of the Reich. Bavaria promulgated its own decree for the protection of the Reich 'instead of' the amendment passed by the Reichstag. A major bone of contention was the judicial autonomy of the states – now threatened, for one thing, by a new centralizing bill governing the powers of local police forces that was indubitably aimed at Bavaria. After all, the tracks of nearly all those involved in attempts at political assassination had petered out south of the Danube. The main threat to local judicial authority, however, was Berlin's decision to transfer jurisdiction in the case of political offences to a new State Court. Bavaria still had its People's Courts that had been set up 'temporarily' following the summer of 1919 in order to deal with the deeds and misdeeds of the Soviet Republic. Ever since then they had continued to function without let or hindrance, persecuting and harrying the political left – and only the left, of course – often handing down sentences of draconian severity.

The Reich, lacking any executive machinery of its own, was unable to enforce laws that had been legitimately passed, other than by the use of military force. Such a step would not only have imperilled the country's unity, but also severely tried the loyalty of troops called upon to enforce Reich legislation. For these reasons a compromise was once more arrived at, with Ebert acting as mediator. Bavaria agreed to give up its separate decree in return for the restriction of the State Court's jurisdiction to major cases involving more than purely regional issues. In addition, there was to be a separate south German division of the court, with three (out of four!) Bavarian lay justices, and an equal number of professional judges (all of them Bavarian). There were also further concessions regarding location, the power to grant reprieves and a number of other topics that had been drawn into the debate.

For a third time the final settlement of political differences between the Reich and Bavaria – long since overdue – had been postponed. The Republic could now be defended on a uniform basis throughout its entire territory, as far as that was feasible with the administrative apparatus at its disposal. But it had become clear in the meantime that right-wing agitation hostile to the Republic could no longer be dealt with by bans and police state methods. The foundations on which the Republic rested had become far too weak as regards its own citizens.

5

From the battle of the Ruhr to the stabilization of the mark

Rathenau had been dead no more than a matter of months when the political consequences of the failure of the policy of fulfilment backed by him and Wirth began to be manifested. During the discussions on the law for the protection of the Republic the Centre Party and the Democrats had already made an attempt to include the People's Party in the government, because the latter, under Stresemann's influence, had opposed terrorism and supported the law. This attempt had failed when the Social Democrats turned it down. Now, however, in the autumn, more inflexible relations with the Allies, and especially the recent intransigence of the French, also seemed to call for a broader-based government, for reasons of foreign policy.

Before the Reparations Commission two opposing views faced each other over an apparently unbridgeable gap. Even those Allies who did not share the French intransigence towards Germany called for a stabilization of the currency from Germany's own resources: only then could a revision of reparations be discussed. Germany, on the other hand, argued that international assistance, in particular a postponement of payments, was an absolutely essential precondition for the stabilization of the mark. As 1923 was to prove, this particular sequence was *not* necessary, and even from a subjective point of view the German contingent were inclined to look on their claim that stabilization was impossible under the unrelenting pressure of reparations simply as a useful argument in the fight against reparations, an argument that was particularly acceptable to Anglo-Saxon ears. In any case there was no doubt that there would be tough international arguments in the near future and a stronger government was desirable.

At the end of October a front extending from the People's Party was formed. At the same time Ebert's period of office was extended until the middle of 1925 by means of a law which changed the constitution. In fact, popular election of the President should have been carried out as early as 1920, but the government parties had time and time again shied away from an election of this kind, in view of the continuing uncertainty at home and the complications abroad that might ensue – much to the displeasure of the President, who would have been glad to see his position strengthened through a plebiscite. It was mainly Ebert who wished to see this party grouping, which had extended his period of office, turned into a government coalition. Wirth's efforts to obtain a corresponding commission from the President failed once again because the Social Democrats refused. The latter did not believe that their new party colleagues, the rump of the Independent Socialists who had just joined them, could be expected to associate with the People's Party, which represented big business. This concern on the part of the Social Democrats for their new left wing tended to make them less flexible and more wary in all their dealings with the middle-class parties. The result was ultimately Wirth's resignation in the middle of November: he was unwilling to govern without the Social Democrats. He was succeeded by a 'business administration' of experts under the managing director of HAPAG (the Hamburg–America Steamship Company), Wilhelm Cuno, which was more or less outside the usual parliamentary framework.

Cuno belonged to no party. Politically, he had formerly been close to the People's Party, but was now associated with the conservative right wing of the Centre Party which was once more growing in importance. Wirth's failure, as the latest in a long line of mishaps to befall the Republic, had not in fact led to breaches in the ranks of Centre Party voters, who were united by their religion. However, within the party the democratic trend initiated by Erzberger in 1917 began to give way to a ready acceptance of conservative, and ultimately authoritarian, 'renewal campaigns'. The Centre Party, whose policies were not dictated by the usual, generally more or less political, class interests, but by the essentially cultural and otherwise more flexible concerns of a religious community, turned out to be a good barometer registering any impending change in the political climate. A number of other members of the government had no party affiliations, but leant to the right: those figures in the economy with 'discountable' signatures, from whom much was expected and who, it was thought, would impress opponents abroad more than the politicians.

Although by no means unusual under the rules of the parliamentary game, this cabinet of business experts signified the first obvious symptom of political lassitude in the public under a *German* democratic regime that had only just been installed and was distinctly unstable. The public was still not aware of the imperative need for parliamentary compromise, for a balance between economic and other interests. They attributed many of the evils of the last few years to trivial squabbles between the parties and to 'horse-trading' for influence and jobs, and placed their hopes of a remedy in a 'strong', non-party political, 'national' government. The authoritarian state had fostered illusions of government by capable experts who were above party affiliation: they would act with paternal impartiality at home to ensure that everyone got their due, play their part on the international scene with a firmness and determination befitting the nation's dignity – and be rewarded with the success they deserved. Such illusions were only fleetingly realized in the parliamentary intermezzo that lay between the Empire and the advent of Brüning. Time had not yet run out for the parties, but for the first time they seemed incapable of assuming responsibility in the face of an impending crisis and were prepared to hand political power to others. This was surely a warning signal that the machinery of this state was no longer functioning as it was meant to. Its adversaries on the right and the left were still too weak to threaten it other than by a *coup d'état* or an insurrection that would have little prospect of success, but the signs of the times suggested that this situation might change very soon.

In fact Cuno's government was not totally outside the party political sphere. It had ministers from the People's Party, from the Centre Party and the Democratic Party. The Social Democrats, however, were left out. On the other hand, Cuno could boast of support from the Nationalists on his right. Altogether his cabinet represented a perceptible swing to the right when compared with its predecessor. Nevertheless, the new bold policy in response to French demands that was expected of the 'big business' government was also backed by the Social Democrats – and even, up to a point, by the Communists.

Cuno submitted to the Allies' suggestions for a five-year moratorium, which would be bridged by a system of internal and external reparations loans, and which would involve deliveries in kind. The proposal called in effect for a temporary suspension of reparations, but promised at least an attempt to stabilize the currency from the country's own resources, with the aid of part of the internal loans. Moreover, France's need for security was to be met by the offer of a kind of anticipatory Locarno, i.e. by an undertaking on the part of the Rhineland powers not to commence hostilities against each other without first holding a national referendum. The tone which the 'national' German government had now adopted, however, made it easier for Poincaré to insist stubbornly on his legal rights. His British and Italian allies had put forward compromise proposals, but if they were not prepared to join him, as he told the Chamber, he was determined to go it alone and take steps to insure France against loss by seizing 'productive pledges'. Such measures, he argued, should on no account be construed as punitive action: Germany was attempting to disguise a prosperous and solvent economy by staging a state bankruptcy. Any creditor was entitled to take such action. Germany was perfectly capable of paying, but was simply unwilling to do so. And as his British friends actually did refuse to join him, Poincaré went ahead on his own.

The threat of sanctions against the Ruhr, the industrial heartland of Germany, had already been on the table several times. So far, however, the hostile sanctions, which had been followed by concessions in the fulfilment of reparations on Germany's part, had been limited to less important areas on the right bank of the Rhine. But now the hour of the Ruhr had struck. A delay which justified sanctions could readily be found, although the pretext was somewhat flimsy. Because a short-term moratorium on reparations payments had been in operation since August, the famous 100,000 telegraph poles – part of the Allies' massive demands for timber – which had not been delivered punctually to France had to serve as an excuse. Against the vote of the British, the Reparations Commission adjudged the delay in delivering the telegraph poles to be a formal breach of the peace treaty, and France declared that these deliberate infringements called for territorial sanctions. A delay in coal deliveries which was detected shortly afterwards lent a little more plausibility to the French measures: after all, there was not much timber to be had from the Ruhr. Coal, however, was a different matter.

In order to fetch this coal, French and Belgian troops marched into the Ruhr on 11 January 1923. This step was explained to the German government in thoroughly modern terms: the five French and one Belgian division were only there to protect a commission of technical experts who were to supervise the operations of the coal-mining syndicate in the Ruhr, to ensure the strict implementation of the programme laid down by the Reparations Commission and to take all necessary steps to see that reparations were paid. There was no thought 'at the moment', the statement went on, of a military operation or an occupation of a political nature.

As usual, the government of the Reich registered 'a solemn protest before the entire world'. This time, however, it did not stop there: it recalled its ambassadors from Paris and Brussels and discontinued all payments in cash and kind to France and Belgium. The Ruhr coal syndicate had in fact made its escape in good time before the French invasion and moved, together with all its records, to Hamburg, so that a centralized registration of coal stocks by the occupying forces was prevented. Now individual pits received instructions not to deliver coal to the French, even if they offered to pay for it. A number of industrialists, including Fritz Thyssen, were arrested by the occupying authorities and brought before a court martial. They were joined by German civil servants who had refused to obey the instructions of the French, for the government had ordered the civil service to obey only *German* instructions and to refuse to obey orders from the occupation troops or authorities that conflicted with these instructions. In particular, railwaymen were told not to transport confiscated coal. Even the police force refused to go on duty after the French had forbidden them to wear uniform or to bear arms. And the German population, united as they had not been for years following this French intervention, responded unambiguously to the resistance slogans, even in the occupied territories.

Poincaré, of course, was not prepared to be deprived of the fruits of his Ruhr campaign in this way. A state of siege was succeeded by even more stringent measures. Fresh troops marched in. Civil servants who had refused to obey orders and remained loyal to their oath were arrested together with representatives of local authorities and expelled along with their families – a total of 140,000 souls. Still more towns, such as Dortmund and Gelsenkirchen, and also the area round Offenburg on the Upper Rhine, were occupied, as were Emmerich and Wesel on the Lower Rhine. Branches of the Reichsbank, other public banking facilities and a good many private accounts were confiscated, customs barriers separated the Ruhr district from the rest of the Reich, the railways were placed under French management, German ministers were refused entry, and local people were required to carry passports. On both sides each measure was met by a countermeasure; only the most important of these are mentioned here.

The mood of the country, already anything but friendly towards the French, naturally became more and more inflamed. There were clashes between Germans and Frenchmen, either deliberately provoked or simply as a result of the tense atmosphere; fatalities occurred on a number of occasions when French troops opened fire. The gravest incident of this kind took place in Essen on 31 March, when French soldiers attempted to drive away vehicles belonging to Krupp. On the instructions of the management the workers abandoned their benches, the troops opened fire and left eleven dead on the Krupp premises; two more workers later died of their injuries. Krupp von Bohlen und Halbach and eight of his leading managers were sentenced by a court martial to between ten and fifteen years in prison and fines of 100 million marks each.

There were also occasions when *passive* resistance turned into *active* opposition. This was in fact less the case for the local population of the Ruhr itself; they were sufficiently occupied with the effects of their passive resistance. The protagonists were activists from nationalist circles elsewhere in Germany who made their way to the Ruhr to initiate a kind of guerilla campaign against the French invasion. Their acts of sabotage on bridges, railway lines, canals and so on, and their attacks on French sentries were naturally followed by severe reprisals, fresh arrests and deportations and eventually even death sentences. One of these was actually carried out by the French: a former member of a volunteer corps, now a National Socialist, Albert Leo Schlageter, was shot by a French firing-squad near Düsseldorf on 26 May. The battle against the incursion into the Ruhr had found its martyr.

The government had not instigated active resistance, indeed it had warned against it and described it as pointless, but it could not stand aside from the glorification of Schlageter as a national hero which embraced all factions, from the extreme right to the Communists.

In the meantime there was confusion and disorder in other parts of Germany and the political unity of January was slowly beginning to crumble. The national elation could not last for long; it could make people forget the trials and tribulations of everyday life for a brief spell only. And these were indeed bad enough, for it was now that the great currency delirium set in. The problem of reparations had been shelved for the moment: the government had resolved not to deliver reparations in cash or kind to powers involved in the occupation of the Ruhr. However, the campaign of passive resistance was costing far more than the reparations, in terms of lost production and the compensation which had been guaranteed by the government.

The Reichsbank was able to hold the mark stable for about three months by support purchases at the expense of its gold and currency reserves, i.e. what was left of the mark. When the French occupied the Ruhr on 11 January, 10,000 marks were needed to buy one dollar. As a consequence of the incursion into the Ruhr the paper mark at first fell drastically. Then, following the introduction of supporting measures, the exchange rate of the dollar stayed at an average of 25,000 marks until the end of April. In April, however, the Reich abandoned its attempt to prop up the mark. There was no sign of the Ruhr business ending, and no one wished the country to be totally stripped of its gold and foreign currency, especially as they were obviously being thrown into a bottomless pit. Besides, speculators who thought very little of a mark which rose only fitfully and minimally in exchange value, now stabbed the government in the back by submitting foreign currency cheques for encashment. Stinnes and his like might well gloat, for now the inflationary spiral moved into that hectic phase that ultimately turned today's money into tomorrow's wastepaper. In May the average exchange rate was 50,000 marks to the dollar, in June 110,000, in July 350,000 and in August finally 4.6 million paper marks.

The well-nigh universal enthusiasm that had greeted a response to French greed that was – for once – more than just empty words was obviously bound to flag under the ordeal. As far as Poincaré was concerned, the undertaking was not proceeding exactly as he had imagined. The gains were at first minimal and, even later on, not exactly spectacular. In the course of time, when the situation had settled down and signs of weakening began to appear on the German side, more could be extracted from the 'productive pledge' on the Ruhr. The Anglo-Saxon allies, however, waxed indignant on legal, political and economic grounds. Shortly after the French had marched into the Ruhr, the Americans withdrew from their small occupation zone in the Rhineland as a mark of protest. This was no gain as far as Germany was concerned, for their place was taken by the French – much to the disgust of the local population.

Suggestions which Cuno submitted at the beginning of May were little calculated to persuade the Anglo-Saxons to offer active opposition to the French. They were concerned once again with the 30,000 million marks that had once been mentioned, but this time the figure was so hedged about with ifs and buts that it was easy to see that there was no intention of paying even that sum. Moreover, Cuno's government stated that passive resistance would go on until the evacuation of the Ruhr. This gave Poincaré the excuse he was looking for to break off all negotiations until the passive resistance stopped. Any compromise solution was thus blocked, and it was only a matter of who could hold out longer: Germany or France. Since the Germans were the underdogs, while Poincaré had an overwhelming vote of confidence from the French nation in his pocket, the issue could not be in doubt for very long.

At first sight it seems amazing that the Weimar state, in this dismal situation, did not more readily once again become the target for assaults by radical groups which had brought it to the brink of disater on various occasions and now might have engulfed it altogether. Never had the situation so favoured a seizure of power by the Communists, especially as they, like everyone else, were now unashamedly riding on the tidal wave of national indignation against France. However, the political line taken by Moscow and international Communism at that time was opposed to any such action. Besides, Rapallo was already paying dividends. Such a policy was in keeping with the fact that the revolutionary zeal of the German workers, in so far as it had ever existed, had been exhausted in the fruitless attempts of the years 1919–21.

It is true that there were disturbances here and there in 1923, and once even an attempt at a localized general strike. However, the radical left was concerned more with consolidating its collaboration with the Social Democrats, so as to be able to take over once Cuno's right-wing cabinet had come to the end of its tether. The exclusively Social Democratic governments in Thuringia, and especially the government under the lawyer Zeigner in Saxony, had concluded alliances with the Communists, acknowledging their support in the state parliaments by setting up proletarian defence organizations in common. In the Communist camp this was reckoned to be a first, impressive step in the right direction.

The Social Democrats in Saxony and Thuringia had thus formed links with the Communists under the leadership of Brandler, who was committed to a more right-wing course, but they were only a new left wing of their party. The Social Democratic leadership clung to its traditional aversion to a Third International that was in bondage to Moscow. At this time Bebel's party was weaker than it ever had been, or ever was to be in the future. Its parliamentary representation, admittedly, had swelled to huge proportions following the merger with the rump Independent Socialists, but this was nothing but a deceptive façade, a gigantic corps of leaders without an adequate following. The party had been paralysed when its chief supporters, the trade unions, were shorn of their power. Faced with membership dues that shrank to nil in a matter of days, and lacking even a short-term financial cushion, they found themselves in no position either to finance a strike or to conduct meaningful wage negotiations. For this reason the gravely debilitated Social Democrats were not in the least interested in experiments. Would they be prepared to assume governmental responsibility at some stage with their former middle-class coalition partners, if they were called upon to do so? Yes, certainly – but no more than that.

Even more perplexing than the tranquillity on the left was the momentary lull on the right. But after all, Cuno's cabinet was unsullied by Marxists, it was rather a businessman's government supported by the Nationalists and politically located all along the line dividing black, red and gold from black, white and red, with the centre of gravity situated on the latter side. No longer were there generals with ambitions to launch a putsch, at least not on the active list or in influential positions. For in the Reichswehr, obedience in the Prussian tradition was once more the order of the day – at any rate as long as those who commanded it were wearing uniform. Beyond that, however, who could say? 'I would like to know,' the President of the Reich once asked his Chief of Staff at that time, 'where the Reichswehr actually stands?' And Seeckt replied with sturdy self-confidence: 'The Reichswehr stands behind me.' But where did Seeckt stand? As always in those days, he stood with ordered arms waiting for the time when a real 'Reich', a greater Prussia, would emerge from this Republic. He himself would be prepared to participate in this transformation, in so far as it took place 'legally'.

For the moment the situation called for military preparedness towards the outside world, as far as that was possible, given the weakness of the available forces. There was of course no question of opposing the French in the Ruhr. But what if they were to extend the occupation? After all, everything so far had happened in the demilitarized zone. When the French marched into Dortmund, the German government warned the Allies that any further advance would bring them into areas garrisoned by German troops. But what could the Reichswehr have done about it? Things were different in the east, where it was feared that the Poles – either on their own initiative or at the instigation of the French – would try to assert their unsuccessful claims, in Upper Silesia, say, by the employment of regular troops.

Even to counter this possible threat, it is true, the leadership of the Reichswehr, including their minister, believed that their army of 100,000 men was inadequate. The Allied Military Control Commission no longer existed de facto; the German government had refused to allow inspection by the French and the Belgians following the entry into the Ruhr, and the British officers had thereupon also ceased to act. The time seemed ripe to cast off the restrictions that had been imposed on German rearmament. This was done by the creation of the so-called 'black Reichswehr': by recruiting surplus 'temporary volunteers' and also by forming additional units that were stationed in barracks or on farms, masquerading as 'labour squads'.

In this way began a range of hectic activities outside the legal limits set by the Versailles Treaty, which had become the law of the land, but it was all so respectable and in the national interest that no 'good German' could possibly object. Nevertheless, people who were concerned about the democratic constitution had misgivings such as were expressed in that question of Ebert's to Seeckt: wasn't all this patriotic activity on the part of the military not perhaps directed against the Republic rather than against any external enemy? In particular, there were incidents involving an institution which, for want of other candidates, was increasingly playing the part of a republican defence force: the Prussian police force, which had been under the leadership of the Social Democratic Prussian Minister of the Interior for a period of fourteen years (apart from a break of four months in 1921). They had uncovered arms caches of a totally unpatriotic kind, and had seized docu- ·ments clearly relating to the military underground and its aims. Agreements were arrived at between the Reichswehr Minister, Gessler, and the Prussian Minister of the Interior, Severing, which were calculated to prevent the worst abuses and dangers, although in fact nothing much changed at lower levels.

It was not only the underground political activities of the Reichswehr which gave cause for concern: even more alarming were the links which were discovered time and time again between army formations and the volunteer corps, which, although formally disbanded years ago, were still ready, even in mufti, to go into action against the French or the Poles, the Communists or the Democrats. The ambition of the volunteer corps to be incorporated into the armed forces had already been disappointed once (in 1920) and their hopes were not to be fulfilled on this occasion either. It is true that the Reichswehr liked to recruit its temporary volunteers from the pool of man-power represented by the demobilized volunteer corps: they were reliable in the 'national' sense – they were anything but reliable in a republican sense, but who cared about that? The leaders of the Reichswehr, however, who had contrived to hold on to their posts had not the slightest intention of adopting the Free Corps, complete with their commanders. For, quite apart from all sorts of personal animosities and rivalries, this increment of personnel would naturally have gravely imperilled the whole 'apolitical' political concept of the Reichswehr leadership.

It even came to an open conflict between them and the men of the volunteer corps. The dispute had smouldered ever since the period of the latter's disbandment, and it had been latent even before then, for these soldiers of fortune scorned any rank above lieutenant-colonel as bourgeois and hidebound. In 1923, here as elsewhere, the rift in the political right which had been apparent in previous years now widened to breaking-point. Alongside conservatives intent on a restoration, there was another group, still divided within itself, which sneered at ideas of restoration and reaction. The Empire with its 'good old days' meant little more to them than the despised 'Jewish Republic': they were steering a course towards new nationalistic and authoritarian shores. This distinction was clearly and publicly expressed in the way in which the leaders of the Free Corps and their followers renounced the parties of the right in 1922/23. They thought that things were moving too slowly in these parties, everything was too 'dull', too 'senile', too backward-looking. Three deputies in the Reichstag who had hitherto been Nationalists were now sitting as members of the new Freedom Party of the German Race (Deutschvölkische Freiheitspartei).

Having been rebuffed by the Reichswehr, the racial nationalists and the Free Corps tried an approach via the Chancellor: they claimed that the Reich needed strong defence units against the external enemy, but also against the enemy at home – of whose existence, admittedly, there was no evidence. It was high time, they argued, to consolidate these forces under the supreme command of Ludendorff. Whether this appealed to Cuno or not, he could not very well take up a position in opposition to the Reichswehr. Seeckt's support for any such project was hardly likely to be gained by the mention of Ludendorff's name. The leader of the volunteer corps, Rossbach, chief of the 'Gymnastic Associations' (i.e. the new party's defence organization), was arrested out of hand and prosecuted under the law for the protection of the Republic. Only one man was entitled to pursue Reichswehr policy and that was Seeckt. 'In Germany no one can carry out a putsch but me', – so the general assured the ministers of the Reich in that year, 'and I declare to you that I do not mean to do so.'

In this way the part that the Free Corps had intended to act had been cut out of the play. This did not mean, however, that the rift between the conservative camp and the extreme nationalist opponents of the Republic was so ideologically deep that it could not be bridged, nor that all contacts and links between them had been broken off. The path to a common front, such as helped to shape the last years of the First Republic, remained viable, and the Reichswehr was glad to go on using various bands of freebooters wherever it seemed appropriate to local commanders. Besides, there was a state in 1923 where the two nationalist camps still clung together, where conservatives and racial nationalists could still work together ever more openly in their efforts to bring about the downfall of the Republic. This was, of course, the so-called 'nucleus of order': Bavaria.

In 1921 Kahr's Home Guard government had been forced to resign because the Bavarian People's Party had been too intransigent in its attitude to Berlin. Lerchenfeld's cabinet practised parliamentary government and pursued a policy of moderation and appeasement, but it was too feeble for this environment and in the following year it suffered the same fate as its predecessor for the opposite reason. In the argument surrounding legislation to protect the Republic, it had indeed gained a series of concessions on the part of the Reich, but the victory was only a partial one. It had been unable to achieve the Bavarians' principal aim, which was a constitutional guarantee of Bavarian sovereign rights as the prelude to a federalistic revision of the Weimar constitution more or less on the lines of the situation before the war. Lerchenfeld's government collapsed amid the furious clamour and scurrilous abuse of the patriotic organizations as well as the Count's right-wing party 'colleagues'. A right-wing putsch, which had long seemed imminent, was avoided, but largely because Catholic and legitimistic circles refused to join in.

The disbanding of the Home Guards had left a positive jungle of all kinds of radical organizations which profited from this legacy, forming an umbrella organization in November 1923 under the name of 'United Patriotic Associations' (Vereinigte Vaterländische Verbände, or VVV). In the course of 1922 one of these little groups forced its way increasingly into the foreground: the National Socialist German Workers' Party (National-Sozialistiche Deutsche Arbeiterpartei, or NSDAP, commonly known as National Socialists, or Nazis). It could be distinguished from the others, first, by its particularly aggressive and uncommonly anti-Semitic rhetoric, and, second, by the fact that it was not a patriotic club, or a so-called defence force: it was organized as a political party, although it did have its own armed contingent, the 'Storm Troopers' (*Sturmabteilung*, or SA for short). Finally, it possessed a leader who towered head and shoulders over his rivals in the Munich National Park in political instinct, in his psychological insight into the soul of the masses, in his fanatical dedication to his mission and in his sheer rhetorical power: Adolf Hitler. His following was still numerically of little account, but it was active and was constantly kept on the go by its leader.

Hitler had originally been the party's press agent, but in the summer of 1921, after working in the party for eighteen months, he had it totally under his thumb and had risen to be the absolute ruler of his faithful followers. By that time the party had changed from being an obscure political club and become a force to be reckoned with – in Munich politics at least. It had benefited from the patronage of the Kahr government and the Munich headquarters of the Reichswehr, which offered its benevolent support to any organization on the political right. Its welfare had been a matter of personal concern to the Munich chief of police, Pöhner, and the head of his political section, Frick, so that it was now considered a suitable partner for the major right-wing organizations. Even the right-wing Catholic Bavarian People's Party had been eager to take this chicken under its wing, along with others of the nationalistic brood; it was only later that Hitler's burgeoning anti-Catholic zeal was noted with disapproval.

The NSDAP, however, no longer needed the shelter of an incubator. The Lerchenfeld government indicated that it proposed to get tough with the unruly rowdies and their talk of 'Berlin Asians', 'lackeys of the Jews', 'parliamentary hookworms and arse-lickers'. This would not have been difficult, since Hitler, who had moved to Munich from a series of hostels and dosshouses in Vienna, still had Austrian citizenship and could have been deported from Bavaria and from Germany in a matter of days with the help of a simple administrative order. Faced with threats by the National Socialists that if their party leader was deported, 'the Jews in Munich would die by the dozen like dogs', as well as by the furious indignation of the other right-wing associations, Lerchenfeld's Minister of the Interior did not dare to carry out his intentions; instead, he climbed down meekly.

So Hitler was able to carry on. His party celebrated the murder of Rathenau with a poster encouraging fresh acts of the same kind: 'Rathenau is dead, Ebert and Scheidemann are still alive!' After Kahr's heirs, still mourning his departure, had induced Count Lerchenfeld to resign in disgust, a new Bavarian government under Eugen von Knilling was sworn in during November. It was the old coalition of the Bavarian People's Party and the Nationalists posing here as the 'Bavarian Party of the Centre' (because a majority for the Concordat was required). Only the head of the government was new: he represented the right wing of the Bavarian People's Party, and was once again a civil servant, a man of straw put up by the real leaders of the Bavarian People's Party, a figurehead who could be replaced if necessary. He allied himself with the right-wing radicals and, in the Landtag, subscribed to the 1920 programme of the 'Bavarian Roland', Kahr, who had been sullenly waiting for his hour to come in self-imposed rural exile. He did not have much longer to wait. For the events of 1923 triggered off the Bavarian problem for the third time, and actually brought about a solution at last.

At first, however, nothing much happened. As long as Cuno's right-wing government was at the helm in Berlin, no danger threatened from the Bavarian quarter. For the common denominator of all the right-wing rag, tag and bobtail elements amounted in their view to a conflict between a Christian, patriotic Bavaria and a Marxist Berlin infested with Jews. Only if the Berlin government turned 'Marxist' again – and as Munich understood it, this meant if the Social Democrats were represented in the cabinet, even as Post Minister – would the time be ripe for action. And for the white and blue adherents of the Bavarian cause this meant that it would be time to pull out of the Reich; for the black, white and red party it would be the signal for a march on Berlin, after the fashion recently set by Mussolini with his march on Rome. There was one individual, however, to whom the Cuno government was anathema: Adolf Hitler. Having parted company with his associated patriotic comrades, he was now aiming for a radically right-wing 'association of militant organizations'. Immediately after the French entry into the Ruhr he was declaiming that the slogan should not be 'Down with France!' but 'Down with the November criminals!' A man of action, he had scorned and derided passive resistance from the very beginning.

His attitude here casts some doubt on the claim of his party to be 'national'. Its claim to be 'socialist' was greeted with derision – at least by Marxist Socialists; and even if some members of the party, particularly among Hitler's 'old guard', were still infected with 'anti-capitalistic' notions, the party itself, encouraged by support from the capitalists that was not merely moral, blossomed over the years into a splendid capitalist enterprise. The NSDAP was not even 'German', at least until 1923, hardly even Bavarian, but almost exclusively a local Munich phenomenon. And it was only during the pre-Hitler months of 1919 that 'workers' constituted the sociological core of the party: in fact its founders had come from the central railway workshops in Munich. The NSDAP as such was always, first and foremost, a party of the *petite bourgeoisie*, of white-collar employees, the unemployed and other rootless individuals. Its mighty surge in popularity came about because it served as a catchment area for those classes and groups who had been thrown off course by the war, inflation and the economic crisis, who had been dispossessed and whose economic existence and social standing were threatened. Finally, from the very start Hitler had never had the slightest inclination to lead a 'party' in the sense of *pars* – a mere part. He was not interested in being a big fish in a small pond. His thoughts were consistently focused on a dictatorship, an authoritarian state, whether he was claiming the leading role for himself, or – in the early years – was drumming up support for someone else. There was no need in any case for parties other than his own, because – apart from the Jews and some numerically insignificant splinter groups – Hitler promised everybody exactly what they wanted. He did so quite blatantly in addressing himself to various individual groups, but he also did it sufficiently obviously before mass audiences: whoever had ears to hear might have heard. But Hitler had the gift of stopping up men's ears and closing their minds. He had a comforting faith to offer all those who were frightened, turning them into unquestioning believers by virtue of that sovereign remedy used by every founder of a religion or pseudo-religion.

Admittedly, there were not many who believed in Hitler at the beginning of 1923. Still, in Munich at least he was a force to be reckoned with. With the aid of the Reichswehr Regional Commander-in-Chief, von Lossow, he was able to stage a dozen open-air mass meetings. Lossow, the general commanding the 7th Division, held his title of Commander-in-Chief as a relic of Bavaria's former reserved rights, and he had a special relationship with the Bavarian authorities: he could be appointed only on their nomination, and the government could call on the Bavarian division in case of emergency. Hitler's meetings 'went off extremely well' – in spite of the state of emergency, originally imposed expressly to prevent them but now invoked only against counter-demonstrations. Some six weeks later, on 11 March, Hitler had reached the point where General von Seeckt condescended to talk to him. The meeting was timely: three days later, the Supreme Court endorsed decrees enacted by most of the German states ordering the dissolution of the NSDAP as an unconstitutional organization. Hitler had to share the territory of the Reich with the Freedom Party of the German Race. He was content for the moment with the south as his sphere of influence, for in Bavaria no one was likely to harm a hair of his head.

With the 'Association' he had organized he embarked on an armed demonstration against the socialists' May Day celebrations. Whether he meant to attempt a putsch, no one really knows; the Bavarian police force was on the alert at any rate, with the Reichswehr standing by in reserve, and they ultimately disarmed Hitler's forces, which had paraded for the first time bearing arms (one wonders who had supplied them). When nothing happened, apart from some drill, a procession and a rally, the Ministry thought it had won a trial of strength and had returned a fitting answer to Hitler's question as to who was actually master in the state. In fact the incident, which came very close to a treasonable act, was not penalized in any way, and a half-hearted investigation begun by the Public Prosecutor was soon dropped. In spite of this fiasco Hitler enjoyed a great deal of sympathy locally. And, besides, he might turn out to be useful sooner or later, for who knew what might come after Cuno in Berlin.

In 1923, however, the danger from the right was mainly a problem for individual states. In the Reich outside Bavaria, the right were quarrelling among themselves and the Reichswehr had little interest in embarking on any sort of venture. But here, too, the paramilitary organizations had begun to flourish once more, the almost forgotten Pan-Germans had also begun to weave their plots again and succeeded here and there in attracting a circle of junior officers or a general who was tired of Seeckt's wait-and-see policy. The leadership of the Reichswehr, however, declined to be involved: no unconstitutional action, if you don't mind! All the military had in mind was a constitutional dictatorship, such as was – allegedly – provided for under Article 48. This, it seemed, was the only way out of the dilemma. For Bavaria was not the only threat to Berlin that had surged up in a particular area.

Things were also happening on the left, in Thuringia and Saxony, although there had been no disagreements or acts of open defiance on the Bavarian scale. Armed 'proletarian squads' had emerged, been activated or recognized, as a result of the pact between the Social Democratic governments and the Communist Party. They were used occasionally as special constabulary and in some areas, especially in Thuringia, they were coming increasingly under Communist influence. The more critical the situation in Bavaria, the closer the authorities in central Germany drew to their Communist allies. Zeigner began attacking the Reich government openly in his speeches. The Saxon government, already at loggerheads with the Reichswehr, accused the latter of being politically unreliable, and also charged big business with being corrupt.

The aim of this popular front in central Germany was indeed to preserve the Republic, just as the express aim in Bavaria was to eradicate it. Since the French entry into the Ruhr the Communists had been beating the patriotic drum loudly enough to gladden the most stalwart heart, but this could hardly be more than a tactical interlude to match the approach adopted by the Third International. Besides, the Republic, as it had developed in the meantime, could not be saved by the socialist side. Even with the best will in the world and the greatest possible devotion to the Republic, the regime was just as likely to be driven into chaos and dissolution by any action launched from a socialist base as by any similar move coming from the Bavarian 'nucleus of order'. In 1923, as opposed to 1919–21, the balance of forces was so finely matched and so entrenched that the constitution and the unity of the Reich could be preserved only by Berlin's steering a careful middle course.

Besides these two territorial pseudo-problems, there was a third, genuine, problem which was, however, largely beyond the influence of Germany. In the occupied zone, as one aspect of French activity on the Rhine and the Ruhr, separatism, which had been smouldering since 1919, now burst into flame. At this late stage, when similar impulses had long since subsided elsewhere, the separatist cause experienced its most dangerous revival. Separatist associations and parties flourished under the patronage of the French occupying power. They armed themselves (or were provided with arms), which was not otherwise permitted for Germans, they demonstrated, occupied town halls – all with the aid of a foreign backer. All the same, it was not much fun being a separatist in the Rhineland: if the French were not actually standing close by, it was not uncommon for these people to be beaten up or even killed, for the overwhelming majority of the population was not in favour of their cause.

The separatists were a pretty mixed bunch. They included a good proportion of riff-raff, but also some very respected citizens, supporters of the Centre Party as well as Social Democrats. But what they wanted under their red, white and green banner was not entirely clear. The 'Rhenish Republic' and the 'Autonomous Palatinate', which the occupying power actually tried to set up in October, were initially intended to mark a secession from Prussia or Bavaria. The professed intention was to remain within a federation of the Reich, although the association would be distinctly loose – after all, this was occupied territory. Who really wanted this, and who simply pretended to want it, is hard to say. The French at any rate do not seem to have taken these assurances seriously, but no doubt felt that they had come a good deal closer to their ultimate aim of a Rhenish buffer-state between France and Germany. The response was similar in Berlin, where the subversive activities of Dorten, Smeets, Matthes and Heinz were watched with considerable concern, and attempts were made to counter them with declarations, appeals and protests.

All these problems were, however, more or less outcrops of the main problem: the campaign of passive resistance in the Ruhr and the total collapse of the currency, which was one of its consequences. If relations with France could be normalized once more, then the German administration could be restored in the occupied zone and the separatists' mills would be deprived of their French grist. And if the monetary flood of the inflation receded, then the more lunatic right-wing organizations would find themselves in financial difficulties; without money the *condottieri* of the counter-revolution would be unable to keep their squads together. And if the danger of the Whites in the south evaporated, then the Red coalition in central Germany would also collapse. So far, so good. But how could the Gordian knot on the Ruhr be unravelled? It could certainly not be done to Germany's advantage, for in 1923 Germany was at the end of her tether: Poincaré had, of course, been able to hold out longer.

If we assess the balance of forces between Germany and France with the benefit of hindsight, it is clear that passive resistance was bound to fail. It is less simple to assess its significance. Some commentators say that it was a psychological necessity, and that something had to be done. The Allies should have stayed within the limits of what was acceptable to Germany at that stage and not carried things to extremes. And they examine the question as to which measures were appropriate and effective. Others take a diametrically opposed view, arguing that if there was to be passive resistance, then it should have been consistently carried through and not stopped at half-measures. In practical terms it had been farcical to stop the railways transporting coal while allowing the pits to go on producing it and stacking it for the French to take away with their own labour and transport. It is true that every time the gangs appeared to fetch the coal, the German colliers and their officials vanished from the pits, only to return afterwards and pile up new supplies for the French to help themselves.

This criticism is not without a germ of truth, and one conclusion may be drawn from it: this is what the bosses are like, quick to respond with grand speeches, but it is another matter if it is a question of their profits. But realistically, for how long would it have been possible to maintain a total shut-down of the economy, involving, as it would have, massive unemployment and in effect total support of the Ruhr at least by the remainder of the Reich? True, France would not have received any coal at all once the existing stock-piles had been exhausted. But why should Poincaré have felt obliged to retreat for this reason? In the light of previous experience the opposite would probably have been the case. Germany, on the other hand, would doubtless have had to climb down and raise the white flag eventually, as in fact it had to now, but in a matter of weeks rather than months.

For it could no longer be denied that Cuno had simply got himself into a
jam with his passive resistance. He knew it too; he wished to resign and made
no secret of his wish. In August, when the Reichstag reassembled after the
summer recess, everyone was sure that things could not go on in the same
way. The nationalists were calling for a dictatorship, the Communists wanted
to prosecute Cuno's government in the Supreme Court for having conspired
with the employers to betray the workers' struggle in the Ruhr. The other
parties were agreed that a government of various parties on the broadest
possible basis would have to take over the helm. They were looking for a
man to head the cabinet who was 'forceful to the point of unpopularity'.
And, when the Social Democrats brought down the government by a vote
of no confidence, they found him.

Gustav Stresemann, the son of a Berlin publican, an individual of barely
concealed ambition, had risen to become leader of the People's Party. He
had waited a long time for his hour to come. For years he had suffered from
being overshadowed by that other rising star of German parliamentarianism,
which was not exactly studded with talent – Matthias Erzberger. In the
spring of 1921, following Fehrenbach's resignation, it had seemed that the
way was open for him at last. But his parliamentary party had hesitated and
had been reluctant to 'face up to the – republican – facts of life'. In the
meantime Ebert, who did not quite trust the 'chameleon' and was put off by
such ruthless ambition, had called on Wirth. And along with Wirth, a new
luminary had arisen who threatened to push even further into the background the representative of the People's Party, who was eager to prove his
mettle as a statesman. But fate was kind to Stresemann: both Erzberger and
Rathenau were removed from his path, so that he got the green light to go
ahead on 11 August 1923.

Stresemann had recommended himself for his new office as Chancellor by
speeches of statesman-like moderation. But he had also managed to force his
recalcitrant parliamentary party to adopt his policy and he kept their support
in spite of constant disputes which by no means abated as time went by. He
had no qualms about his ability to conciliate his nationalistic colleagues and
keep them in line by means of bombastically chauvinistic speeches which
hardly differed from the tone he had assumed in wartime, for his position in
the party was based on such contacts. However, we may leave aside the
question as to how far the 'republican' and 'European' Stresemann was
sincere, or how far these qualities were simply vehicles to further his
ambitions. Like any other man, his life no doubt contained its share of mixed
motives, rational factors on the one hand and emotional predilections on the
other. All that need concern us here is the result, and that justifies us without
any doubt in singling out Gustav Stresemann as one of the few important –
and successful – statesmen and servants of the Republic. He has been
described as the only bridge between the black, white and red and the black,

red and gold Germany. The trouble was that no one used this bridge. Its fate was not as dismal as the fate of the bridge that had been erected in the opposite direction under Noske's auspices, but here too the foundations on the near bank turned out to be unsound. For respectable conservatives, their former spokesman, 'Ludendorff's young man' of yesteryear, was to be numbered in future among the 'November criminals'.

Stresemann's cabinet was the first administration of the grand coalition that embraced the People's Party, the Centre Party, the Democrats and the Social Democrats. The fact that the Social Democrats had not only entered a government along with the People's Party (which they had declined to do under Wirth only nine months previously), but were prepared to serve under a Chancellor from that party, was in itself a triumph for Stresemann. All the same, the political situation in the country now called for a Chancellor who was as far to the right as possible to counter the growing clamour among the middle classes for a 'strong man'.

Of the two portfolios that were of special importance in view of the situation, the Chancellor himself took over Foreign Affairs, while the Ministry of Finance was allocated to the Social Democrat Rudolf Hilferding. These two were thus responsible for the two major problems that called for instant solutions: the ending of passive resistance in the Ruhr and, once this had been achieved, the stabilization of the mark, which was still cavorting like a will-of-the-wisp through the exchange rates. Both these tasks were accomplished in the bare 103 days that Stresemann's chancellorship lasted. A thousand million more or less in gold marks was not a matter of life or death, he had said in April (which was remarkable, considering that the other right-wing party, the Nationalists, were unwilling to pay any reparations at all), nor did it much matter whether economic revival came about a year or so sooner or later. What did matter was that the Rhine and the Ruhr should remain German.

There was less hope than ever now of a victory in the Ruhr. With the burdens imposed by the situation there, there was no chance of salvaging the currency. If the government held out against submitting to Poincaré, what choice was there but to abandon the Rhine and the Ruhr to their fate and to the French, in the hope that, in some way or other, they might find their way back into an association with the Reich at a future date? It was not only the captains of industry in the occupation zone who seemed likely at that stage to yield to overtures by the French and accept some kind of special regional status in order to protect their interests. Even in the unoccupied parts of the Reich, there were influential individuals, some of them actually in the government, who toyed with the idea of choosing this way out of the calamity. At the time, separation of the occupied areas from the Reich seemed unavoidable, at least temporarily, and in some such way at least an attempt might be made to salvage Germany's prestige. Stresemann opposed this 'sagging policy', and subsequent events proved him right.

So, if no one was prepared to write off Rhine and Ruhr, the only alternative was to give up passive resistance. The third possibility, continuing with passive resistance, was ruled out. In the occupied territories symptoms of exhaustion were beginning to multiply. Every day of passive resistance was costing the Reich 40 million gold marks – in one month they were paying out more than half of each of the two annual reparations payments. Leading figures in the economy were calling on the government to give way, as were politicians of the moderate right. The nationalistic rowdies in the People's Party and further to the right were unmoved by the catastrophe towards which the country was manifestly drifting. If a change was needed, they argued, then it could only be in the opposite direction, towards active resistance.

It is not surprising, then, that it was Bavaria which urged Stresemann's new cabinet not to raise the white flag, and threatened 'the gravest political consequences within the country' if they did so. On the blue and white or black, white and red chequered political chessboards in Bavaria, the transition from Cuno to Stresemann and the grand coalition had been greeted with fury and 'chilly disdain'. The capitulation on the Ruhr was the final straw. A proclamation to the German nation by the President and government of the Reich, two days after a cabinet decision, announced the termination of passive resistance. This was enough to trigger off in Munich the action which had been threatening for some time.

During the preceding weeks Stresemann had been trying in vain to come to an arrangement with the French which would have allowed Germany to save face and to negotiate at least some small concession on the part of the French. He had explored the possibility of a Rhine pact as a security guarantee for France, and had also reduced the side-effects of the diplomatic boycott, resuming talks with the French representatives. Poincaré, however, was not willing to see diminished the victory which was now within his grasp. The hopes which had been placed in Britain, whose Foreign Minister had firmly opposed French policy in the Ruhr, also led to nothing. When the British Prime Minister, Stanley Baldwin, had a meeting with Poincaré in Paris on 19 September, a communiqué was published that was framed as a warning addressed to Germany and was in fact taken as such. There were no fundamental differences, it read, which might threaten the collaboration of the two countries.

A week later Poincaré had his triumph in his pocket. Stresemann, for his part, had offered proof that he was brave enough to risk the unpopularity called for at this juncture – as it was so often called for in Germany during those years. The peace arrived at in the Ruhr was a peace of capitulation, and it was during the following weeks that the French policy of secession displayed its most alarming features; nevertheless, the solution of the most urgent topical problem, the stabilization of the mark, at least came within the range of possibilities. And simply because it was a peace of capitulation, the twin threat to the unity and the constitution of the Reich which had developed in Bavaria approached what was to be, for the moment at least, its critical climax. In spite of the dismal situation of the Reich, this crisis diminished the threat from the 'nucleus of order' for some time to come.

The Bavarian seismograph, which reliably recorded the temper of the political right, had responded with a convulsive leap to the capitulation in the Ruhr. The nationalistic faction in Munich called for resistance to the Ruhr traitors and seized this useful opportunity to stoke up the fire under their anti-Marxist and federalistic brew and to express their disgust with Stresemann's government, decrying it as Marxist and tainted with democratic ideas. The Bavarian authorities had already declared a state of emergency the previous night (although the Bavarian Prime Minister had consented to the Ruhr capitulation), partly under the pressure of this public mood, partly in order to stem the danger from the extreme right, and to isolate it. They had appointed the 'Bavarian Roland', Gustav von Kahr, General Commissioner with full executive powers: this was a gesture calculated to appease the 'Patriotic Associations', who were backing Kahr, although of the Munich volunteer corps they were the least dangerous.

The government of the Reich thereupon declared a state of national emergency and imposed martial law throughout the country, assigning executive powers to the Minister for the Reichswehr, Otto Gessler; the latter delegated his authority to the officers commanding the military districts. So now it was the Reichswehr that ruled. Seeckt, with whom Stresemann had sought refuge from the impending Bavarian tidal wave, was not actually in possession of full executive powers, while the minister who had been inserted into the chain of command counted in fact for very little. Now it was a question of who would prove to be the stronger: the semi-dictator in Berlin or his opposite number in Munich; the leadership of the Reichswehr or their less privileged comrades, now mainly concentrated in the Bavarian defence units, whom Kahr was trying to bring under his control in order to serve his own ends.

What were Kahr's aims? Or rather, which factors were dominant in these aims: the blue and white element, aiming at a more or less sovereign Bavaria under the restored Wittelsbachs? Or else the black, white and red faction, which was determined to march on Berlin, clean up the 'Marxist pig-sty' there, save Germany and put things to rights at long last? They meant to create a new and powerful, 'national' Reich that would once more show the world the German fist. The slogan 'Via Bavaria to the Reich' could certainly be implemented in a harmonious alliance of blue and white with black, white and red. The succeeding phase, however, 'A strong Bavaria in a strong Reich', was liable to set blue and white federalists and red, white and black unitarians at each others' throats. Still, only implacable protagonists of their own position, like Crown Prince Rupprecht of Bavaria on the one side and

Ludendorff on the other, were inclined to make an apple of discord of this issue. For their more pliable allies this was a problem that could be settled later on. To begin with there was a fair degree of agreement, and where there was not, people pretended that there was – like Hitler, say, who promised to leave His Wittelsbach Majesty and Herr von Kahr to shape their strong Bavaria as they pleased, provided it was within a strong Reich. What dominated the Munich scene more than objective issues were personal animosities and rivalries. The rivalry between Kahr and Hitler turned out to be the most important of these.

What aims Kahr was pursuing were not ultimately so very important. They were also hard to define. It was Rupprecht's supporters who had put Kahr in the saddle, and it was from the house of Wittelsbach that he continued to receive his most powerful support. On the other hand, for instance, he had summoned Captain Ehrhardt to Bavaria, and this hero of the Free Corps had stationed defence units on the borders with Saxony and Thuringia. What was the purpose of these units and of General von Lossow's troops, who were also massed in the area, other than preparations for a march on the north? They would first clean up the Red stronghold of central Germany, then, with their helmets decked with these fresh laurels, they would put things in order in Berlin.

The troops General von Lossow commanded were, to be sure, Reichswehr troops – but *Bavarian* Reichswehr. The conflicts inherent in the twin appointments of a Bavarian regional commander and – simultaneously – a divisional general in the Reichswehr now came into the open. If we wish to form a proper judgement as to the reasons why the manifest facts of real life in Munich triumphed over Berlin, which made its impact only via radio and telephone links, we have to bear in mind that the Bavarian defence units were considerably stronger than the 7th Division of the Reichswehr, and Lossow had informed his military superiors some weeks previously that he was not prepared for a trial of strength with them. Seeckt, however, wanted his subordinate in Munich to make his position clear.

The pretext was provided by personal attacks on the Chancellor and the Chief of Staff of the army which appeared the day following the imposition of the state of emergency in Hitler's party newspaper, the *Völkische Beobachter*. Lossow was ordered to ban the paper. He tried to worm his way out of the predicament, but the army command was firm. The general did not obey the order, however: although he had executive authority in Bavaria under the terms of the state of emergency proclaimed in the Reich, he passed Berlin's order on to Kahr, who had executive powers under the *Bavarian* emergency regulations. Kahr declined to act: he was on the point of uniting all the 'nationalist forces', and was therefore anxious not to offend Hitler. Berlin then ordered the use of armed force. Kahr once more refused to act, and Lossow merely shrugged his shoulders regretfully: there was nothing he could do, for he was determined at all costs to avoid a conflict with the General Commissioner. Berlin reprimanded Lossow and called for his resignation. Bavaria asked why: the general had behaved absolutely correctly. Shortly afterwards, the *Völkische Beobachter* was in fact banned – not on account of Stresemann and Sceckt, but because Hitler had extricated himself from Kahr's embrace and had begun to compete with him in his efforts to rally support, publishing appeals to this end in his paper.

The Lossow case dragged on, however, now divorced from its initial pretext. Bavaria wished to use him as a lever to advance its old federalist interests, which included the command structure of the Reichswehr. Admittedly, there was no great fear of Kahr in Berlin: he had shown himself as not equal to his hour and had dithered backwards and forwards like Buridan's ass between his bundles of hay. But then there was also the deployment of radical right-wing forces on Bavaria's northern border, and finally there was Adolf Hitler in Munich with his followers, by now 40,000 stalwart party members. Hitherto the vacillating Kahr had held them in check – but when would they break loose? The idea that the Reich might impose its authority on Bavaria was utterly crazy: Bavaria was too large and the government of the Reich too feeble, its forces too unreliable in a confrontation with the right. Even if Lossow's and Ehrhardt's troops were to march, 'mop up' in Saxony and Thuringia and enter Berlin with Zeigner's scalp at their belts – who knows, perhaps Seeckt would now find for his part that *his* troops would not fire on their comrades. For the Reichswehr did not back their Chief of Staff all that unanimously.

That had become obvious when, at the end of September and beginning of October, a Major Buchrucker (retired), who was in charge of the 'labour squads' in the Third Military District, had attempted to launch a putsch in the fortress of Küstrin. His intention was to effect from the east the march on Berlin that was so much in the air at the time, and remove Seeckt and Gessler. Buchrucker's move had not been originally planned as an isolated action. Plans of this kind were intended to force the leadership of the Reichswehr and the government of the Reich along the path towards a nationalist dictatorship, and they represented the ultimate aim of the policy pursued by the clandestine 'black Reichswehr'. In so far as the plans entailed a reinforcement of the armed forces, they served the interests of the plotters, namely the security of their own careers. Senior ranks in the Reichswehr, indeed the most senior ranks, had watched this ploy for some time with expectant sympathy and had tolerated it.

This had not prevented the illegal units from following a policy of their own. The leadership of the Reichswehr consequently had to walk a tightrope between them and the thoroughly justified suspicions of the Prussian Ministry of the Interior, which had consented to the secret strengthening of its forces in this way only on condition that such 'organizations' were eliminated. At the end of September Severing's protests – but even more the Bavarian mutiny, which had roots similar to Buchrucker's action – abruptly put an end to this forbearance. Deserted by most of his erstwhile comrades-in-arms, Buchrucker had plunged into a desperate enterprise not unlike that which was to be staged five weeks later, on 9 September, in Munich. The Army Command coped easily enough with the Küstrin amateur, but Seeckt's joy in his 'black Reichswehr' was blighted for good.

The comic opera in Küstrin had not affected the problem in Bavaria, where the danger was as menacing as ever. One thing could be done, however: under the emergency regulations the Berlin authorities were able to deny Zeigner's scalp to their rivals in Munich, the forces at their disposal being adequate for that purpose at least. Saxony and Thuringia were smaller than Bavaria and geographically more conveniently situated. And, whereas the White Guards were armed to the teeth, the ill-organized proletarian battalions in central Germany could muster no more than the odd rifle here and there. Above all, since it would be a campaign against the left, Lossow need have no qualms of conscience. True, in Dresden and Weimar the local governments had been nothing like as obstreperous as in Munich. For that reason even Cuno's Minister of the Interior, Rudolf Oeser, had been reluctant to take unilateral action against Saxony and Thuringa, as long as he was forced to stomach all manner of insubordination on Bavaria's part.

All the same, there were sufficient grounds for complaint in what Zeigner had said in his speeches. Developments in Saxony/Thuringia, on the one hand, and Bavaria on the other, had of course led to further radicalization on both sides: on 18 October diplomatic relations between these states had been broken off! On 10 October the Communists had in fact joined the Saxon government; a week later they entered the Thuringian government. They were well versed in the appropriate vocabulary, and in the Third International it was noted that revolution in Germany might be on the cards after all. On 22 and 23 October a rising was attempted in Hamburg. It found little response and was quickly suppressed, although at considerable cost in human lives. In Saxony, in the meantime, the Reichswehr general in Dresden, representing the authorities under the emergency regulations, had disbanded the proletarian companies. They had defied his order, and Reichswehr regiments had thereupon marched into a number of towns in Saxony. Zeigner had retaliated by publishing revelations about the 'black Reichswehr'. Although he had acted on the basis and in the spirit of the constitution, he was reckoned to have crossed the threshold into the area of high treason, a step that was anathema to all good patriots.

During the second half of October the situation developed further. Following Lossow's dismissal by Berlin, the Bavarian government reminded the Bavarian Reichswehr units of their duty to remain 'true to the sublime task of restoring the internal liberty of our German fatherland' – and reinstated the general. All that happened as a result was that Bavaria was disowned by a conference of the states, and the government of the Reich politely requested Munich to restore the constitutional command structure in the Bavarian Reichswehr units. Saxony, on the other hand, was confronted with an ultimatum demanding the resignation of Zeigner's government, because, it was alleged, Communist ministers were not compatible with the terms of the constitution. After the twenty-four-hour deadline had expired, the Reichswehr marched into Dresden with bands playing, escorting the Commissioner of the Reich, Rudolf Heinze, who was armed with Ebert's emergency decree. The Commissioner, who had been Prime Minister under the Saxon crown only five years previously, intervened somewhat too forcefully, so that he had to be called to heel now and then. But it worked. The Saxon assembly was cowed and appointed a new government. There was no resistance whatsoever. In Thuringia, where the most recent development had been the appointment of a Foreign Minister, the same performance was repeated on 5 November.

Among supporters of the Republic, it is true, there was indignation over this one-sided use of force. The leaders of the Reichswehr declared that they were not in a position to take action simultaneously against the right *and* the left. In other words: they were not prepared to act against the right (as Seeckt stated, he was in command of the Reichswehr, not the proletarian companies). But the government of the Reich was guided in its decision not merely by political likes and dislikes but more by the realization that it was powerless in the face of subversive activities by the right. These were concentrated in Bavaria, but also went on elsewhere in the Reich, where various 'organizations' were merely waiting for the 'call from Bavaria'. The campaign against the left also had the advantage that it improved Berlin's image in the eyes of the right. Thus, the initial objective of the hostile forces massed in northern Bavaria – the springboard, as it were, that was to catapult them into the capital – was no longer relevant. Besides, the nationalists had been deprived of one of their most effective propaganda weapons. It was indeed extremely unfortunate for the fate of the Republic that the Social Democrats had left the coalition following the campaign against Saxony and the refusal of their demand for similar action against Bavaria, leaving Stresemann with a rump cabinet. However, as far as that went at least, the Chancellor could only be pleased that his government had been purged of the stigma of Marxism that so offended the right.

And so the whole affair might have been amicably settled in a third compromise between Berlin and Munich had it not been for Hitler. Lossow had committed himself so far that he could not possibly survive any such agreement, and Berlin was demanding his head as the first condition of any settlement. The Prime Minister, Knilling, and the leaders of the Bavarian

People's Party were considering dropping him, when the leader of the National Socialists tried to stop all his hopes being thus dashed. One thing seemed certain after the example set by Mussolini in Italy and Kemal Pasha in Turkey: whoever first gave the signal, 'à Berlin', would be able to establish himself there after his victory. And Hitler meant to be that man, although possibly after an interregnum under 'Field-Marshal' Ludendorff, with whom the National Socialist leader was working hand in glove at that time.

But the triumvirate of Kahr–Lossow–Seisser (chief of the Bavarian police force) also had ambitions to march on Berlin and proclaim a dictatorship there. Lossow, who had nothing to lose, was already working out his march on Berlin with General Staff precision, assisted by the Patriotic Associations. But he and his friends were still hesitant: they felt that they were too weak on their own. On the other hand, they had no desire to join the march simply as the tail to Hitler's comet. Besides, they meant to be part of a campaign only if it had a 51 per cent chance of success. But there was no such assurance. Hitler, with his 'Defence League' (*Kampfbund*) was also too weak on his own, and he tried to force his faint-hearted allies to risk the leap, starting the action himself and thus dragging the waverers with him.

A good opportunity to strike the first blow was offered by a meeting in the Bürgerbräukeller on the evening of 5 November, the fifth anniversary of the revolution and two days in advance of the deadline originally foreseen. Everyone who mattered in Munich would be present at a demonstration against Marxism, and Kahr was to give the keynote speech. He did not get very far with his speech in fact. Suddenly Hitler appeared with his supporters. After entering flanked by machine-guns and firing the famous pistolshot into the ceiling, he held a meeting in a separate room with the triumvirate, alternately threatening and pleading with them to join him. They at last agreed. What tipped the balance was the influence of Ludendorff, who had been hurriedly fetched and who was somewhat vexed at the minor role assigned to him by Hitler in the great revolution: Minister for the Reichswehr and Commander-in-Chief of the national army. The first to give in was Lossow, the famous Field-Marshal having appealed to his honour as an officer, then Seissner, and finally the governor presumptive of Bavaria, Kahr. The latter would in fact be no more than the representative of the monarchy, as Hitler – glib as ever – assured him: the Nazi leader would personally inform 'His Majesty' (i.e. the Crown Prince Rupprecht) that the rising in Germany had put right the injustice done to 'His Majesty's late father'.

The new government of the national revolution then shook hands before the delighted audience, like the Swiss confederates on the Rütli meadow. Then, however, as members of the Bavarian government and other notorious reactionaries were being dragged from the meeting and arrested by Storm Troopers, Hitler, the amateur revolutionary, permitted his reluctant colleagues to go home. They for their part could hardly wait to denounce the whole undertaking, declaring that their consent had been obtained under duress and taking countermeasures that same night. Next morning Hitler found himself alone with his band of paramilitary forces on board his revolutionary flagship flying the battle ensign of the Reich. He immediately called on the Crown Prince to act as mediator, but his comrade Ludendorff wanted no help from the house of Wittelsbach. He organized a march intended to mobilize local support for the putsch which had so ignominiously ground to a halt. The tables might still be turned and the defectors brought back. However, the demonsstration was fired on and dispersed by the local police who were stationed by the Feldherrnhalle in order to cordon off the city's administrative centre.

In contrast to what he subsequently made of the occasion, Hitler was no more than an extra on that 9 November. He did not assume a leading role until his trial before a court in Munich in February and March 1924. For the principal actors in the show on 8 and 9 November were not charged before the High Court in Leipzig: Bavaria meant to discipline her own over-zealous sons. Treason for patriotic motives could count on finding sympathetic judges anywhere in Germany at that time – especially in Munich.

All the same, the upshot of the affair was the elimination of Hitler from politics for a full year. Moreover, he had compromised Kahr and Lossow to the point where they reluctantly departed from the Bavarian scene in the middle of February. The alliance between the white and blue faction and the black, white and red faction, an alliance that had thrust the Republic to the edge of the abyss, had been shattered. The danger had been contained for the moment – and, indeed, for a number of years to come, given the stabilization of the economic situation. The so-called 'Angora solution', i.e. the removal of power from the 'diseased' capital by 'sound' forces from the provinces on the model set by Kemal Atatürk, was no longer a subject for debate.

The conflict between the Reich and Bavaria was finally laid to rest in February 1924, over the political graves of Kahr and Lossow. The ultimate crisis that might have arisen from a knot tied during the autumn did not in fact eventuate. Seeckt handed back to the constitutional bodies the executive authority granted to him in view of the threatening situation on the day of the Hitler–Ludendorff putsch. He had not after all seized his chance to carry out a putsch, as many had hoped or feared.

Seeckt had long toyed with the idea of a non-parliamentary emergency 'directorate' based on the Reichswehr, the business community and the civil service. At the end of October he had even drafted a sixteen-page document outlining a governmental policy. He was reluctant, however, to go ahead with the support of the Reichswehr alone and against the letter of the constitution. For one thing, he was sufficiently clear-sighted to envisage the international complications which would be certain to follow: the victor of the Ruhr, Poincaré, for instance, would hardly be prepared to tolerate a

German military dictatorship. He was also inhibited by a characteristic reluctance to do anything that was not legally sanctioned, although in the Republic this was not much more than a matter of form. He would certainly have liked to become Chancellor or 'Director' of the Reich, but only with the voluntary or quasi-volunary assistance of Ebert. When the President did not co-operate, but retained Stresemann's government, Seeckt's plans came to nothing. That had become obvious during the first few days of November, when the President explicitly refused to appoint the General as Chancellor. Since then Seeckt had been in political retreat – a tactical retreat. For during the preceding months the regime of Article 48 had strengthened the position of the President, as well as that of the Reichswehr. But the President in 1925, following the elections that were due in that year, might very well have been called Seeckt; his chances were not all that bad. Could he not attain his goal in that way, without a *coup d'état* and without international complications?

In the meantime the decline of the mark had been brought to a halt. The resistance in the Ruhr with its concomitant collapse of the currency, to which the inflation in general was commonly attributed, had in fact brought about a recovery in three respects. First, it had been made obvious to trade and industry that the inflation, although it was so profitable, could not be allowed to continue indefinitely. Second, the conservative financial bureaucracy was made to realize that the outworn recipe of supporting the mark as best they could, and otherwise granting credit and printing banknotes, would no longer do, even as a way of patching up the situation. And third, it was now understood abroad, especially in the Anglo-Saxon countries, that help from outside was needed to stabilize the mark, if the whole process was not to start up all over again, in spite of the most strenuous efforts on the part of Germany to prevent it.

The issue had become particularly urgent in the autumn of 1923, because there were rumours of plans for separate currencies in Bavaria and the occupied territories. And not only that: there were fears – and indeed the first alarming indications – that the farmers would not bring their harvest to market in return for the worthless rubbish of paper marks. Haste, then, was essential. In the middle of October the Stresemann government had an enabling act at its disposal, and issued a decree concerning a new unit of currency called the 'Rentenmark'. This was conceived from the outset as a stop-gap, and was hence declared to be an additional type of legal tender, which would be accepted by all public financial institutions and which could be redeemed for gilt-edged securities. At this point the exchange rate of the mark was already staggering into the hundred thousands, and the stabilization in the following month was effected at the absurd rate of one billion old marks for one new mark. The paper mark, now called for convenience the 'Billmark' (i.e. one billion marks), nevertheless continued to fall; in the end, however, its decline was arrested, it recovered and was brought into line with the Rentenmark. Ever since then there has been dispute as to who should be given credit for this remarkable feat. Already in the electoral campaign of the following year, every party which could possibly do so, was claiming vociferously that their own man had fathered the idea. Thirty or forty years later the surviving fathers were still quarrelling amongst themselves in the correspondence columns of newspapers and journals. The basic idea for underwriting the new currency – for sufficient gold was lacking – came from the Nationalist Helfferich, and was in the form of a mortgage on all German real estate which would take precedence over all other charges. In the final version the charge was to be divided equally between agriculture on the one hand, and industry, trade and commerce on the other, with real estate bearing the major burden even in the case of the latter. The new feature was that the currency could be liquidated in the form of fixed interest securities. This meant that anyone with banknotes of the new auxiliary currency could exchange them at will for such fixed interest securities. Of the commodities which were increasingly used at that time as stable auxiliary currencies, rye was to be adopted as the standard for the new money, with the aim of inspiring confidence in the farmers, as custodians of the harvest.

Hans Luther, the Minister of Food, who had no party affiliation, as a member of Stresemann's first cabinet had modified the project in regard to the standard of the new currency: instead of the 'rye mark', which fluctuated with variations in the price of grain, he had created the 'real estate mark' (Bodenmark), with its value fixed against gold, and the latter was ultimately issued under the name of the 'Rentenmark'. Finally, the Social Democratic Finance Minister, Hilferding, had cut by almost half the credit limit of 2,000 million marks allowed to the Reich under Helfferich's original plan, and had set an example by preliminary action in his own Ministry. In a cabinet reshuffle which was necessitated at the beginning of October by Stresemann's ultimately successful battle to get his enabling law passed, Hilferding, who was slow to take decisions, had been obliged to vacate his post. He was succeeded by Luther, who introduced a balanced budget – the first precondition, apart from strict economy measures, for salvaging the currency.

The fourth figure involved in the transaction was Hjalmar Schacht, one of the founders of the Democratic Party. First as Currency Commissioner and then, from the end of December, as President of the Reichsbank, he had supervised and guided the introduction of the Rentenmark and the following year the Reichsmark, which was based on the gold standard. He succeeded to the latter appointment following the timely death of Havenstein, who was seen as a symbol of the inflation and who consequently inspired little confidence; he could not be dismissed, however, having been appointed for life. And finally, although he is often overlooked, the fifth in the list was Stresemann himself, who as the head of the government responsible, and backed by the enabling law he had forced through, had risked the experiment that was put to the test on 15 November with the issue of the first Rentenmark.

It is important to remember, however, that the introduction of a new currency is no great feat in itself. What is vital to the whole plan is some device that will engender the greatest possible degree of confidence in the new money. If more than a few individuals had turned up asking to change their Rentenmarks into fixed interest securities, the bubble of this uniform emergency currency would have very quickly burst. For the whole thing was not much more than a bluff – new banknotes on which only a dozen zeroes had been cancelled. There was actually no obvious reason (at least if one stuck to the line of argument put forward hitherto) why the whole performance should not start all over again.

And the slightest slip would be bound to have fatal consequences at home and abroad. The credit for preventing this must unquestionably go to Schacht. He did it by rigorously banning the issue of emergency currencies, mostly by local authorities, in spite of the uproar on the part of interested parties; by stringently controlling the circulation and keeping to the credit limits that had previously been set (120,000 million marks apiece for the state and the economy), even at the cost of grave slumps in the economy with all their consequences, as for instance in April 1924.

It helped, of course, that even the captains of industry had become convinced in the interim that the good times of the inflation could not continue for ever in that form, if the entire fabric of the state and of industry, along with themselves, were not to be swept away. Most of them were therefore prepared to join in the stabilization game. The Stock Exchange speculators, on the other hand, who wanted to keep the inflationary merry-go-round going suffered heavy losses in consequence of the stringent policy pursued by the currency managers: on the black market the paper mark fell to 12 billion to the dollar, against the official stabilization rate of 4.2 billion. In industry, too, during the next few months a number of speculators went bankrupt, because they were unable to adapt to the new policy. They included the heirs of Stinnes, who had died at the beginning of 1924. The rest settled down to live with deflation, for which they had prepared by taking preliminary measures designed to improve productivity during the final palmy days of the inflation.

That this rationalization was carried through largely at the expense of the work force was a consequence entirely in keeping with the division of power within society that had come about. Not only were wages, up to and including civil service salaries, considerably reduced and signal breaches made in the eight-hour day legislation; with the ending of inflation and its concomitant full employment, the unemployment problem instantly reappeared. From a peak in the first post-war years, the unemployment figure had declined by 1923 to nearly negligible totals in five figures – and so might have been said to have vanished. But in the cause of austerity the Reich alone dismissed 330,000 of its employees. In the occupied areas in December, almost overnight, a million and a half unemployed workers thronged the unemployment relief offices (the figure in the same month of the previous year had been a mere 43,000!).

It is true that the unemployment problem soon receded again, at least for a time, thanks to foreign loans. That credit system collapsed, however, and the economic crisis doubled – and ultimately quadrupled – the number of jobless there had been at the end of 1923. That is why the Weimar state perished.

6

The Dawes Plan and the presidential election

Before it reached that point, however, the Republic was vouchsafed a few more years of convalescence. In February 1924 things quietened down at last, and at the end of the month the President revoked the state of emergency. The mark had been stabilized, and if the hard-won equilibrium was not called in question abroad by ruthless demands for reparations, then the 'miracle' could be reckoned to have succeeded. Here, too, there was some prospect of a sensible arrangement, since the view of the English-speaking countries had prevailed – namely that the whole matter of reparations should not be regarded primarily from a political point of view but that economic experts should play a leading part. The end of the conflict in the Ruhr had paved the way for the success of these efforts and for a review of Germany's solvency, which Stresemann's governments had asked for on 24 October.

Two expert committees of economists had been convened in December to examine possible ways of bringing the German budget and the German currency under permanent control, and of stemming the flight of capital from Germany. These were issues which inevitably involved Germany's obligations by way of reparations, which were linked to the establishment and maintenance of her solvency. France had, of course, objected to the inclusion of economic experts, but Germany's capitulation over the Ruhr had deprived Poincaré of the most categorical objection he had raised up to that point. More important, however, was the fact that the Americans had emerged from their isolation and were powerfully represented in the committees. The chaos in Germany that was so closely bound up with the repayment of Allied war debts, and with the international system of payments in general, had demonstrated that the problems could not be solved without America's participation, that they were not just European but world problems.

Not to mention the fact that Germany, hungry for capital investment and with great economic reserves, attracted Wall Street as an absolutely ideal field for expansion. For that purpose, however, the country had first to be put back on its feet.

On the Rhine and in the Ruhr France had in fact gone on giving the Reich the cold shoulder even after the end of passive resistance, and had negotiated only with industry in the Ruhr, dictating delivery quotas in November in 'Micum' contracts, so called after the abbreviation for the Franco-Belgian Ruhr authority. In February there was still no mention of the Ruhr being liberated. It was in that month, however, that the last remnants of the separatist movement in the Palatinate collapsed. Here, as in the Rhineland, the separatists had received a boost after 28 November and had set about seizing power under the wing of the French occupation forces. Whereas the 'Rhenish Republic' had breathed its last on 28 November, the 'Autonomous Palatinate' under the protectorate of General de Metz had survived until the middle of February – largely owing to the events in Munich, which offered the French a cover for their plans (the Palatinate, after all, was Bavarian territory).

Now Poincaré had to admit he was beaten, at least on this issue. Nothing came of a codicil to the Versailles Treaty in the form of a proposal for a Rhenish buffer state, nor of a modified project for a dependency of the Reich, possibly with its own currency, an international police force and prerogatives for the occupying power: even this was no longer a topical issue. Poincaré's Rhine and Ruhr policy had thus been deprived of its ultimate real aim, and public opinion in France was growing tired of the issue. At that time it was obvious that it was not only the passive resistance of the population that was credited with this outcome. Specific acts of terrorism had underlined the otherwise legitimate defensive measures – most strikingly in the murder of the separatist President Joseph Heinz and his entourage in Speyer on 9 January.

In February 1924, therefore, this chapter of Germany's post-war history was finally brought to a close: the unity of the Reich was no longer called in question. In February, too, the dispute with Bavaria was finally settled. Thus the dispute between federalists and centralists vanished from the list of urgent problems: in future there was to be no 'nucleus of order' and no 'Angora'. With the failure of the Munich putsch the extreme right had run out of steam for the immediate future, just as the extreme left had done previously with its various abortive attempts. But neither of these extreme wings had been destroyed, and the democratic forces did not emerge in any way strengthened from these critical years. After all, the democratic Republic had been able to hold its own on both fronts only thanks to the support of the Reichswehr – actively as regards the left, and tentatively or passively vis-à-vis the right.

It was the reactionary right, the conservative black, white and red faction, that was the gainer in every respect during these years – and this was confirmed by the elections. But the right also had its problems. In 1919 it had been the Republic's Public Enemy Number 1; now the state was faced by an uncomfortably vigorous new right, which did not look back to the good old days but was striving towards an uncertain future. The conservatives had fallen out with this new right, and were consequently somewhat more tolerant of the Republic. For some time to come the old right accepted the Republic – the Nationalists rather more, the People's Party rather less hesitantly – according to the influence wielded by industry in these two parties. Capitalist big business did in fact influence both, although the Nationalist Party also included many landowners and civil servants. Businessmen had observed that it was possible to make arrangements to suit oneself in this Republic, once socialist influences had been eliminated. It was early days yet, but for the moment at least the political scene was relatively tranquil.

What followed has entered the history books as the 'Stresemann era'. Throughout his 'era' the leader of the People's Party was never in overall charge of the policy of the Reich, but was only its Foreign Minister. This fact suggests where the political accent lay during this second phase of the Weimar Republic. By February 1924 Stresemann had long since ceased to be Chancellor. He was bitterly hated by the Nationalists as the man responsible for capitulation in the Ruhr, and Seeckt had long been working to bring about his downfall. Indeed, the General had declared openly at the beginning of November that the Chancellor no longer enjoyed the army's confidence and that he ought to be replaced. The Social Democrats could scarcely find it in their hearts to pardon the distinction Stresemann had drawn between Bavaria and Saxony, although it was hard to think what other policy he might have followed. In order to justify themselves in the eyes of their supporters, the Social Democrats in the Reichstag had brought in a vote of no confidence, which was in fact so framed that the Nationalists could not vote for it. Having declined to make his exit through the back door, Stresemann had insisted on an open confrontation. On 23 November the Reichstag refused to give him the vote of confidence he needed, and his rump cabinet collapsed.

His successor in office was Wilhelm Marx of the Centre Party, but otherwise everything remained the same – government policy and the coalition, and, to a large extent, the cabinet, including Stresemann as Foreign Minister and Luther as Finance Minister. Under its new signboard this minority cabinet was given the parliamentary support of the Social Democrats that it needed. By the middle of February the latter had even granted Marx's government a new enabling act, which it used for a sweeping legislative programme by decree. Many on the left regarded this programme as hostile to the working class. The eight-hour day, for instance, was so eroded by a decree on working hours issued on 23 December 1923 that it virtually became the exception, although it was retained in principle. This achievement of the revolution had been linked to a proposed international convention that never in fact came about. It had been attacked by the employers as not feasible in view of international competition. The Social Democrats insisted on changes to the decree, but the middle-class government believed that its policy of economic recovery would be endangered if the legislation were to be trimmed, and refused to give way. They were rescued from defeat only when the President dissolved the Reichstag – something he had refused to do for Stresemann's benefit.

The elections took place on 4 May 1924. Following the chaos of inflation and in a period of deflation with widespread loss of jobs, the Republic suffered a new setback. On the right the Nationalists gained twenty-five seats more than in the elections of 1920/21, and thirty-one more than in the previous Reichstag at its dissolution. Together with the right wing of the People's Party, the 'National Liberal Union', which had broken away in protest against Stresemann's policy, and an associated agrarian list, this made them the strongest party in the Reichstag (106 seats). Still further to the right, the National Socialist Freedom Movement gained thirty-two seats at its first attempt – ten of these delegates were Hitler's National Socialists. On the extreme left the Communists rose to sixty-two seats, having had no more than four in the 1920 poll, and ultimately seventeen in the previous Reichstag.

Amongst the losers, on the other hand, were all those with their home ground somewhere between the extremes. While the Centre Party just about held its ground with sixty-five seats, compared with sixty-six (sixty-nine), the Democrats lost eleven seats: what had once been the middle-class republican party of consolidation was represented in the new Reichstag by no more than twenty-eight delegates. The greatest losses were suffered, however, by the next-door neighbours of the radical winners. One-third of the People's Party rewarded Stresemann's courageous refusal to court popularity by not voting for him: of sixty-six members of the People's Party, only forty-four were returned to the Reichstag. The reunited Social Democrats were even more shabbily recompensed for their policy of tacking backwards and forwards between government and opposition: they were able to claim no more than 100 seats, eight fewer than the Social Democrat right wing had gained in 1920/21. At the time of the schism the supporters of the Independent Social Democratic Party had moved to the left, almost to a man. In purely mathematical terms, of 472 seats in the new Reichstag, a Weimar coalition could count on 193, a grand coalition on 237, a middle-class bloc with the Bavarian People's Party, but without the Nationalists, on 153, and – with the People's Party – on 269 seats.

So this is what the new Reichstag looked like: in practice, more Nationalists than Social Democrats, with the extreme racial nationalists stronger than the Democrats. There could be even less thought than before of broadening the government towards the left by including the defeated Social Democrats. On the other hand, the People's Party was doing its best to burden with the responsibilities of government its victorious rival, which had done so well in opposition – and hence to retard its triumphant advance. The Nationalists, for their part, would dearly have loved to join the government benches, but as Foreign Minister Stresemann was bound to make it a condition that the new partners should accept the foreign policy he had followed hitherto. How little they were inclined to do this was shown by the individual they put forward as their candidate for Chancellor: the Emperor's Minister of the Navy, Grand Admiral Tirpitz, the man responsible for unrestricted U-boat warfare and co-founder of the Patriotic Party. So even now everything remained as it had been, and Marx's minority cabinet returned almost unchanged, supported in its foreign policy by the Social Democrats.

The elections and the formation of the government had, however, for the most part been affected by a political issue which favoured the election victory of the Nationalists but at the same time prevented them from joining the government. Between the dissolution of the Reichstag and the election, on 9 April, the experts on the Reparations Commission had submitted their reports. The commission, the Allies and, shortly afterwards, the German government had accepted them *in toto*. In this way these reports and the proposals they contained had become a central issue in the elections to the Reichstag.

The Dawe's Plan, so called after the American chairman of the (first) expert committee, was of course bitterly attacked by the right, like everything connected with reparations, as a new chapter in the detestable policy of fulfilment, and as a further step along the road to the perpetual enslavement of Germany. However, those who took a less bigoted view (and they included the Foreign Minister of the Reich) saw beyond the letter of the report the chance of a final stabilization of the German currency and a step towards the liquidation of the ill-starred year 1924, as well as the recovery of political freedom, the liberation of the Ruhr and the restoration of a unified Reich, which was still divided by a customs and administrative frontier.

Taken out of this general political context and regarded purely as part of the reparations problem, the Dawes report in fact did not signify any improvement in Germany's situation. The experts wished Germany to be aware that her burden was onerous, but on the other hand they took an optimistic view of Germany's economic development, which at the time seemed justified. Eschenburg says that the position before the London ultimatum of spring 1921 had once more been reached by an extremely expensive and roundabout route. There was no discussion about the total amount of the debt or the period of repayment, which had proved to be very explosive topics hitherto (the London payment schedule of 1921 remained formally in force). The German reparations payment, including occupation costs but without deliveries in kind, was fixed at 2,000 million marks – higher than hitherto – plus an eventual corrective liability. The sources from which these sums would be derived were precisely specified, so that the debtor would not be tempted to procure the money simply by increasing the money supply and hence starting the inflationary process over again. The Reich budget was to raise 1,250 million plus the transportation tax, while the remainder was to come from the interest on 11,000 million marks in railway debentures and the interest on and redemption of 5,000 million marks in industrial debentures. This was therefore another version of the 'productive pledges' demanded by France, but this time they were to be not merely 'local' but 'general'.

There was to be a running-in period of four years, with a moratorium on the state contribution in the first year, followed by rising levies – altogether one of 1,000 million marks, two of just under 1,250 million and one of 1,750 million marks in the four transitional years. There were a further four points in Germany's favour. First, the report called for restoration of German economic unity as a first condition. As a further condition it demanded that the launching of the plan should not be handicapped by any sort of punitive measures. On the contrary, the continuity of payments should be secured by a mechanism that was not dependent on political fluctuations. Third, the Reich was to be granted a foreign loan of 800 million gold marks to support the stabilization of the currency, in practice to pay the first instalment of reparations. What was intended as a pump primer would then be developed into a system, a cycle, on which the operation of the entire Dawes plan would depend. Fourth, Germany's obligation would be regarded as fulfilled once she had raised the money; its transfer was the responsibility of a reparations agent in Berlin with an associated Allied committee. In the process of transfer, account was to be taken of the stability of the German currency. If the German economic and financial situation did not permit the transfer of certain sums, they were to be invested in the country – and if they exceeded a certain level, the levies were to be correspondingly reduced.

These concessions – above all, the loan and transfer protection – had to be paid for by grave infringements of German interests and sovereign rights. For one thing, there was the general agent, who would set up his camp in Berlin along with a number of commissioners and trustees, acting as supervisor of German payments and finances. He – the American Parker Gilbert – consequently became one of the most powerful men in Germany. Second, the Reichsbank was to be turned into an institution independent of the government and placed under the control of a supervisory body, half of whose members would be foreigners, so that it could not become once more an instrument of credit liable to ruin the currency. Third, the state railways (*Reichsbahn*), which the authors of the report had unearthed as a lucrative pledge in the course of their survey and on which they had imposed a major part of the levy, were to be privatized and also made subject to the controlling influence of the reparations creditors. All this provided the parties of the right with plenty of ammunition for the electoral battle. It soon turned out that it was in fact no more than ammunition for the election campaign and that it was not backed by any political alternative.

An international conference was planned to put the Dawes Plan into effect. It began on 16 July 1924 in London and initially involved only the Allies, together with the Americans. On 2 August an invitation was sent to the German government, and their delegation, including the Chancellor, the Foreign Minister and the Finance Minister, took their seats at the conference table three days later. The atmosphere was pleasanter than it had been previously – it could clearly be sensed that parliamentary elections in December 1923 in England, and in May 1924 in France, had brought parties of the left into power. An important decision had already been taken when the Germans arrived – in keeping with this atmosphere: it had been decided, against French opposition, that sanctions should not in future be imposed by one country alone. The final judgement as to whether Germany had fulfilled her obligations or not, and possible punitive measures or sanctions, would be made in future by an impartial court of arbitration under American chairmanship.

What mainly concerned the Germans in London was not this or that modification of the Dawes Plan, but the withdrawal of occupation troops fron the Ruhr. They wanted to bring this concession back to Berlin, so as to have something tangible at least with which to counter right-wing agitation. However, the French Prime Minister, Herriot, had made it a condition that the Ruhr should not appear on the London agenda. Herriot personally was certainly no chauvinist of the Poincaré stamp, but the fate suffered by Briand in Cannes was a clear warning against undue leniency. Stresemann could then quite rightly reckon it a success when, thanks to the good offices of the British Prime Minister, he obtained from Herriot an assurance at least that the Ruhr would be evacuated within a year, while Dortmund and Offenburg would be evacuated at once, more or less as a goodwill gesture.

This, admittedly, was not much, but it was still something with which Stresemann and Marx could face the Reichstag on their return from London in the middle of August amid howls of fury from the right. They were able to introduce and have passed nine new bills necessary for the implementation of the Dawes Plan. This was not in itself all that difficult, given the aid of the Social Democrats, who supported the foreign policy of the minority government. The bill on the new railway company, however, required a change in the constitution and hence a two-thirds majority. Even with support from the Social Democrats and the Bavarian People's Party this could not be achieved in the face of opposition from the Communists, the populists and the Nationalist members. And then something strange happened. All nine bills passed their second reading with about 250 votes to 170 in each case. At the critical third reading on 29 August – the chamber was rather more crowded on this occasion – eight bills were passed by the same majority: about 260 votes to 175. But the railway bill, by which the entire Dawes Plan could have been blown sky-high – the vociferously declared aim of the opposition – suddenly received 311 votes, with only 127 against. Forty-eight Nationalist members had voted for the bill.

What had happened here? The railway vote was regarded even then – as the *Frankfurter Zeitung* wrote – as the 'disgusting triumph of party political tactics', and is still generally regarded nowadays as a perfect example of the irresponsibility of the parliamentary opposition during these years. And that is certainly the case up to a point: when they were suddenly called upon to assume their share of responsibility, instead of recklessly heckling the government, the Nationalist members saw things rather differently. They were against the plan, but they were not sure how they should actually set about opposing it.

But there was another factor. Of the groups making up the Nationalist Party, one had emphatically and officially spoken in favour of the Dawes Plan – the group that would have borne the brunt of what would follow should it be rejected: industry. The fact that the Nationalist group in parliament allowed its members a free vote on this vital issue reflected the divergent interests of their supporters, and the pressure exerted by the industrial lobby. As a catchment area for all manner of enemies of the Republic, the Nationalist Party was in a more difficult position than the People's Party, who were blatantly capitalistic. The Nationalist rank and file often differed in their views from the party leadership, and it was with their help that one individual who was destined to play a part in the history of the Republic began to fight his way to the top in the party: Privy Councillor Alfred Hugenberg. A former managing director of Krupps, he had profited from the inflation and had managed to keep his gains, investing them to financial and political advantage in various press enterprises, such as the Berlin *Lokal-Anzeiger*, a press agency, and the Ufa film company.

There was a further factor besides the internal tensions in the party. The government had up its sleeve a presidential decree dissolving parliament, which would be used if the bills failed; another election, however, was not in the interests of the victors of 4 May. And, third, the People's Party and the Centre Party had promised the Nationalists that they would be included in the government and given an appropriate number of seats in the cabinet if they dropped enough white 'yes' cards into the ballot-box when the vote on the railway bill was taken. If it was a question of lack of moral fibre, then the deficiency was not confined to the Nationalists, as is sometimes claimed.

The protocol of the Dawes Plan was signed in London on 30 August. France evacuated the first stretches of territory in the Ruhr, and where they remained the occupying forces made themselves as inconspicuous as possible, in keeping with Herriot's promise. The expulsions were cancelled, an amnesty was declared, a new commander of the French Army of the Rhine was appointed, and the so-called economic occupation was dismantled. On 27 October the Reparations Commission confirmed that the economic and fiscal unity of the Reich had been restored. In October 1924, too, Germany obtained her loan, which made possible the return of the mark to the gold standard, and hence finally secured its stability.

This first loan attracted others: the enormous demand for capital led to high rates of interest, and this, together with confidence in the German economy and German efficiency, had a magnetic attraction for foreign capital. Germany recovered rapidly from the symptoms of deflation, and unemployment declined equally rapidly – almost as quickly as it had appeared. Suddenly, there was money everywhere, although the reparations for the ensuing years were punctually paid. For the 7,000 million marks which were delivered under the Dawes Plan were balanced by more than twice as much, 16,000 million marks in – mostly American – foreign loans.

The stream of dollars also gave a tremendous boost to domestic investment. During these years there was building, extension, expansion in Germany – there was a huge demand following the war and the post-war years. Industry expanded and concentrated, new firms and cartels sprang up which kept prices high and left the businesses and businessmen with the profits derived from increased efficiency which had been financed by investment credits. 'Rationalization' was the great slogan of the day. It meant cheaper production through mechanization – with a consequent reduction in the work force. As long as business was booming that did not matter, and no one had any thought of a slump.

The German domestic market with its great need of replenishment expanded on a massive scale, but there was little in the way of export trade to match it. With one exception, the German trade balance was in the red: the deficit was made good through foreign capital. In most cases it was a question of short-term financial operations, aspects of a new wave of speculation, which carried along with it financial jugglers at home as well as abroad: for them industrial enterprises served only as stakes in their game of roulette. Even the work force gained to some extent from the boom: wages rose from their starvation level during the winter of 1923/24 and almost doubled, while the cost of living hardly rose at all.

Nor did the state prove to be tight-fisted: it handed its civil servants hefty increases in salary. The public sector, especially local authorities, followed the example set by private industry, and began to build and redevelop furiously. A decree of March 1925 making the raising of credit abroad subject to approval by the Ministry of Finance did indeed do something to stem the flood, but not nearly enough. Long-term projects were embarked upon everywhere – lavish cultural amenities and housing estates. Apart from making good the neglect of the preceding decade and putting right some of the architectural and town-planning sins of the closing decades of the nineteenth century, these projects had the further advantage of creating new jobs.

This was all very well and good; life had once more returned to normal, poverty and distress in all their manifold forms had been done away with. These were the 'Golden Twenties', the 'Roaring Twenties', as they were further glorified in hindsight. But the whole business had one great flaw: all this splendour was based on credit. Industry, agriculture and the public sector – all those institutions that had managed to get rid of their debts at the expense of the small and medium saver, now acted like a dry sponge, soaking up new loans and mortgages recklessly and almost in the style of the inflation.

Things might have gone on in this way indefinitely; there was no real cause for concern, apart from a growing indignation over black marketeering and speculation, for a system of this kind in itself is not bound to lead to disaster. If the system were to short-circuit, however, then there would be a whole series of chain reactions. And these were likely to be particularly damaging because the German economy, especially the local authorities, had manipulated the credit system with such criminal recklessness, in spite of warnings by experts. They were in the habit of making long-term investments with money borrowed on short terms. If the creditors were to withdraw their money suddenly and *en masse*, then bankruptcies on a large scale would be unavoidable.

Nevertheless, at that time no one gave a thought to this possibility. People thought that foreign lenders would withdraw their money if there were doubts about Germany's stability and her solvency – if their investment no longer looked safe. For that reason the widespread view was that Germany could not afford to default on her reparations payments. That, Stresemann argued for the benefit of the French, was a much better pledge than the whole of the Rhineland. So this bogus boom even had its foreign policy advantages – although not for everyone in Germany. The Marxist historian Rosenberg has written that in this period Germany was little more than a colony of the New York Stock Exchange – and the analysis of the situation was practically identical on both left and right. Even if this is taken with a pinch of salt, what other way out could there have been, apart from that which Stresemann took?

In the middle of January 1925 a cabinet under Dr Luther, who had no party affiliation, took over, and Stresemann was once more appointed

Foreign Minister. Marx had quitted the Chancellery after the arrangement agreed with the Nationalists had fallen through and an attempt to bring the Social Democrats into the government had also failed. Admittedly, the Social Democrats had backed the government's foreign policy, but they had understandably been in vigorous opposition on issues of domestic policy. This came to a head on 30 August 1924, during a debate on a new bill regulating customs duties and purchase taxes, when the Social Democrats walked out of the chamber along with the Communists. On 20 October, when all efforts to broaden the basis of the government had failed, the President dissolved the Reichstag, which had only just been elected, and on 7 December the citizens of the Republic were summoned to the voting booths for the second time that year.

Now that the economic situation had perceptibly improved, the radical parties on both wings suffered considerable losses – about one million votes in each case. On the left the Communists retained only forty-five of their sixty-two seats, while, on the right, the National Socialist Freedom Movement was left with no more than fourteen seats – but unlike in May, most of them were National Socialists. The racial nationalists in Northern Germany were almost completely wiped out. On the other hand, the Social Democrats won back thirty-one seats, Stresemann's People's Party registered a gain of seven delegates, while the parties of the bourgeois centre were reinforced by three or four seats apiece. The Nationalists gained seven seats (however, their country cousins lost two seats).

This election in effect implied endorsement of the Dawes Plan, its advocates gaining votes all along the line whereas its opponents lost votes. The main object of the election, however, a parliamentary majority for the government's policy, had not been achieved. With a total of 493 seats, a bourgeois grand coalition extending from the Democrats to the Nationalists would have been backed by 299 votes, but the Democrats could not be persuaded to join that kind of right-wing alliance. And in numerical terms a grand coalition extending from the Social Democrats to the People's Party would now have had a solid majority of 283 votes, but neither of the parties on the wings was inclined to join such a coalition. In association with splinter groups like the *Landbund* (Rural Union), with its eight members, which inclined to the Nationalists, and the ominously growing Economics Party (Wirtschaftspartei) with seventeen seats, a purely middle-class lobby, other combinations might have been devised, but they remained in the realm of mere theory.

Marx's cabinet resigned immediately after the election. The tug-of-war over the formation of a new government lasted over a month. What emerged in the middle of January was a cross between a party cabinet and a cabinet of experts *à la* Cuno. It was quite obviously a right-wing government, however, for the determination of the People's Party representatives to join none but a middle-class cabinet had settled the issue. The 'outside-left' in the coalition was now the Centre Party. The latter had called for a 'government of the whole national community', by which it meant a broadening of the government to include the Nationalists, such as had been debated for so long. As far as the Nationalists were concerned, the national community had in fact been constituted – but the Democrats had got lost in the process.

The Centre Party, the Bavarian People's Party, the People's Party and the Nationalists now each had an 'agent' in the cabinet. The remaining ministers, like the new Chancellor, had no party affiliation, although they may have had leanings towards one or other of the coalition parties. An exception was the permanent Minister for the Reichswehr, Otto Gessler. The Centre Party had made their participation conditional on his retention. Gessler's presence did not imply in fact that his party (the Democrats) supported Luther's govern-ment, but it had assisted at the birth of this shaky minority cabinet, simply by abstaining. They could afford to do so, since the black, white and red faction had paid lip-service at least to recent foreign policy, and also to the recognition of the Republic, together with its national colours. Business interests had demanded that the Nationalists make this sacrifice and enter the government. By way of recompense, a Nationalist took over at the Ministry of the Interior.

This did not pose any threat to the Republic as long as the Social Democrat Severing was in charge of the *Prussian* Ministry of the Interior. And there he stayed, although simultaneous elections to replace the Prussian Landtag of 1920 had considerably strengthened the Communists on the left, and the Nationalists and National Socialists on the right, largely at the expense of the Social Democrats. When the People's Party broke up the grand coalition, a ludicrous muddle ensued, in which a Centre Party member of the Landtag, Franz von Papen, made his debut as a subversive opponent of the government. Eventually a new Braun–Severing cabinet emerged, another Weimar coalition. This time it had no majority in the Landtag to back it, but it was destined to have a long life – thanks no doubt to the disarray in which its opponents found themselves. One reason was that in Prussia, unlike the Reich at large, the Centre collaborated well with the Social Democrats, who allowed them more influence – especially in the Catholic provinces – than they might have expected from the Nationalists.

In the Reich, however, the 'bourgeois bloc' ruled unchallenged until this Reichstag was dissolved in 1928. Sometimes it ruled with the Nationalists, sometimes without them – but always in a sound conservative spirit. The People's Party did not dare to challenge their Nationalist rivals openly; instead, they tried to smother them in a passionate embrace. Unsuccessful as the attempt was, it had dire consequences in that it entailed the isolation of the Social Democrats. The new policy of the bourgeois bloc was made easier by a swing of the Centre Party to the right in an attempt to ensure the loyalty of their right wing – an unnecessary manoeuvre, as it now appears. The fact that the most prominent representative of the left in the Centre Party, the former Chancellor Wirth, resigned in 1925 from the parliamentary group, was rather more than just a symptom.

The governments of the bourgeois bloc, pursuing Stresemann's policy of mutual understanding, had inherited an indubitably democratic legacy from the early period of the Republic, and they might well have followed, under the aegis of the country's current prosperity, a social policy that was sensible and acceptable to the workers; nevertheless, a stiff conservative breeze prevailed. In the interests of big business and major landowners, for instance, they pursued a policy of protective tariffs that was detrimental to the consumer, because the agricultural sector, unable to compete at world market prices in spite of rationalization and investment credits, clamoured for such a policy. And a good many other things served the same interests, up to and including fiscal policy. The effect was that, in these circles and in the lower middle class generally, the Republic, was accepted – for the moment at least; for just as long as one could live well in it and enjoy a decent income.

Another election was imminent in 1925, for in the middle of the year the President's term of office, which had been extended by parliament, finally expired. Enacted at a time when Ebert's re-election by the nation for a further term of seven years seemed beyond doubt, this extension was in fact a curtailment. For the first President to stand for election again seemed hopeless, not only because the present bourgeois coalition would hardly allow a Social Democrat to occupy the office, but also because even in the ranks of his own party the advocate of compromise had lost ground. It appeared that he had sacrificed the interests of the workers to those of the employers, including the eight-hour day, the great achievement of the revolution. The former saddler's apprentice, now President of the Reich, was demonstratively expelled from the saddlers' association. What was worse, at the last conference of the Social Democratic Party a local branch even submitted a motion to expel Ebert from the party. In the meantime the right-wing hate campaign raged on with its countless insults. The campaign reached its climax on 23 December 1924, when a jury court in Magdeburg declared that the President was guilty of treason because he had taken part in a strike of munitions workers in January 1918.

The case dated back to a visit Ebert had made to Munich in 1922. He had been greeted by a populist rowdy called Gansser with a shout of 'Traitor!' Ebert sued, but dropped the case when the court in Munich insisted that he should appear before it in person. Dr Gansser then challenged Ebert in an open letter to clear himself in court of the charge of treason. With financial support from interested parties an obscure newspaper in Stassfurt reprinted the letter with spiteful comments. Thereupon the Public Prosecutor brought charges, with the President of the Reich as joint plaintiff.

Now, the Social Democratic leadership had not instigated that wildcat strike in 1918, nor had Ebert played any leading part in it. On the contrary, he had tried to pacify the strikers, and that was the only reason he had taken part in meetings of the strike committee and addressed the strikers. True, when they responded sullenly to his appeal to them to do their patriotic duty, he had, for purely tactical reasons, uttered a few words of encouragement. The general tendency of Ebert's involvement in the strike was therefore perfectly obvious, and the court was deliberately ignoring every political, historical and moral criterion when it found the offending editor guilty of formal slander, but declared the President to be a 'traitor within the meaning of the criminal law'.

The Magdeburg verdict was condemned at the time by the left-wing press, and has been condemned since as a scandalous miscarriage of justice of the worst possible kind. As far as that goes, we may demonstrate that a bourgeois presiding judge with nationalistic leanings was acting with malicious intent, but in the final analysis it was a petty, legalistic mentality that won the day (we may discount the peculiar delight which expert commentators took in the case). Nothing can be expected, after all, from a judicial system except judicial verdicts; it is not competent to make any other kind of judgement, and in Magdeburg in 1924 it declared its incompetence. The fault lies rather in the political role which tends to be thrust on the judicial system, and in the practice of making political capital out of judgements that inevitably stick to the letter of the law.

The parties of the right were jubilant and called on Ebert to resign. The President himself thought briefly of taking this step, but numerous messages of sympathy – mostly, it is true, from intellectuals, democratically minded professors and politicians – encouraged him to hold out. Particularly impressive was a statement of their confidence in the President endorsed by the whole government, which, after all, included only bourgeois parties (it was still Marx's cabinet, and did not include Nationalists). Otto Braun, on behalf of the Prussian government, associated himself with this vote of confidence.

Only a few weeks later Ebert found himself facing fresh accusations. Among the firms that had flourished during the inflation but were beginning to wilt by 1924, had been that owned by the Barmat brothers, Jews from the eastern provinces. During the war they had been based in Holland and engaged in the grocery business, which was obviously of prime importance at that stage. In the course of business they had made useful contacts with German politicians which they put to good use during the inflation, when everyone was avid for credit. Thanks to these connections the Barmat brothers had received from the Prussian State Bank, and later from the Post Office, substantial sums of money, which were lost when the firm collapsed under a huge burden of debt at the end of 1924. The Public Prosecutor was called in, and leading figures in the firm were arrested. Politicians of the Centre and Social Democratic parties who had been implicated, including the former Chancellor, Gustav Bauer, came under fire from their political opponents – partly because they had mixed politics with business, partly because they had simply been negligent. Some of them even ended up in the clutches of the law – the Post Office Minister, for instance, a member of the Centre Party, who died in custody after hastily resigning.

But the Barmat brothers had also been on friendly terms with Ebert's family, although the President was in no way implicated in their shady dealings. On 9 January, at the request of the Nationalist Party, the Reichstag appointed a committee of investigation, which the Nationalists, with the support of their press, turned into a tribunal. In order to meet these renewed attacks on his integrity, Ebert delayed treatment of an inflamed appendix. When he was finally operated on it was already too late. On 28 February 1925 the first President of the First Republic died – literally hounded to death by his enemies, despised as a renegade by many of his old friends and unappreciated by his nation. Nevertheless, he was sincerely mourned by all who had sufficient insight and understanding.

The question of the presidency had thus become urgent sooner than anyone had expected. The poll took place on 29 March and involved seven candidates, for almost every party had nominated its own man. Only the People's Party and the Nationalists had been able to agree on a joint candidate: the Mayor of Duisburg, Karl Jarres, who belonged to the right wing of the People's Party. An attempt to nominate the Democrat Gessler as the candidate of the bourgeois bloc had failed because Stresemann had exploited doubts among the diplomatic corps, suggesting that elevating the Minister for the Army to the presidency would cause offence abroad. Naturally none of the candidates gained an absolute majority in the first round of voting. Significantly, Jarres was in the lead, with 10.8 million votes, followed by the Prussian Prime Minister Braun as the Social Democrats' candidate, with 7.8 million votes. The National Socialists' candidate, 'Field-Marshal' Ludendorff, brought up the rear, well beaten with no more than 211,000 votes.

The second round of voting that was thus required was critical, for the candidate who gained most votes would be elected. If this was not to be Jarres, the 'Weimar' parties would have to agree on a single candidate. It was characteristic of the political climate that a compromise was arrived at, not in the centre, but on the right wing of the right wing. The joint candidate of the 'popular bloc', consisting of the Centre Party, the Democrats and the Social Democrats, was the former candidate of the Centre Party and former Chancellor, Wilhelm Marx. With the votes cast in the first round for the candidates of the three parties, he was bound to win. But there was one other possibility: Jarres was scarcely known, and his place might be taken by a name with more drawing power.

The People's Party were reluctant to drop their candidate, but the Nationalists over-ruled their half-hearted objections and put forward the legendary hero of Tannenberg, Hindenburg. The leader of the People's Party once more raised doubts about the possible effects of this choice abroad, but he did not do so in public, nor with the same insistance as in the case of the Democrat Gessler. True, Hindenburg's former Quartermaster-General had just suffered a humiliating defeat, but during the war Ludendorff had been altogether overshadowed by his chief as far as the public was concerned. Besides, he had since contrived to make a thorough nuisance of himself through all sorts of absurd antics. Hindenburg's prestige, however, sedulously shielded from disparagement (at Groener's expense), had, if anything, increased since the time when he had been regarded as Germany's secret Emperor. But Hindenburg was not willing to stand. He had felt competent to act as His Majesty's politically active General, but not as President of the democratic Republic. Only after his comrade Tirpitz had argued with him long and insistently was he finally persuaded to stand as a candidate.

It worked perfectly. The German people, as Stresemann remarked at the time, did not want a President in a top hat, but one in uniform and with strings of medals. It was not only the National Socialists who approved of Hindenburg; even the Bavarian People's Party preferred the Prussian Protestant to the Catholic from the Rhineland. Animosity against the party from which they had seceded was doubtless strengthened by the fact that the middle-class Bavarian heart had experienced a greater than average shift to the right: after all, one simply could not vote for a man to whom the Social Democrats had pledged their support, even if he were a Catholic ten times over. So now the 'popular bloc' was faced by a 'Reich bloc'. Following the Brandler fiasco of 1923 and the sacrifice of Brandler by the Kremlin, the Communists once more had a left-wing leadership. They stood by their candidate, Ernst Thälmann, although Moscow wished Communists to cast their votes for Wilhelm Marx. Shortly afterwards, Stalin split the leadership of the German Communist Party: henceforth, with the aid of Thälmann's group, he was able to subject it totally to Moscow's control. The Communists have been reproached to this day with acting as lackeys to the imperial Field-Marshal, but they cannot have been all that eager to heave the right-flanker of the Weimar coalition into the saddle.

And so, thanks to the Communist candidature, and the support of the Bavarian Catholics, Wilhelm II's Field-Marshal was elected second President of the Weimar Republic on 26 April 1925. The suggestion that anti-Catholic sentiment in Protestant circles may have adversely affected Marx's chances is not borne out by the voting figures. With 13.75 million votes, Marx had gained no less than 350,000 more votes than he, together with his two predecessors, had won in the first round. Thälmann's 1.93 million had been boosted by an extra 45,000, presumably Social Democratic, supporters. But

– apart from the 12 million who had previously voted for Jarres, Held and Ludendorff – Hindenburg's name had attracted to the ballot-box no fewer than 2.66 million voters who had abstained in the first round. This is what tipped the balance.

On 11 May the new President of the Reich moved to Berlin from his retirement home in Hanover. The streets were decked out almost exclusively in black, white and red bunting provided by right-wing organizations. The era of the Free Corps had passed; their place had been taken by the great nationalist veterans' organization, the Stahlhelm, which now ousted or absorbed all that was left over from earlier years. During the preceding year similar veterans' associations had begun to make their appearance on the left as well – somewhat belatedly, it is true. The Social Democrats founded their Reichsbanner with reluctant and dwindling participation on the part of the Centre and Democratic parties. The Communists had founded their own Roter Frontkämpferbund (Red Veterans' League). But these organizations were not represented when Hindenburg made his entry into Berlin. The following day the Social Democrat Paul Löbe, as Speaker of the Reichstag, administered the oath on the constitution to the Marshal. Fortunately, the word 'Republic' did not occur explicitly in the text.

The ominous forebodings were not realized, however. In spite of the traumatic experience of 9 November, the flight to Holland of the Emperor on the advice of his Commander-in-Chief, and regardless of his longing to see his 'imperial master' make his entry into Berlin castle once again, Hindenburg remained by and large loyal to the Republic – more loyal, at any rate, than might have been expected of him. It might be termed a sergeant-major's sense of fair play, when in his first period of office, having been elected by the right, he gave the impression of being an almost pedantic republican – and *vice versa*, in his second period of office. However, if we survey the politicians of the Republic, it is difficult to find one who would have defended the Republic and democracy on their deathbed against Hitler more vigorously and successfully than this stubborn old royalist. It would not be strictly correct, then, to claim that the election on 26 April 1925 dug the grave of the First Republic. But its blunder, the choice of this 'surrogate Emperor', as Eschenburg calls him, was a symptom both of the widespread longing in German middle-class circles for the 'good old days' and of the weakness of the Weimar state.

It cannot be said that it was a good thing for that state when, after only five years, a dyed-in-the-wool monarchist, the most prominent representative of the military caste, was invited to occupy its supreme office. On the other hand, as Werner Conze points out, Hindenburg's election might even have helped to strengthen the First Republic, precisely because of his loyalty to it: in his own person he might have narrowed, if not closed, the gulf between black, red and gold and black, red and white. It is in fact conceivable that, if the President-cum-Marshal's second term of office had been passed in more peaceful times, it would have made the Republic more or less respectable in the eyes of the conservative right. However, it proved impossible to put this to the test.

7

The policy of the bourgeois bloc

As far as Germany was concerned, the other significant event of 1925 was the initialling of the Locarno Pact. This took place in that small town in Tessin on 16 October, following a two-week conference. As already mentioned, it was Cuno, at the end of 1922, who first suggested the idea of a security pact on the Rhine. In February 1925 Stresemann, encouraged by the British – and taking his cabinet, especially his Nationalist colleagues, by surprise – had revived the proposal in a note to the Allies. His motive was the same as Cuno's: to meet France's desire for greater security by acknowledging the western frontier laid down in the Treaty of Versailles. In return, France would find it easier to give up her territorial pledges on the Rhine. The first thing was 'to get the stranglers from our throats', the Foreign Minister wrote at the time in a letter to the Crown Prince (which was later to play a large part in the Stresemann controversy). In order to achieve that, German policy would have to go in for a certain amount of delicate manoeuvring.

There was another, urgent, reason for a move of this kind: on 5 January the Allies had informed the German government that they did not intend to proceed with the evacuation of the first Rhineland occupation zone (Cologne), which had been due to start in five days' time. The reason given was that Germany had not fulfilled the Versailles disarmament conditions as 'faithfully' as had been specified in the treaty as a condition for the evacuation.

The Reichswehr and the government had been trying since 1923, with good reason and a host of ultimately futile ruses, to prevent the Inter-Allied Military Control Commission from resuming its activities. Before the Dawes conference the German side had been obliged to permit a 'general inspection', which they attempted to interpret as putting an end to the whole process of arms control. On the Allied side, however, termination of control was made dependent on the result of the inspection. Given the attempts made by Germany to reinforce her army during 1923, it looked very much as if the Allied refusal to evacuate the Cologne area was justified. But Stresemann suspected – quite correctly – that the issue of French security was once again behind it. In fact, following Locarno and Germany's admission to the League of Nations, the whole question of military inspection had very rapidly petered out. In January 1927 the Commission was finally withdrawn.

After a certain amount of hesitation France had responded to the Luther–Stresemann cabinet's 'peace offensive'. The so-called 'Geneva Protocol' of the League of Nations, which guaranteed the status quo of 1919, had just collapsed because Britain opposed it. This made Paris, where Briand had returned to the Quai d'Orsay in April, more responsive to the German offer. The main point of dispute concerned the demand by France and her allies in central and eastern Europe that frontier guarantees of this kind should apply also to Germany's eastern borders.

At that stage, however, it would have been impossible for any German government formally to recognize the eastern frontiers stipulated in Versailles, and such recognition was not in Stresemann's programme. From the west the situation looked quite different. Alsace-Lorraine had always been regarded as France's legitimate booty, while Eupen-Malmédy offered no cause for major agitation. Incidentally, negotiations had soon started with the effective aim of buying back these two provinces from Belgium – and at times had even looked like being successfully concluded. The German territories that had been lost in the east, however, had an almost mystic status in Berlin, which was not all that remote from them. Almost every German was convinced that the 'bleeding' frontier in the east would have to be revised at some stage, one way or another. The government's view, as well as public opinion in Britain – and even more so in the Dominions – was much the same. Unease about Germany's eastern frontiers in central Europe, and reluctance to be committed to them, had already swept the Geneva Protocol from the table.

This issue ended in a German offer of German–Polish and German–Czech arbitration treaties, an offer which had already been made at the outset. Similar treaties had been annexed to the main treaty concluded with Germany's western neighbours. Moreover, France concluded mutual assistance pacts with both states, assuring them of military aid should Germany attack them. The Rhine pact between Germany, France, Belgium, Great Britain and Italy, however, embodied an additional undertaking that they 'would not go to war against each other'. Backed by the two powers not directly involved, Britain in particular, it guaranteed the inviolability of the Versailles frontiers in the west, as well as the demilitarization of the Rhineland.

Locarno, however, did not mean the advent of a new era (as Mussolini said of the completed treaty at the time), even before Hitler tore up the pact on 7 March 1936. The 'spirit of Locarno', which Stresemann was so fond of invoking, was only the run-up and not the jump. All the same – and that was presumably the Foreign Minister's main aim – Germany once more joined the ranks of the great powers. The first fruit of the pact to which the Luther government could point was the evacuation of the Cologne occupation zone. It began on 1 December 1925, one day before the ratified Locarno treaties were signed in London. Considerable relaxation of the regime in the remaining occupied areas soon followed. The evacuation of the Ruhr and of the cities affected by sanctions, Düsseldorf, Duisburg and Ruhrort, had already taken place; in the middle of September Hindenburg had been able to celebrate their liberation between Bochum and Düsseldorf.

All this, however, was still not enough for the loud-mouthed nationalists. Stresemann had indeed managed to persuade the Nationalist members of the cabinet to back the policy which led to Locarno (although at times he stood virtually alone, and at one stage even the Chancellor would have been glad to see the last of the security pact and to pack his Foreign Minister off to the London embassy). For, on the one hand, the Nationalists stuck to their seats in the cabinet on account of a protective tariffs bill that was important for agriculture, and, on the other hand, industrial interests were affected: the United States had suggested plainly enough that the security treaties and the credits urgently needed by the German economy constituted a package deal. For those reasons the Nationalists in the cabinet had finally given the green light for the expedition to Lago Maggiore. Nevertheless, only Luther's vigorous commitment to Stresemann's policy had prevented the luggage for Locarno being crammed with unacceptable conditions: it would have been impossible to retreat at that stage without loss of face.

When it came to ratifying the treaties after the return from Locarno, however, the Nationalist rank and file rebelled against this betrayal and against the renewed policy of fulfilment being pursued by a pack of disreputable scoundrels. In fact, the German signatories saw the Locarno pact as a step along the road to a revision of Versailles, a road which could only be trodden with extreme caution: they had the same goal in view as the extreme right. The latter, however, were demanding a foolhardy policy of all or nothing that would doubtless have been catastrophic at that stage. Under pressure from their party organization the Nationalists left the government on 25 October. In so far as this was not simply a matter of internal dissension but a tactical move, it worked: with the votes of the Democrats and the Social Democrats backing them, the Locarno treaties sailed through the Reichstag on 27 November, along with the approval of Germany's membership of the League of Nations.

The validity of the Locarno treaties was bound up in fact with Germany's joining the League in Geneva; on this depended everything which the sponsors of the treaties had hoped from the 'spirit of Locarno'. As compared with 1919, the situation had now been reversed: at that time Germany had not been permitted to join, now she was obliged to do so. And, as far as possible, without any preconditions. But this the German government was no longer prepared to do, mainly for reasons of internal policy.

At first nothing much had changed on the domestic political scene. Following the final signing of the Locarno treaties Luther's cabinet resigned, as he had already announced they would do, on 5 December 1925. The formation of a new government ran into major difficulties, however. The broadening of the rump coalition to include the Nationalists was out of the question, because the government parties had insisted hitherto that Stresemann's foreign policy must be pursued unconditionally. Consequently, the only possibility was to include the Social Democrats, if a majority government was to be maintained. They, however, refused. For one thing there were the arguments about compensation for Germany's former rulers which were just beginning, and for another there still remained the old disagreements with the bourgeois parties on social issues, with the focus on the eight-hour day and its reinstatement.

When various attempts to form a grand coalition government had failed, the only possibility left was a minority government of Democrats, Centre Party, Bavarian People's Party and People's Party, once more under Luther's chairmanship, and, of course, once more with Stresemann at the Foreign Office. For somehow or other, as the Chancellor had shouted, heckling a speaker in the Reichstag, Germany *had* to be governed. Thus, almost everything stayed as it was, with the parties' wheeling and dealing and their apparent inability to compromise on minor differences for the sake of larger issues, once again earning the parliamentary system of government bad marks in the eyes of the public. It even looked (and this was in fact largely the case) as if the 'depressing sight of incessant government crises', as Hindenburg had put it in an ultimatum addressed to the parties, might have continued *ad infinitum*, had the President not vigorously intervened.

Luther's second cabinet, which gained no more than 160 votes in a vote of confidence and which survived only thanks to abstentions by the Social Democrats, could, of course, not provide even a moderately lasting solution. And it governed for barely four months. The issue on which it finally fell was a decree on the flying of the ensign issued by the President on 5 May 1926, according to which embassies and consulates overseas and in European ports would in future hoist the black, white and red commercial ensign alongside the national colours. This innovation has been attributed to Hindenburg's fondness for the old colours of the Reich, and the President had mentioned in a letter to the Chancellor that it was his most fervent wish to achieve 'in the foreseeable future a compromise on the flag question by constitutional means'. This would correspond to 'present-day Germany and its aims' and also 'do justice to the historical development of the Reich'. Nevertheless, the decree seems to have been Luther's idea in the first place: he thought it appropriate – so at least he claimed – to eliminate the anomaly, incomprehensible to the simple foreigner, that German vessels entered port under one flag only to be greeted by the other. It may well be that he was also paying his respects to the stalwart German communities abroad and their allegiance to the old colours.

The Social Democrats and the Democrats were justifiably indignant at this deliberate assault on the symbol of the republican constitution. Following a debate in the Reichstag, a vote of no confidence brought down Luther's government – which was possible because the Nationalists abstained. The government crisis ended with the old cabinet returning under a new head. Thanks to Stresemann's predilection for a not unduly powerful 'co-ordination Chancellor' (Eschenburg), Wilhelm Marx entered the Chancellery for a third time as leader of the old bourgeois minority cabinet of the centre that was viable only as long as it was tolerated by the Social Democrats. *De facto* it was a grand coalition government, with a sleeping partner. The flag regulations that had tripped up Luther remained in force – partly because they suited the two-faced behaviour of the People's Party, but mainly because they had been signed and were favoured by the President. *His* position was so secure that there could be no serious thought of repealing them, once the first wave of anger had subsided and the storm had claimed its victim.

The fact that there was no grand coalition – for which, amongst others, the Mayor of Cologne, Konrad Adenauer, had taken soundings – was due to the refusal of the People's Party, for reasons of social policy, to have any truck with the Social Democrats. It was also due, however, to the dispute about the property of the German princes, which had been confiscated in 1918. The fact, on the other hand, that the bourgeois bloc remained incomplete, with the Nationalists – for the moment – remaining in opposition, was a result of the latter's rejection of Stresemann's foreign policy. For the latest developments were still in the balance: Germany's admission to the League of Nations had not yet taken place. Of the three conditions laid down on the German side in 1925 the most awkward issue had been defused – i.e. the reopening of the war-guilt question – because the Nationalists were no longer in the government.

This problem which so excited German passions had never vanished from the agenda of the First Republic at any stage and would not do so in the years to come. Lately, pressure from the right at the time the Dawes legislation was being passed had led to a declaration by the government that it did not acknowledge Germany's war guilt and that Germany should be freed from the burden of this false accusation. The delivery of this declaration in the form of a note to foreign capitals had fortunately been prevented, mainly because of objections by the Secretary of State at the Foreign Office. The issue of war guilt had ceased to be topical for the moment, but it was obvious that Germany's entry into the League of Nations would once more turn the latent issue into a vital problem. Since the League's Statutes were incorporated into the Treaty of Versailles, it might be expected with certainty that Germany's accession to the League would be interpreted as a voluntary admission of that burning topic, the 'lie of Germany's war guilt'. As long as the Nationalists were not on the government benches, this could be tolerated. The matter might have ended with an appropriate disclaimer, of which Germany's foreign partners would not have taken much notice, had not Stresemann felt it necessary at the end of September, after Germany's appearance in Geneva, in deference to his own feelings and to the right wing of his party, to grasp the nettle once again. The applause he earned in Geneva he then tried to convert into an exoneration of Germany from war guilt. The result was an obvious, embarrassing and avoidable rebuff in London and Paris.

A second German request referred to Article 16 of the Statutes of the League of Nations, which obliged every member to participate in any measures which the League might take against a particular state. Since this might involve military support, Germany had pointed out that she had been demilitarized and would be unable to comply. The concrete case which the League had in mind was assistance for Poland against the Soviet Union. Now, whatever one might think of Rapallo and Germany's secret contacts with the Soviet Union, getting involved in a conflict with the Soviet Union for the sake of the Poles, Germany's hated neighbours, supporting them, even if only by granting them the right to march through German territory, against the one great power who shared Germany's opposition to Versailles – that was something that no German politician was prepared to do. A compromise had been worked out in Locarno, an interpretation of Article 16 which made the extent of participation in such measures dependent on the military situation and the geographical location of member states. This limited the scope of the Article considerably, to Germany's benefit.

Third, the government of the Reich had asked for a permanent seat on the League of Nations Council along with the four main Allied powers. No one had any objection to the inclusion of the Reich in the circle of great powers. However, other states seized the opportunity to claim the same status for themselves. This would mean an inflation in the number of permanent seats on the Council and a depreciation of concessions already gained, which Berlin for its part was not willing to accept. Every increase in the number of seats on the Council (i.e. Germany's seat as well) had to be unanimously approved in the full assembly, so that a proposal could be torpedoed by any single member. This is not the place to discuss the details of this to-ing and fro-ing. Suffice it to say that all attempts to find a compromise in this issue failed, and when, in the middle of March 1926, the assembly took place at which Germany's membership was to be approved, the problem had to be postponed until the following meeting.

This failure of Stresemann's policy was used by the right in Germany to trigger a new wave of agitation, which culminated in the demand that the government should withdraw its application for membership. A vote of no confidence on this issue, it is true, did not command a majority in the Reichstag, but Stresemann found it advisable nevertheless to distract attention from the débâcle in Geneva by taking a step which had been in his programme already, but which he had been trying to postpone until after Germany's entry into the League.

The imminent integration of the Reich into the common front of the western powers had naturally made the Russians uneasy. Since the weeks preceding the Locarno conference they had been urging Berlin to extend the Treaty of Rapallo. Right-wing circles among German politicians, in the civil service and the army had no qualms about collaborating with the otherwise hated Bolsheviks whenever it was a matter of breaking the fetters of Versailles. They now sensed that their chance had come: an alliance between Germany and Russia of whatever kind with the aim of partitioning Poland for a fourth time and thus destroying an important pillar of the French system of alliances in eastern central Europe was a project dear to the hearts of the Nationalists and Seeckt. And in discussions between the two powers there had actually been talk to the effect that 'it was a matter of pushing Poland back within her ethnographic boundaries'.

Leading German politicians, however, Stresemann especially, remained sensible enough to bank on gradually dismantling the Versailles fetters by a cautious alignment of German policy westwards rather than bursting them with the aid of the Soviets, who were still weak and whose embrace entailed certain internal political risks. That did not exclude the possibility of a reinsurance treaty, however, on the Bismarck model, although inevitably on a smaller scale. After all, a revision of Germany's eastern frontiers, which was a *sine qua non* for virtually all Germans, could hardly be envisaged without the support of Russia. In Stresemann's original timetable it had been planned that the insurance phase was to precede the reinsurance. There was no desire to prevaricate in Geneva when it came to questions about links with Russia. What would happen afterwards was another matter altogether, and was not meant to go anything like as far as Moscow hoped. When the first approach to Geneva failed in the spring of 1926, the Russians were jubilant and became even more insistent – backed by their friends in the black, white and red camp. Amongst other things, the pact provided for mutual neutrality in the case of an attack by a third party; it was signed in Berlin on 14 April 1926. The Russians had reason to be satisfied that the Locarno club had thus lost the appearance of a common front against the Soviet Union. On the other hand, it is true, the 'Berlin pact' had been modified by the German side so that it contained nothing that was not consistent with Locarno or with Germany's imminent admission to the League of Nations. Nevertheless, it was obvious that it was not exactly received with enthusiasm in western capitals, and it was only thanks to Stresemann's diplomatic skill that it was not felt to be an affront and did not block Germany's way to Geneva. This way was eventually smoothed during the succeeding months by a study group in which Germany was represented. The creation of three 'semi-permanent' seats on the Council provided a compromise that saved face all round. On 10 September 1926 Stresemann entered the assembly of the League of Nations to loud applause.

While all this was happening in the field of foreign policy – with continual repercussions in domestic policy – within Germany itself the arguments about the property of the former German princes, which had been confiscated, but not expropriated, in 1918 were coming to a head. Quite apart from the fact that it was not always easy to distinguish between genuinely private and fiscal property, restitution, which was incumbent on any non-socialist state, entailed a political handicap. The lower classes of the population had been robbed of their savings and fobbed off with a few wretched per cent by way of revaluation. There was bound to be bad feeling if the public purse dispensed vast fortunes in stable assets to those very individuals on whose account the path to inflation had been taken.

These matters had been dealt with hitherto by the individual states with varying degrees of success. The attempt to regulate them by a national law at once brought the Communists into the fray. The issue was one that gave them a good opportunity to put their Social Democrat rivals on the spot and to push the latter into conflict with the bourgeois camp, for the Social Democrats could not afford to fall down on this question. The parties of the left laid before the Reichstag a bill which called for the radical expropriation of the former princely houses without any form of compensation. The bill was of course defeated, and its proposers on the left then initiated the procedure for a plebiscite, as provided for in the constitution. The first stage was a resounding success: during the first half of March 1926, 12.5 million voters signed the plebiscite lists – considerably more than the 10 per cent stipulated for a referendum. The next step was a second reading in the Reichstag, where, as expected, the two working-class parties were defeated.

Now a referendum had to be held. It took place on 20 June, after both sides had campaigned vigorously, and even the President of the Reich had not hesitated to state his view of this 'grave infringement of the constitutional structure of the lawful state'. The initiators of the referendum on 20 June did not in fact obtain the necessary majority, namely 20 million, but they were able all the same to record an impressive degree of success, with 15.5 million 'yes' votes. This was far more than the 10 million that had sent socialist deputies to the Reichstag at the end of 1924, and even more than had been cast in the other camp for Hindenburg as President.

In the question of compensation for the princes, then, the situation remained the same: since the bill in the Reichstag had failed, it was still up to the states individually to come to terms with their former rulers. But that was not the most important thing. Even the apparent strengthening of the left-wing parties was to turn out, in hindsight, as not particularly significant. More important was the fact that the Social Democrats took a further step away from government and were kept in that disastrous semi-opposition which did so much to prevent a consolidation of the First Republic. It is true that it was mainly disagreements on economic and social policy which prevented the gap between the Social Democrats and the conservative and liberal parties being bridged in a way that would have secured the stability of the Weimar state in the long run. To these disagreements were added – as the quarrel over compensation for the former rulers showed – constant ideological differences which made it hard for the different factions to co-operate. And it would soon be desperately necessary for these factions to stand together.

Before 1926 ended there was another surprising event. The man on whom the weal or woe of the entire nation had depended barely three years previously, and who at that time seemed to be on the verge of taking over as dictator, made his exit from the political scene: in October General von Seeckt was dismissed. It goes almost without saying that it could not have been a politician or politicians who forced him to retire, although the pretext was highly political. The Chief of Staff had granted the request of the eldest son of the Crown Prince, on his return to Germany, to take part in man-oeuvres; this meant that the Hohenzollern claimant to the throne had made his appearance in Reichswehr uniform without having sworn the oath of allegiance to the constitution – which, naturally, he could not have done. Seeckt had granted this request, which was likely to cause alarm both in Germany and abroad, without feeling it necessary even to inform his Minister, Gessler.

When this became known (as a result of a public statement which Prince Oskar foolishly made), and when the democratic press raised a hue and cry, Gessler could see no way of 'coping with the Reichstag and the Entente'. He had been criticized, not without justification, at home and abroad as being a mere tool of General von Seeckt, and following this sensational disclosure he was virtually forced to take an uncompromising stand. By a miracle (bearing in mind the balance of power), it was not the Minister who resigned – although he offered to do so – but the General. This was solely due to the animosity that the President (and Field-Marshal) had felt ever since the war towards the Chief of Staff, who had been a close colleague of his rival, Mackensen. In an interview on 7 October Hindenburg refused to support the Chief of Staff and also turned down a compromise that would have allowed Seeckt to stay in office, because the cabinet was disinclined to accept it. Seeckt went, and his successor was General Heye – although Heye's appointment had little more than the title in common with Seeckt's.

The Chief of Staff of the army, who had once been so powerful, now became no more than a link in a chain of command descending from the President and the Minister for the Reichswehr – as had actually been provided for in the constitution. The pace of this decline in influence quickened when, at the beginning of 1928, Hindenburg's former Quartermaster-General, Groener, took Gessler's place at the Reichswehr Ministry. If the basic reason for Seeckt's fall was the impossibility of getting the army to serve two masters, the Chief of Staff's position was bound to lose its authority rapidly once it was subordinated to such massive military potential. Seeckt had had two civilians over him; since 1928 Heye and his successor had to deal in practice with the Army General Staff in its legendary final combination: what else could they do but toe the line?

Power and influence was gained, however, by another officer: Colonel (later Major-General) von Schleicher, first as head of the Wehrmacht department, then of the Ministry which developed from it. He, too, had played a part in Seeckt's downfall. Schleicher was friendly with Hindenburg's son and adjutant, Oskar, and had come from the school of Groener, who called him his 'adopted son', even at a time when he – like many other fathers – had little reason to be proud of that son. Schleicher's office became a kind of political switchboard in matters concerning the Reichswehr. This was even more the case once his patron Groener – not without some help from Schleicher – had taken over the Ministry.

With this triumvirate, Hindenburg, Groener and Schleicher, a conception of the Reichswehr emerged which differed radically from Seeckt's notion. There have been fierce arguments ever since as to which of these conceptions was more beneficial to the Republic; in Wheeler-Bennett's book *The Nemesis of Power*, Seeckt's circumspect loyalty is put in an unjustly favourable light as compared with the opportunistic political scheming of the 'evil genius' Schleicher. German historians have rightly accorded a more positive assessment of Schleicher's activities, which were certainly hectic and not very propitious in the long run, and, above all, to Groener's sympathetic attitude to the Republic.

In practice, Seeckt's doctrine of a Reichswehr 'above and beyond the parties', a state within the state, was retained even after his departure. In spite of maxims of this kind, Schleicher was by no means the first general to dabble in politics. What did change, however, was the dislike of, indeed hostility to, democracy and the Republic as such that lurked behind all Seeckt's political ducking and diving. With Seeckt a policy of wait-and-see and the hope of a restoration – albeit not by *coup d'état* – had been dominant.

But Groener, and Schleicher too, saw the Weimar state at least as a viable foundation on which the nation could build a new life, and where the army too could find a place.

This is a point to which we shall return. Following Seeckt's downfall, the first thing that happened was a fresh government crisis, set off this time in the field of military policy. It was instigated by the Social Democrats, who were pursuing two goals which could not in fact be reconciled without a certain amount of friction. On the one hand, they were tired of being sleeping partners in the responsibilities of government: they now wanted either to play a part in making political appointments and the other pleasures of government, or else to act as an active opposition. Marx was not disinclined to create a parliamentary majority for his cabinet by taking in a number of Social Democrats as ministers and thus forming a grand coalition, but the right wing of the People's Party dug their heels in and defied their party leader: collaboration with the Social Democrats was impossible, especially in view of their disagreements concerning the length of the working day and the Reichswehr. It was the latter issue in particular that offered grounds for dispute.

The Social Democrats had wished – and this was their second major concern – to use Seeckt's resignation to raise once again, and to settle once and for all, complaints about the Reichswehr, which in some cases dated back a number of years: the 'black Reichswehr', which had still not disappeared, the army's contacts with right-wing organizations and its recruiting methods (which there was now little point in changing, given the shortage of applicants for the profession of arms). Whether Gessler's assurance that everything would be different under the new leadership of the Reichswehr would have dispelled the suspicions of those Social Democrats who were inclined to come to an understanding, could not be put to the test, however. In December 1926 a number of incidents occurred which provided grist for the mill of the more radical wing of the Social Democrats.

A confidential and detailed memorandum from the Junkers aircraft factory had fallen into the hands of the British. It demanded compensation for the failure of a project initiated by the Reichswehr that would have provided factories in Russia for the construction of aircraft, which was of course forbidden in Germany. Now people could read in the foreign press – and in the Social Democrats' paper *Vorwärts*, which reprinted the story – to what lengths German–Soviet co-operation had gone in the military field. There was another incident which the Social Democrats also hoped to use as ammunition against their opponents at home – on the right as well as the left. Three ships containing Soviet shells for the Reichswehr had been secretly unloaded in the port of Stettin, and the dockers had been paid extra, more or less to keep their mouths shut. This had been made possible by an understanding with the relevant Communist cell – a good example with which to pillory the Communist Party and show how their interests harmonized with those of the Reichswehr.

And so, when negotiations about a broadening of the government were finally bogged down (mainly because of the intransigence of the Social Democrats, who demanded Gessler's head), the socialists put forward a vote of no confidence in the Reichstag on 16 December and it was backed by Scheidemann in an uncommonly aggressive speech. His criticism extended to the Reichswehr's links with big business and the financial support it was receiving from that quarter, to its contacts with right-wing organizations, its collaboration with the Soviet Union and the various ruses used to camouflage it, and a number of other issues − not forgetting, of course, the collaboration of the Communists in Stettin.

There was uproar on the right. To discuss the armaments conspiracy with the Soviet Union was regarded as treasonable, and in Germany one had to have parliamentary immunity even to mention the subject without risking a formal prosecution. While Scheidemann was speaking, the indignant Nationalists left the chamber, along with a large number of members from the other bourgeois parties. However, when a vote was taken on the Social Democratic motion of no confidence, based on the sins of the Reichswehr, the black, white and red faction chose to ignore the reason for the motion and joined the Social Democratic 'traitors' in bringing down Marx's third cabinet.

They knew very well what they were doing. For, when the President, after a government crisis lasting for weeks, was finally able to appoint a new ministry on 29 January 1927, it was the Nationalists and not the Social Democrats who were on the government benches. In November this would have seemed absurd, for even Hindenburg had spoken against a Nationalist government and had hauled the party leaders over the coals on account of their opposition to Stresemann's foreign policy. Now, however, after the Social Democrats' fierce assault on the Reichswehr, and especially following Scheidemann's speech, which was not exactly auspicious in a tactical sense, the bourgeois parties were no longer so keen on extending the government towards the left − and the President was even less keen. He was working for a bourgeois bloc including the Nationalists, with a right-wing People's Party member as Chancellor.

When that plan failed because it was opposed by the Centre Party, which did not wish to relinquish the reins of government and was still lamenting the failure of its original intention of forming a grand coalition (i.e. from the People's Party right through to Social Democrats), Marx was once more commissioned to explore the possibilities of forming such a government of the centre. But his efforts too remained fruitless because of the inflexible attitude of the parties on both wings, especially the People's Party, who were striving with all their might for the inclusion of the Nationalists. In the end, in response to urging by the President and the People's Party, Marx's fourth

cabinet emerged. It was a different kind of cabinet: the first purely parliamentary cabinet of the right, extending to the Nationalists, but forfeiting
both the forbearance of the Social Democrats and the participation of the
Democrats.

True, the Centre Party did not feel entirely at ease acting the part of
'outside-left' to the new government coalition. The black, white and red
faction had paid a price for their entry into the government – but with a
considerable rebate: they had indeed acknowledged the validity of the Locarno
treaties, but they had managed to water down the 'unconditional recognition
of the Republic' to a noncommittal 'recognition of the validity of the constitution'. Apart from the common interests of economic – above all, agricultural
– circles, the cement which held these two sociologically mixed major parties
together was their identical interest – on the one hand Catholic, on the other
Protestant – in a religious bias within the Education Bill, which Article 146
of the constitution had laid down as a guideline for the states. Following an
abortive attempt to pass a bill in 1922, the issue was back on the agenda.
The revival of religious interests was bound to be a thorn in the flesh of the
more liberal partners in the coalition, so it was obvious from the start that
Marx's new government could not lay claim to much stability.

Nevertheless, a number of major bills were passed during the eighteen
months it held office. Its activities had positive results – paradoxical as it
may seem – mainly in social legislation. This was because the government
was very keen that the political elimination of the Social Democrats should
be compensated for by concessions in the social field. Even Hindenburg had
exhorted the bourgeois bloc to assume 'a particular duty to care for the
legitimate interests of the broad mass of working people'. And other
advocates of right-wing government had also proclaimed that they had no
intention of creating a 'bloc of well-to-do bourgeois', but would concern
themselves with the welfare of the community and social needs just as much
as the government of the centre had done hitherto. This is why, for instance,
there was at last a step forward in the tiresome business of working hours:
in future, work that extended beyond the normal working day had to be paid
for by a supplement to the standard hourly rate.

Even more significant was the bill on unemployment insurance which was
passed by a large majority on 7 July. In the hard times which set in only a
few years later, but which hardly anyone reckoned with at this stage, the
principle here established of self-financing by contributions from employer
and employee very soon became illusory. State loans, originally intended only
as a stopgap, and emergency assistance, likewise provided from public funds,
then became a mainstay of the system. What had been intended as an
intermittent low level of subsidy expanded into a perpetual major drain on
public finances and gave rise to conflicts, for which, however, the 1927
sponsors of the institution cannot be held responsible.

Another well-intentioned measure led to adverse consequences. A number of states had taken preliminary steps to increase official salaries, and this rise was now embodied in a bill covering the country as a whole. After the wishes and interests of all the salary grades, and of all the parties vying for the electors' favour, had been taken into account, the substantial rise in salaries had gone up from an initial 10 per cent to almost 25 per cent. The Republic now had to pay for having, in an excess of republican puritanism, prohibited the use of official appointments and titles as an effective – but less expensive – substitute for rises in salary. Generosity on this scale after years of economizing and cutting back was in any case unsound, and there was certainly no lack of criticism of the new Salaries Bill while it was being debated. The President of the Reichsbank, Schacht, protested against the government's spendthrift policy, as did the reparations agent, Gilbert, in an official memorandum. The final outcome was even worse than these warning voices had imagined: in the bleak years ahead the increases had to be clawed back through cuts in salaries, and this caused more resentment and bad feeling than could possibly be earned now in terms of gratitude.

The reparations agent's memorandum of October 1927 had not merely criticized the rise in civil service salaries; it had referred generally to the 'rising tide of government expenditure', as well as the financial policy of the states and local authorities and their addiction to borrowing. All this was bound to lead sooner or later to severe economic setbacks and slumps. On this occasion, too, it was pointed out that no one had even thought of trying to streamline the administration of Germany. This criticism, backed by big business in Germany, which feared higher taxes and consequent price rises that would affect Germany's competitiveness in world markets, was aimed mainly at the complex and often entirely superfluous administrative arrangements entailed by German federalism. It fuelled the discussion that had gone on for years about changing the relationship between the Reich and the states. This had been laid down constitutionally in a compromise that satisfied neither side. Not only was the longstanding dualism, Prussia and the Reich, to be resolved, according to plans evolved by the Centre Party, by turning the largest German state into a 'Reichsland' directly subject to the Reich government, the Reichstag and a Reichsrat; but also, in a state like Hessen, which was not exactly small, there were signs of frustration and a propensity to get rid of financial problems, the thorny aspect of independence, by converting its territory into a 'Reichsland'. A whole series of projects was planned, some by prominent politicians like the former Chancellor Luther, and the former ministers Koch-Weser and Hoepker-Aschoff. Their plans were either purely unitarian, or else aimed in one way or another at a unitary state in the long term, via an 'extended Prussia', say, or by the gradual sapping of the financial and administrative powers of the states. Resistance to such dangerous plans was offered primarily by that federalist stronghold, Bavaria, followed by the other two south German states, and Bavaria had all the more say in this matter in that the Bavarian government party was also a coalition partner in the Reich.

Between 18 and 20 January a 'conference of states' met in Berlin at the Chancellor's invitation. The chief ministers of the states who met under the latter's chairmanship, it is true, could only agree that the current situation was far from satisfactory. But the views of unitarians from Berlin, Darmstadt or Hamburg, and federalists from Munich or Stuttgart were diametrically opposed as regards the direction in which change might proceed. It was to be made easier for tiny states to join their larger neighbours (i.e. Prussia) – but the south German states were unwilling to let Hesse go, although it was tired of being independent. The absorption of ailing states by the Reich was expressly rejected, but otherwise the whole problem was handed over to a committee, which did a certain amount of work in the succeeding years without coming any closer to an overall solution. In any case Germany would soon have other worries.

Two days before the conference of states met, the government of the Reich lost an important member: not just any minister, but the perpetual Minister for the Reichswehr. When the Democrats refused to join Marx's fourth cabinet, Gessler had stayed on, but this time – tired of continually changing from party minister to go-between and then to departmental expert – he abruptly left the party. What brought about his sudden downfall after nearly eight years in office was not in fact politics, but a scandal.

A Captain Lohmann, chief of the marine transport department of the naval staff at the Ministry of the Reichswehr, had used illegal funds which had come the way of the Reichswehr during the crisis year 1923, to assemble a fleet of tankers, set up a separate naval intelligence service and direct various other useful undertakings. He had also been given responsibility for certain links with the Soviets. In order to pursue these necessarily secret projects in times which were financially less propitious, the captain had gone into business, had embarked on audacious financial deals and had been involved in all manner of, mostly shady, enterprises. It was claimed that Lohmann's superiors had no idea of what was going on, but, given the scale of his operations, there was in fact a strong presumption that many people were turning a blind eye to them. Be that as it may, the enterprising, albeit distinctly simple-minded mariner never had the slightest difficulty in obtaining official guarantees whenever this was required in the course of his financial juggling act.

When the Phoebus Film Company, in which Lohmann had shares, collapsed, however, the whole string of speculative investments fell apart. Lohmann's business was wound up with a deficit of 200 million marks, and the left wing, seeing all its suspicions of the Reichswehr strikingly confirmed, raised a howl of indignation. Gessler did not dare face the Reichstag in connection with the Lohmann affair: on 14 January 1928 he submitted his resignation, and five days later Groener – summoned and appointed by Hindenburg – took over his office. Henceforth it was not a party politician who ruled in the Bendlerstrasse but a general – a general in fact who had served as Minister of Transport in four republican cabinets between 1920 and 1923 and who, because he was open-minded in regard to the new state, was more warmly welcomed by the left than by the right. Now, however, he was Hindenburg's agent, as he frankly declared on taking up his post.

Groener's appointment, like that of his predecessor, was doubtless meant to be a long-term affair, but Marx's fourth cabinet was already on its last legs. Intransigent Nationalists had been in the habit of making speeches in which they ripped to pieces the foreign policy of their coalition colleague Stresemann, and this had naturally not improved the climate in the cabinet. However, the reason for the coalition being dissolved on 15 February was the Education Bill that had led to its creation. When it came to the crunch, the People's Party felt that it was impossible for them to follow the path of their three partners. The latter wished to have, along with the nondenominational school stipulated as the norm in the constitution, religious schools of equal standing (and – in theory – purely secular schools). According to Article 146, parents only had the right to ask for a denominational school more or less as an exception to the rule; now they would be allowed a free choice of school.

When the Centre, the Bavarian People's Party and the Nationalists gave notice on 15 February that they were ending the coalition, they were acting in defiance of an admonition by the President, who had written to the Chancellor asking for the argument about the Education Bill to be postponed until a number of other important issues had been dealt with. Along with the budget Hindenburg mentioned a number of other matters, including support for the agricultural industry, which concerned him particularly. However, all the parties were now keen that these issues should be decided through the ballot-box.

The government came to an agreement with the democratic parties in the opposition to deal first of all with outstanding issues in an emergency programme; the parliamentary session was in any case nearing its end. Once this programme had been completed, or had been rejected, the Reichstag would be dissolved and the cabinet would resign. During the second half of May, the government promised, new elections would be held. The emergency programme was in fact concluded on 30 March, and the Reichstag was dissolved the following day. The main theme of the elections, which then took place on 20 May, had been provided in advance by the old Reichstag. It was not the Education Bill (which never became law), but, oddly enough, a ship – and a ship, in fact, which did not even exist: the notorious 'Cruiser A'.

The Treaty of Versailles had left Germany with six old capital ships, which might be replaced by new building, although only in units of not more than 10,000 tons. The favourable financial situation and technical developments which made possible the construction of ships with considerable battle potential even within these limits, had prompted a desire in the navy to lay down the first new ship of that kind, to be followed be three others. The Minister for the Reichswehr and the President were both very taken with the plan. During the budget debate the government had accordingly introduced draft legislation to cover the first financial instalment. It had been supported by Groener in a very good speech which in general advocated 'sensible pacifism'.

The Social Democrats, however, saw in the new cruiser nothing but a highly expensive toy without any practical value. They pointed to cuts in social spending undertaken by the government and declined to stretch the Versailles Treaty to the limit at such great expense. They were outvoted, but on the day following the dissolution of the Reichstag the Reichsrat had passed a motion proposed by Prussia which called for unfinished business to be postponed until September. In theory this gave the new Reichstag a chance to re-open the issue, so that the Social Democrats were able to conduct their electoral campaign under the effective slogan 'No cruisers – food for our children!'

On 20 May the expected shift to the left did in fact come about. In a relatively low poll roughly 40 per cent of the electorate cast their votes for the two socialist parties: the Social Democrats gained 152 (formerly 131) seats, while the Communists were able to increase the number of their seats from forty-five to fifty-four. The losers were the middle-class parties in the centre and on the right. The Democrats were still further decimated, losing seven of the thirty-two seats they still had, and even the stable Centre Party was reduced from sixty-nine to sixty-one seats, while the Bavarian People's Party went down from nineteen to seventeen seats. The heaviest defeat was suffered by the Nationalists, whose see-sawing between fear of their radical rivals and the share in government demanded by business interests cost them twenty-five seats: no more than seventy-eight Nationalists were left in the new Reichstag.

The ultimate result of this Nationalist electoral setback was to have fateful consequences for the Weimar Republic. The right wing of the party now came to the fore, and in October 1928 the press and film magnate Hugenberg replaced Count Westarp as party chairman. The Nationalists were no longer aiming at a bourgeois bloc but at a right-wing bloc in alliance with National Socialists and, if possible, the right wing of the People's Party. Both the latter groups, in fact, were also among the losers on 20 May 1928. In spite of the growing popularity of their party leader, Stresemann's People's Party had lost six of the fifty-one seats they had held hitherto. And in spite of all the noise the National Socialists made, only 2.6 per cent of the votes had been cast for them: they were forced to relinquish two of their fourteen seats.

As this list shows, the loss of votes on the right and in the centre was considerably greater than the gains on the left. The discrepancy was accounted for by dubious splinter parties and lobbyists. The Economics Party, now calling itself the 'Reich Party of the German Middle Class', entered the new legislative period with twenty-three instead of seventeen seats, while four other lists, including two farmers' parties, also gained a number of seats. No fewer than thirty-one parties had taken part in the election; seventeen of them failed to gain the minimum number of votes and were not represented. In spite of the system of proportional representation, almost 1.2 million votes cast produced no representatives in the Reichstag, and eighteen seats were left unfilled.

At home and abroad the result of the election on 20 May 1928 was hailed as a victory for democracy and the readiness to further international understanding over nationalistic trends. Very few people had any idea of the danger represented by the highly diverse interest groups loosely associated in the middle class and the rural communities. These groups had been deprived of their political home and now formed a potential reservoir of supporters for political adventures. Similarly, hardly anyone was in a position to foresee the strain which would shortly be imposed on the First Republic and which would belie all the tentative signs of its consolidation: the economic crisis.

8

The grand coalition and the Young Plan

The electoral victory of the Social Democrats suggested that one of their number should be entrusted with the formation of a government. And in fact the majority of the party favoured leaving their position in opposition and sharing the responsibilities of government, in spite of the misgivings of their left-wing colleagues. So Hindenburg entrusted the leader of the parliamentary party, Hermann Müller-Franken, with the formation of a new government – and found that he actually got on extremely well with the new Chancellor.

In spite of the Social Democrats' success, the weakness of the bourgeois centre meant that a grand coalition remained the most likely solution, since only such a coalition would be able to provide a sufficiently broad basis. The proposal failed, however, as did so many, because of the attitude of the People's Party. This time the main reason was their demand that, in return for joining the government, they (or, to be more precise, Stresemann) should be taken back into the Prussian government, which they had left in 1924. The Social Democrats in the Reich would have consented to that; in Prussia, however, where Braun's government could at last rely on a slender majority following Landtag elections on 20 May, which had produced similar results to those in the Reich, the Prime Minister as well as the representatives of the Social Democrats and the Centre were opposed to admitting their unreliable colleagues from the People's Party.

The next attempt involved the formation of a Weimar coalition, which would have had a bare majority only if the Bavarian People's Party was included. But this plan also failed, because the chairman of the People's Party was indispensable as Foreign Minister. Müller asked Stresemann, whose health had broken down during the election campaign and who was recuperating in the Black Forest, whether he would join a government of the Weimar coalition in an expert capacity. Stresemann's reply, delivered without consulting his parliamentary colleagues, has become known as 'the Bühlerhöhe shot': he refused to join the government merely as an expert, but declared his readiness to play a part in 'a cabinet of personalities' from various parliamentary parties who would constitute a grand coalition. For, even if the parliamentary groups could not agree on a long-term programme, these 'personalities' would have a better chance as individuals of approaching the Reichstag with a common platform. With a thinly veiled allusion to his own parliamentary group, which constantly made life difficult for him, the chairman of the People's Party declared that the formation of a government in this way was in keeping with the spirit of the constitution, which recognized only the personal responsibility of ministers, not parliamentary parties.

Stresemann, who was still convalescing, was promptly plunged into a feud with the leadership of his parliamentary party, and this was followed by many other disputes. However, his intervention had cleared the way for the formation of a government under Müller. The Centre Party, which had swung over to a mildly right-wing course, now caused difficulties which led to only a single minister from that party being included, pending subsequent discussions on full participation. Nevertheless, the cabinet which set to work on 28 June was undeniably impressive. It had Severing at the Ministry of the Interior, and included also Stresemann, Groener, Curtius, Koch-Weser, Hilferding and Wissell. But the fact could not be concealed that its parliamentary basis – although broader than it had been for some time – was distinctly fragile. Two of the partners – the Bavarian People's Party and the Centre Party – had, as it were, no more than a limited liability, and fierce arguments about various unresolved controversies might certainly be expected, ranging from the ill-starred cruiser to issues of social policy.

The Education Bill, over which *pro forma* the last government had fallen, ought really to have been included in the list of such topics, for now supporters of the school bill from the Centre Party were on the opposite side from the Nationalists, while opponents from the Centre were sitting once more side by side with People's Party representatives on the government benches. However, surprising as it may seem, the dispute over education was not destined to be the subject of discussion in the future: it had finally vanished from the agenda. But there were plenty of other sufficiently explosive issues. It was a manifest sign of weakness that the new Chancellor did not dare ask expressly for a vote of confidence, which would have brought into the open all the latent differences between the half-hearted partners in the coalition. Instead, he had to content himself with approval of a statement of government policy.

After the summer recess Müller resumed his attempts to bind the parliamentary parties more firmly to the government, but without success.

The central issue was clarification of the Centre's part in the government, where the party had been represented so far by a single minister, although he was in fact responsible for two ministries. In February 1929 the Centre Party issued an ultimatum demanding a third ministry. As far as that went, there ought not to have been a problem; after all, the Democrat Erich Koch-Weser at the Ministry of Justice was more or less just keeping a place warm for a Minister from the Centre Party. However, the People's Party were prepared to take part in a grand coalition with full parliamentary support only if they were taken back into the Prussian government – and given two ministerial posts. In their reply the Centre Party proposed to give at best a postdated cheque, and the suggested deal ended with the Centre Party minister resigning from the Reich cabinet.

The international situation, together with support from the President, was what kept Müller's government alive. And in April the knot was unravelled. In the meantime the argument had shifted from the Prussian deal to the problem of balancing the 1929 budget, which was in deficit. When a compromise had been reached, three Centre Party ministers joined the cabinet on 13 April. It thus became, apart from a few reserved areas, a proper coalition cabinet – with all the concomitant drawbacks, amongst which might be reckoned a kind of shadow government in the form of a co-ordinating committee representing the parliamentary parties in the coalition.

What kept Müller's government in the saddle at the beginning of 1929, and in general acted as the elixir that prolonged its life, was a series of renewed reparations agreements that finally emerged as the Young Plan. The same kind of thing had happened in 1923, when the battle for the Ruhr and the inflation had kept alive Stresemann's cabinet, that first experiment with a grand coalition. But the moment the Young Plan had cleared its last hurdle, the overstretched bow that spanned big business and socialism snapped under the strain of the economic crisis. It is not oversimplifying the issue to call the Müller government the government of the Young Plan.

The suggestion of the plan had come from the reparations agent, Gilbert, in December 1927, when efforts were being made to find a permanent sub-stitute for the stopgap Dawes Plan. Personal reasons making it convenient for him to return to the United States combined with objective considera-tions. Financially and economically it looked as if the Reich had mastered the inflation crisis for the foreseeable future. On the other hand, the situation had not changed for the better to such a degree that increased demands by its reparations creditors would make it more difficult to arrive at a settlement.

Similar considerations prompted German politicians like Schacht and the Economics Minister, Curtius, to take up the suggestion. The Dawes instal-ments, which had been paid punctually – thanks to the foreign loans – had reached their peak of 2,500 million marks per annum in 1928. It was believed, however, that this sum far exceeded Germany's ability to pay, and that the time had come for a substantial reduction. But it was the political aspect of the plan that most attracted Germany. For one thing, it was hoped that a revised plan would mean the ending of the trusteeship governing German financial policy. For another, France had let it be known that the evacuation of the second and third occupation zones in the Rhineland would depend on a final solution of the reparations problem.

The 'black shame on the Rhine', however, had an emotional potential in German politics that was in no way proportionate to the true significance of the occupation. It was no longer 1923; the Entente troops had fulfilled the promises made by the French, rendering themselves virtually 'invisible', so that their presence could annoy none but those who were determined to take offence at all costs. Nor did the foreign troops represent a financial burden, since occupation costs were subsumed under the reparations account. Whether the British, the Belgians and the French now stayed in Aachen and Koblenz until January 1930, and in Trier and Kaiserslautern for a further five years, or not, was of no practical significance – and, looking back, we might even say that it would have been better for Germany if they *had* stayed.

But what do rational considerations matter in an issue of such heartfelt concern? Even for Stresemann, the 'liberation of the Rhineland' was the chief immediate aim. Since the signing of the Dawes Plan, Germany believed she had fulfilled all the contractual obligations stipulated in Versailles as the condition for an early withdrawal. Nevertheless, her claim for a return of the pledge was rejected by the western powers. Now, however, the fact that France had linked the issue with a definitive reparations agreement brought within reach the goal that Germany had longed for. No wonder that the misgivings Stresemann and others had about raising the reparations question again were silenced. On the occasion of the annual meeting of the League of Nations in Geneva in September 1928 Germany had agreed with the Allies, who were influenced by the reparations agent, to enter into negotiations on an early withdrawal from the Rhineland, as well as on a definitive settlement of the reparations issue. A new commission of financial experts was to make preparations for the latter problem, and – unlike the Dawes Plan of 1924 – it was to include Germany as an equal partner.

The commission duly met in Paris on 9 February 1929. At that point it was already clear that German hopes of any perceptible easing of the burden of reparations through a new payments plan were illusory. The instalments had been paid punctually hitherto, although the money had been scraped together by borrowing, and this had concealed Germany's inability to pay. Moreover, as far as the creditor nations were concerned, any cut in payments was inevitably linked with a similar concession to them on the part of the United States. The Americans declared categorically, however, that they had been sufficiently obliging as far as war debts were concerned, and there could be no question of further discounts.

Thus the two sides were pretty much at odds when the committee met under the chairmanship of an American, Owen Young. The Allies demanded, in line with their own debts plus a small supplement, a whole series of annuities: 1,800 million marks, rising to 2,400 million over a period of thirty-six-and-a-half years, followed by more or less fixed annuities of 1,700 million marks for a further period of twenty-one years. A counter-memorandum from the German experts offered a fixed annuity of 1,650 million marks for a period of thirty-seven years. But it also linked this offer – in spite of objections by the government of the Reich – with a demand, only lightly hedged round with saving clauses, for the return of colonies and the Polish Corridor. Negotiations were on the point of being broken off when sheer chance – the death of the chairman of a sub-committee – caused a delay and allowed time for renewed discussions. These ended in a compromise by Young which in fact moderated Allied demands only slightly. The period of fifty-seven-and-a-half years remained, but the incremental scale was made less steep in the early stages.

Nevertheless, the German delegation accepted this plan, which was signed on 7 June by all the experts. The German government, too, regarded its acceptance as 'inevitable'; in fact things had reached the point where a breakdown in the reparations negotiations would have entailed the collapse of German creditworthiness, as was clearly shown by the instant withdrawal of foreign capital during the crisis in the expert conference.

Looked at in the cold light of day, the new plan was a pretty dubious gain. Compared with the payments under the Dawes Plan, it is true, it offered an alleviation of 700 million marks on average during the next few years, but the reduction was by no means as large as had been hoped. It also meant the removal of international controls on the German economy, the railways and the Reichsbank, thus restoring the Reich's sovereignty over its own finances. At the same time, however, it eliminated the reparations agent, and hence the transfer protection that German payments had enjoyed hitherto. In the event of an economic crisis, it is true, a proportion of future instalments might be postponed through an appeal to a Bank for International Settlements which was to be set up and given responsibility for 'arrangements for discharging reparations obligations'. In this way, such payments might be protected by a possible moratorium, but the absence of the former comprehensive transfer protection and of the reparations agent was soon to prove disastrous. The flight of foreign capital during the economic crisis would certainly not have assumed such catastrophic proportions in a Germany that was subject to international controls. The old 'improvement certificate' had, however, also been abolished: even given an economic boom, Germany's payments could not be raised any further. On the other hand, she stood to profit to some extent from eventual cuts in American war debts.

There was, however, one major psychological obstacle. The current value of the Young payments might well be 'only' 37,000 million marks, but how could anyone not trained in economics make any sense of that figure? Much more impressive was the fact that the Reich was obliged to stump up a total of 112,000 million marks within a period of almost sixty years, which sounded horrific. Anyone who stuck to hard facts could point out that 7,000 million marks less than in the Dawes Plan would be paid out during the next ten years – and when, in the course of human history, had anyone ever been able to plan sixty years in advance! Besides, it was obvious that the new instalments could only be paid, as always, with borrowed funds. When, shortly afterwards, this turned out to be impossible, the entire reparations merry-go-round promptly collapsed.

Be that as it may, it was still possible, if one were sufficiently determined, to make propaganda capital from the plan for the benefit of later generations, who had allegedly been born up to their necks in debt. And the right-wing German parties were indeed so determined. A furious nationalistic opposition crystallized around the Young Plan, delighting to point out how their children and their children's children would labour under 'the yoke of Young's bondage' to pay their tribute. What the plan's opponents otherwise had in common, it was hard to say. It was simpler to state what they were opposed to: Versailles and the system set up by the 'November criminals'. In these years of economic recovery, the Young Plan offered a new, more topical watchword to replace rather faded slogans.

On 9 July 1929, a month after the Young report had been signed, a 'Reich Committee for a German Referendum' was set up as a rallying point for all those forces on the right who were out to overthrow the Republic (and who succeeded in doing so in the end). The referendum prepared by the Committee was meant to attack the Young Plan and the 'war-guilt lie'. The movement was headed by the leaders of those anti-republican parties that had combined to launch a frontal assault on the Republic: Hugenberg for the Nationalists, side by side with Franz Seldte, head of the Stahlhelm, and a superannuated judge, Justizrat Class, included more or less *honoris causa* for what was still left of the Pan-Germans. But there was also – and *he* was no musty relic from the nineteenth century – Adolf Hitler, on behalf of the National Socialists.

He had a dozen seats in the Reichstag and 810,000 voters, but apart from that his people had been regarded as hooligans, and he himself as slightly mad. But now his name stood next to that of a well-known and respectable Privy Councillor; now he was sitting at the same table as the latter; now he himself had become respectable, and – last but not least – his associations had given him access to the electoral funds of industry and commerce. While he went on belabouring capitalism with his left hand, he was now able to stretch out an open right hand for levies from the capitalists – an excellent posture in which to promise everyone concerned his due – and then to default on his promises.

For in the end he was to swallow up the lot of them; in the end the illusion of 'Hitler the drummer', which was just beginning among his grand new middle-class friends, was to be dispelled. Until that point Hitler had been a negligible quantity in German politics, a Goliath of the beer-cellars, one of innumerable and generally rather ludicrous figures trying to bring their political brews to the boil over their flickering little fires. But now his rise to the national political level was beginning, and events were to take a turn so favourable to his cause that in a matter of a few years he would have reached the very top.

During the last days of September the Reich Committee published its 'Liberty Law', the subject of the plebiscite procedure which was now initiated. It was both foolish and offensive. Paragraph 1 was on traditional lines: it called on the German government to revoke the 'lie of Germany's war guilt'. The next paragraph, however, had already passed into the realm of sheer demagoguery: the government of the Reich, it stated, should bring pressure to bear to have the war-guilt Article 231 formally abrogated and the occupied territories evacuated 'forthwith and unconditionally'. The latter issue at least was precisely the aim of Stresemann's policy. According to paragraph 3, 'no new liabilities or obligations were to be assumed', especially not the reparations arrangements contained in the Young Plan. The authors of the 'Liberty Law' had nothing to say on how these aims might be achieved, and they could well afford to remain silent, since they need not fear that they would ever be in a position to take responsible decisions. On the other hand, paragraph 4 – and this was a pure and original Hitlerite idea – threatened members of the government and 'those authorized by them' who signed treaties with foreign powers in contravention of the terms of paragraph 3 (i.e. agreement to the Young Plan) with prosecution under the treason paragraph (paragraph 92, section 3) of the Criminal Code.* There had been opposition within the Committee, particularly from agricultural groups, to paragraph 4, which had been deliberately drafted as a blow below the belt. Nevertheless, the radical majority had its way – the text was merely emended by the insertion of a phrase to ensure that at least the venerable Field-Marshal and President of the Reich, the Honorary President of Seldte's Stahlhelm, would be excluded from the circle of those who were here certified as, by rights, deserving prison sentences.

*Paragraph 92 of the Criminal Code read: 'Whoever deliberately . . . 3. conducts with another government an official commission entrusted to him by the German Reich or by one of its constituent states to the detriment of his client will be punished by a sentence of not less than two years' hard labour. If there are mitigating circumstances [which would certainly not have been the case in the eyes of those who framed the 'Liberty Law'] fortress detention of not less than six months applies.'

The plebiscite turned out to be a wretched failure, for the time was not yet ripe. The petition for the referendum, for which lists were distributed during the second half of October, only just cleared the constitutional hurdle, with a bare 10.02 per cent of voters putting their names down. It was a hopeful sign that Hindenburg refused to allow his person or his name to be used in the frenzied agitation which now began on all sides, and that he expressly condemned paragraph 4. At the next stage, in the Reichstag on 30 November, the bill suffered a predictably heavy defeat. This was where democracy was able to celebrate its last triumph: when the vote was taken on the paragraph referring to prison sentences the Nationalists were divided. Instead of the eighty votes for paragraphs 1 to 3, Hitler's sorry effort gained no more than sixty supporters, for a number of Nationalist members, along with some representatives of agricultural parties, abstained. A few days later, when Hugenberg tried to discipline the rebels, a group round Schlange-Schöningen, the former Minister of the Interior, von Keudell and Gottfried Treviranus resigned from the party, without, however, achieving anything other than a further increase in the already sufficiently large number of splinter parties, to which they added a 'Popular Conservative Union' (Volkskonservative Vereinigung)

The opponents of the Young Plan were able to compensate for this loss by registering a gain elsewhere. The President of the Reichsbank, Dr Hjalmar Schacht, erstwhile co-founder of the Democratic Party and recently, as one of the two German delegates, a signatory of the exports' report popularly known as the Young Plan, was an individual with a nose not only for financial issues but also for changes in the political climate. Hence, as the expert committee's deliberations approached their end, he had tried – albeit in vain – to say both 'yes' and 'no' at one and the same time, and then to justify his 'yes' as being dictated by government instructions – although he had been appointed as an independent expert. At the beginning of December Schacht published an internal memorandum, written for the benefit of the government, in which he 'categorically refused' to be held responsible for the Young Plan. As a pretext he used an argument which might at first sight be considered adequate: the recent, if marginal, worsening for Germany in the terms of the Young Plan during its preliminary drafting.

An international conference had been held in The Hague during August, with the object of reviewing the experts' report and discussing both it and the other main point: the evacuation of the occupied Rhineland. The first Hague conference did not take place without a certain amount of friction, although – for once – it was not Germany that was to blame. This time it was the British government that had protested against the new scheme for sharing German reparations among the Allies, which placed them at a disadvantage as compared with the Dawes Plan. They had inevitably come into conflict with the French, at whose expense any increase in Britain's share would have to be made.

In itself, this quarrel in no way involved German interests, but there was a risk that the parties to the dispute would reach agreement on the backs of the weakest members of the conference. In order to avoid this, the German delegation had made one concession that went beyond the experts' report: this would adversely affect the proportion of the secured to the unsecured parts of Germany's payments during the early years of the plan. Before this, however, Stresemann had received from Briand the long-awaited assurance that the Rhineland would be evacuated. The withdrawal of foreign troops was to begin in September under an evacuation agreement. The British, the Belgians and the French in the second zone would depart within three months, and the third zone would also be evacuated by the end of June 1930 at the latest.

Gustav Stresemann, who had negotiated these agreements in The Hague with the last reserves of his strength, did not live to see them realized. On 3 October 1929, only a few days after Hugenberg and his vassals had threatened him with prison, he succumbed to a final, fatal stroke. His death symbolically anticipated the demise of a Republic of which he, the chairman of a party originally hostile to republican government, had, oddly enough, become the protagonist. He was the architect of virtually all those coalitions which had governed Germany in the preceding years. We can only speculate as to whether he would also have been able to master the crisis of the succeeding year, which was to put an end to the Republic. In the long run he would not have been able to parry the attacks of the forces opposing him, but perhaps the Weimar state would not have come to such a wretched end. Stresemann had for years contrived to steer the Democrats in the wake of the Republic, keeping them on course in spite of fierce opposition until the very end of his life, but now they at once began to drift to the right, as though they had lost their ballast. It was on their intransigence (and the apolitical thinking of the Social Democrats) that the last government of the First Republic was wrecked, although, or precisely *because*, people knew that it would be the last.

For the moment, however, the grand coalition was still holding together – the Young Plan still needed to be wrapped up and delivered. It was a sheer necessity; it might provoke a shrill cry of 'No!', but no one had anything like a realistic alternative to offer. This is why the referendum on the 22 December produced a result that could only embarrass the progenitors of the 'Liberty Law'. Twenty-one million votes in favour would have been required, but there were no more than 5.8 million in the ballot-boxes – no more than the Nationalists, the National Socialists and the racial nationalist bloc had obtained between them in the Reichstag elections of 1928.

Versailles, a disgust with the multi-party state, a yearning for authority, racist, anti-Semitic or other traditions and emotions, the deceitful language of the nationalists: the referendum on the Young Plan demonstrated that all this together did not at present constitute a serious threat to the Republic.

It formed no more than the foundation for what was to come when economic distress and total hopelessness would seize the masses by the throat. If it had not been for the war, Hitler would probably never have become a politician, if it had not been for Versailles, he would not have remained in politics for long and if it had not been for the grievances of his 'national comrades', his successes would presumably have remained within modest limits – but his *triumph* he owed exclusively to the economic crisis. We can imagine his success with the masses without many of the factors which contributed to it – but not without this one.

In January 1930 a second conference in The Hague took place, the continuation of the negotiations adjourned in August 1929. Now the issues that had been left open were to be settled and agreements signed. Largely on account of German right-wing opposition, there was still one perilous reef to be negotiated, because the French were demanding a clause providing for sanctions, i.e. a renewed occupation of the Rhineland, supposing Germany (under a government led by Hugenberg, say, or Hitler) did not acknowledge or did not fulfil her obligations under the Young Plan. Stresemann's successor, Curtius, managed to fend off this demand. What was left was an exchange of declarations in which the competence of the International Court of Justice in such a case was laid down. The 'creditor governments' would regain their freedom of action in regard to Germany only when the Court established that it was Germany's deliberate intention to 'tear up the plan'. This kind of arrangement was, of course, quite sufficient cause for the right in Germany to raise furious howls of protest.

A number of other disputes were settled in The Hague, while a fresh affront which Schacht permitted himself led to no further consequences. Without the knowledge of the German government he abruptly made participation of the Reichsbank in the new Bank for International Settlements subject to such conditions as acceptance of the Young Plan as it stood and the renunciation of any kind of sanctions. Such matters were certainly not within his competence, but they provided a plausible background to his spectacular resignation from the chairmanship of the Reichsbank, which took place at the beginning of March.

By that time the Hague accord had already been signed and the Reichstag had to ratify it. After certain reservations expressed by the Centre and the Bavarian People's Party had been dealt with, a vote was taken on 12 March 1930 on the hotly debated Young Plan. The principal bill had a smooth passage, being adopted by 270 votes to 192. But now the opposition had recourse to a final disruptive tactic which was to end in a curious manner. The convenient pretext had been offered by the hyperdemocratic Articles 72 and 75 of the constitution. According to them, the promulgation of a bill passed by parliament might be suspended for two months, if this was called for by one-third of the members of the Reichstag. A petition signed not by 10 but by a mere 5 per cent of the electorate would then have sufficed to set the plebiscite machinery in motion once more, leading to a considerable and, in the case of the Young Plan possibly fatal, delay in the bill's implementation.

The opposition, of course, succeeded in getting together the necessary one-third of the Reichstag members. But now the majority in the Reichstag were in a position to declare the disputed legislation urgent – which they duly did. If the Reichsrat concurred in this procedure, Article 72 left it to the discretion of the President of the Reich to promulgate the law or else to delay its promulgation. And Hindenburg, once the hero of the loud-mouthed nationalists who had made him supreme head of the Republic, chose not to avail himself of even a fraction of the month the constitution allowed him to make up his mind: on that same 13 March on which the Reichsrat had joined the Reichstag in supporting the motion declaring the Young Plan legislation to be urgent, Hindenburg signed the bill, 'with a heavy, but also a resolute heart'.

This cannot be explained simply as loyalty to his oath or as legalistic thinking – after all, the republican constitution gave the President a free hand in this matter. The fact that he took this decision in spite of severe pressure from his friends in the right-wing camp, more or less against his own flesh and blood, did not derive from the pettifogging consideration that, after all, a rebate of 700 million marks per annum was better than no change at all. It stemmed rather, in the main, from that one consideration that differentiated Hindenburg from his friends: he bore the responsibility, whereas they need do no more than raise a shout of protest. The Kreuz-Zeitung, the Kyffhäuserbund and the Junkers round Kammerherr von Oldenburg-Januschau made the painful effort to understand their old comrade's motives, but henceforth the Field-Marshal and President was included among the targets of a furious outcry on the extreme right. 'Hindenburg's farewell to Germany' Hitler's party newspaper groaned, for instance, and the former Quartermaster-General Ludendorff declared that 'Herr Paul von Hindenburg' had forfeited the privilege of wearing the field-grey tunic in future, or taking it with him to the grave. Indeed, even in the Stahlhelm it was mooted whether their honorary member should not perhaps be expelled, so deeply was the nation imbued with the hatred surrounding the name of Young.

Now that the Young Plan bore the President's signature, the bond that had held the coalition parties more or less together had been severed – whether the 'new plan' was regarded in a sober commercial light simply as a settlement between a debtor and his creditors, or seen for instance by Dr Heinrich Brüning (rapidly risen to parliamentary honours as the new leader of the Centre Party group) as a further *Diktat* by a superior adversary to which one would have to submit willy-nilly. But, instead of the problems surrounding the Young Plan, the most urgent question became the critical state of the Reich's finances – a burning issue for some time past which had now been aggravated by the economic crisis. Within a couple of weeks this question had split the coalition apart.

From the very start it had never been all that robust, for breadth is not necessarily the same thing as strength, and it certainly was not so in this case. The coalition was an arch spanning a whole range of parties, from the industrial capitalist wing of the People's Party to the doctrinaire socialist wing of the Social Democrats. Both these parties, moreover, had been engaged ever since they were founded in an unremitting defensive battle against their radical neighbours and were practically incapable of taking any decision without considering the possibility of it being demagogically exploited by their rivals. It had been clear from the outset that not much could be expected of Müller's cabinet, in which the adversaries in the class war found themselves, by force of circumstances, sitting side by side: their common ground was too restricted, in spite of, or possibly because of, the breadth of the coalition. It hardly needed a prophet to predict, even in the hour of its birth, that this government would soon be racked by disputes and furious arguments.

This had begun as early as the summer of 1928 and had assumed grotesque forms. A legacy of the bourgeois bloc government was that armoured 'Cruiser A', which had still not been finally approved and against which the Social Democrats had fought their victorious election campaign – only to find themselves sharing the government benches with its progenitors. Following an interim review of its financial feasibility called for by the Reichsrat at the request of Prussia, the cabinet, presided over by the Social Democrat Chancellor, decided to proceed with the construction of the ship. This decision was only logical, if its opponents' sneers about the 'holiday cabinet' were not to seem instantly justified. The parliamentary group and the central committee of the victorious Social Democrats, however, called for construction to be halted – with a look back at their electoral propaganda and a sidelong glance at the Communists who had just staged a petition calling for a plebiscite on the issue. The petition was, incidentally, a miserable failure with something like one million signatures, i.e. barely 3 per cent of those entitled to vote.

The vote on the Social Democrats' parliamentary motion, which took place on 16 November, was made subject to a party whip that included members of the government. And so it was that a farcical scene ensued, as the Chancellor and the Social Democratic ministers of the Reich descended from the government benches and took their seats as members of parliament in order to vote against the decision they had just taken in the cabinet. Of course, the motion, even with help from the Communists, did not achieve a majority – the scene in the Reichstag was pure shadow-boxing. Groener and his friends from the bourgeois parties had raised the cruiser issue to cabinet level, and if the Social Democrats' motion had succeeded, the government would have fallen. But, as the leadership of the socialists expressly stated, nothing was further from their minds, especially as their bourgeois successors would have built the ill-starred vessel anyway. But none of those responsible, it seems, had worried very much about the effect that this circus performance was bound to have on a public who in any case looked sceptically and critically on parliamentary democracy.

That same autumn the 'iron dispute' disrupted the coalition's peace in the field of social policy. Wage demands by workers in the iron industry of north-western Germany had been only partly met by the employers, for good reason in view of the downward trend of the economy. The wave of wage increases thus begun was bound to make exports, on which so much depended, more expensive and reduce their volume. The dispute had gone to arbitration. The employers, however, had refused to accept the verdict of the arbitration commission in Düsseldorf, even after the Social Democratic Minister of Labour had declared it to be binding. On 1 November the employers locked the work force out. The courts delivered different verdicts at various stages of the case. The government could not afford to wait for the end of a succession of hearings; an instant solution was vitally necessary.

In the heated debate on the iron industry dispute the two wings of the coalition were once more seen opposing each other in hostile camps. The significance of the dispute extended beyond its actual cause in the sense that the workers suspected that the employers were intent on mounting an attack on the arbitration machinery as such and were trying to open up a path to wage negotiations free from the restrictions imposed by state intervention in November 1918. If this was the employers' aim (and various statements suggested that it was), then it was not achieved. Their ruthless approach was so ill received even amongst their friends that they were forced to climb down. At the beginning of December both parties accepted mediation by the government, which appointed the Minister of the Interior, Severing, as arbitrator. The parties had agreed in advance that they would accept his award, which followed a middle course – satisfactory to neither side, naturally – between the concessions offered by the employers and the Düsseldorf award, which tended to favour the workers.

Thus, this obstacle had been successfully negotiated, but during that same winter a subject cropped up that was destined to figure permanently on the Republic's political agenda, and on which the government, based as it was on a laborious reconciliation of opposite views, was ultimately to be wrecked. The time (round about 1924/25) when the state's coffers were overflowing – largely because of unduly low estimates of income – had long since passed by 1929. The current situation was not just the result of *force majeure*, but, to begin with anyway, a consequence of financial policy: in 1926, under the Social Democratic Minister of Finance, Reinhold, the prevailing policy of accumulating hidden reserves had been replaced by budgetary estimates 'on the very brink of a deficit'. In the interim, however, the budget threatened to be pushed far beyond this limit, and no amount of rearranging seemed likely to save the situation.

Even the budgetary proposals for 1929, which were to be passed during the winter, were balanced only with the greatest difficulty. Hilferding, once again Minister of Finance, managed to balance his budget through sundry economies and tax increases calculated to bring in 379 million marks. One cause of the country's budgetary plight was the extraordinary budgets of preceding years, which dragged on as a growing deficit. A second cause was the increased reparations instalments under the Dawes Plan, which had for the first time attained the level they would continue at in future. A third cause was the state's increasing need of credit as a result of rising unemployment.

The taxes to be raised had been selected in such a way as to affect the economy as little as possible (beer, brandy, death duties, property taxes). Nevertheless, there was a storm of protest, understandably since, following their defeat in the war, the Germans were numbered among the world's most heavily taxed nations. Inter-party consultations involving financial experts from the five parties closest to the government led to death duties and the tax on beer being left unchanged (after all, the Bavarian People's Party was among the five!) Instead, further cuts were made under various budgetary heads. These consultations also led to the cabinet reshuffle already referred to, so that the 'cabinet of personalities' turned into a proper coalition. Other consequences of the financial calamity were an accelerated approach to the Young Plan, and also the conviction that a fundamental reform of unemployment insurance was essential to stem the ever-growing drain on the country's resources.

For the queues in front of the labour exchanges were growing longer. When we read that just under 2.9 million were standing in these queues in January 1929, this does not suggest that people realized they were standing in the path of an impending avalanche. The winter was particularly harsh, and there had no longer been anything like full employment in the preceding years. There had been 2 million unemployed the previous winter, and in January 1927 there had even been more than $2\frac{1}{2}$ million. In fact the German economy was already in the first stages of the great crisis that was to set its mark mainly on the years 1931 to 1933. A number of factors now came together for the first time in the post-war period of the German economy – some of them direct or indirect consequences of the inflation, of which the true costs were only now becoming fully apparent. The inflation had considerably extended and speeded up the process of cartelization and monopolization, which even before the war had existed on a scale unmatched in any other industrial country. In combination with the regulation of prices and wages introduced during the war, this process resulted in a rigidity of the economic system that in times of crisis impaired the 'recuperative powers' of the economy, in which the prevailing liberal theory still had confidence. By 1928 and 1929, however, the trend towards concentration had initially resulted in a glut on the market, especially in view of the weakness of the domestic market (which was also partly induced by inflation), and this overproduction tended to inhibit the inclination of the private economy to invest.

There was another reason why private and public investment, as well as investment by local authorities, steadily declined during 1928/29. Since the inflation had dealt the German capital market such a shattering blow, investments since 1924 had been financed to an unusually large degree with foreign – especially American capital. In the few years that had elapsed since the inflation the German capital market had barely recovered; dependence on an uninterrupted flow of foreign capital, which reached 20,500 million marks by the beginning of the 1930s, had hardly diminished. In 1929 the export of American capital declined sharply (from 1,000 million to 200 million dollars), because at the height of the speculative fever, many investors believed they could make greater profits in the USA itself. Germany reacted instantly with a marked reduction in investment activity, declining share prices and an increase in the number of bankruptcies. The crash on the New York Stock Exchange in October 1929, which marked the outbreak of the great American slump, meant the end of any hope for Germany. At first the withdrawal of American short-term investments was relatively limited, and in 1930 in fact more American capital actually flowed into Germany than in 1929. But the American crisis made the resumption of capital exports at the level needed by Germany ultimately impossible. Instead, in September 1930 (in response to the first major electoral triumph of the National Socialists) and in the summer of 1931 (when Brüning declared that Germany was unable to go on paying reparations) there followed two politically motivated waves of investment withdrawals, which had catastrophic effects.

To make matters even worse, agriculture was also heading for the lowest point of a grave crisis. The war had forced agriculture into intensive methods of production all round the world, and this led in the post-war years to overproduction and a ruinous fall in prices. In Germany this worldwide structural crisis had been masked until 1923/24 by the inflation, which enabled agriculture to dispose of its debts to a large extent and also assisted efforts to modernize the industry. Since 1927/28, however, inflation had once again had a powerful effect, because German agriculture was operating with very high production costs compared with its international competitors.

The export industries were in no position to help the economy through the crisis; indeed, they also found themselves in the greatest difficulty. Quite apart from the fact that – again not least because of inflation – the domestic market was too weak to support development, the liberal system of world trade had been badly battered by the war and the periods of political, financial and economic crisis that had followed it. Now, in the early stages of the worldwide economic crisis, it collapsed. In the rising panic every country tried to shield its domestic producers by high tariffs levied on their foreign competitors: the truism that no one can sell if no one is prepared to buy was forgotten. Even those who had borne the banner of free trade, the USA and Great Britain, succumbed to short-sighted economic nationalism. This was bound to hit Germany's export industries hard, driving them from markets they had only just regained between 1919 and 1928, and keeping them out of new markets. True, Germany herself was pursuing a policy that was definitely aimed against imports. In fact, it proved possible during the crisis years to maintain a positive balance of trade, but only by rigorously restricting imports and consumption. In absolute terms German exports went steadily down.

After the crisis had started, moreover, certain measures taken by the government of the Reich turned into an important additional factor. The government reacted with a deflationary financial policy and thrifty budgeting, as though it were dealing with a normal downward swing of the trade cycle, or a process resembling the currency crisis in the first half of the 1920s. This was done, in fact, not only in view of the German horror of inflation, but because the government wished to exploit the crisis in order to get rid of its burden of reparations. This policy first of all blocked any way out of the crisis and then added quite considerably to the current deterioration of the economic situation.

After October 1929, when the German crisis merged with the American crisis and all the other national crises to produce a worldwide economic crisis, a decline in world production set in, with output falling to one-third of the 1928 level (in 1932 it was 38 per cent): this was tantamount to a major slump. The loss of political confidence thus brought about was nowhere worse than in Germany, which, along with the United States, was especially hard hit. Even in better years the country had been groaning under the burden of the lost war, with more or less good reason. The democratic republic, which had only just got back on its feet, was floored instantly by this last and most devastating blow. What followed between the spring of 1930 and 1933 was no more than the unconscious loser being counted out.

Up until October 1929, however, Germany was merely in an early stage of this great upheaval, which was hard to diagnose. True, the number of unemployed was still rising, but in comparison with the previous year the level of wages and salaries and the general standard of living was virtually unchanged and gave no hint whatsoever of an impending collapse. It still appeared that this was more or less a German problem, and, in fact, mainly a budgetary problem that might be coped with by a loan for the present and, once the burden of reparations was alleviated, by a reform of unemployment insurance in the foreseeable future. Economic recovery following a period of stagnation would set in once again, as it had done following the critical circumstances of 1926.

If we take the labour market as a barometer, things had seemed much more ominous during the economic depression of 1926, which was later described as an interim crisis. At that time there had been on average for the year 2.01 million fully unemployed persons, compared with only 636,000 in the previous year, 1925. In 1929 the average for the year had been 1.9 million, and the rise compared with the the previous year, 1928, had been far less obvious. Or, to put it another way: in 1926, thirty-two out of 1,000 Germans were unemployed (as compared with ten in 1925), while in 1929 the figure was thirty (compared with twenty-two in 1928). Thus, the situation did not seem to be all that bad; nevertheless a financial reform to salvage the budget was obviously an urgent necessity.

In order to cover the budget deficit, in May 1929 the government sought authority to launch a 500 million mark loan. The terms were extremely favourable – so favourable, in fact, that in the Reichstag debate on the loan bill the right-wing opposition described them as humiliating. A Nationalist member denounced the loan as the 'desperate act of a political system that had demonstrated a genius for borrowing money'. Systematic undermining of German creditworthiness by such subversive talk and by constant prophecies of doom, incidentally, went to show that the system was anything but inspired in its borrowing policy. Although the subscription term had to be extended, the loan brought in no more than a bare 178 million – just enough to tide the budget over to the critical end of May. This was due in no small measure to a boycott by the banks, who were intent on giving the Social Democrat Finance Minister, Hilferding, a salutary fright.

The Reich was so deeply in debt that it could not survive without credit of this kind, and the President of the Reichsbank, Schacht, exploited the situation politically in December, when an insolvent government once more faced a reckoning at the end of the month, and civil servants' salaries were once again at risk. The Finance Minister had tried in vain – and this was characteristic of the political situation in Germany – to raise a bridging loan in the USA. When the attempt failed the government was forced to let Schacht, as head of a consortium of German banks, dictate terms. The terms in themselves – the establishment of a sinking fund from tax income and economies to reduce the national debt – were not unreasonable, but the political consequences were ominous. The Finance Minister and his State Secretary, Johannes Popitz, had to resign, almost as if they were delinquents caught with their hands in the till; the Social Democræt Hilferding was replaced by Moldenhauer, of the People's Party, formerly Minister of Economics (replaced there by a Social Democrat); and Schacht, who had just denounced the Young Plan, had once more demonstrated how easy it was to treat this government in a thoroughly cavalier fashion.

Apart from this development, and apart from the problem of reparations, there was still the question of unemployment insurance. It had been acute ever since the end of May 1929, when the cabinet had instructed the Ministry of Labour to draft a plan for the reform of the insurance scheme. The fact of the matter was that the growing deficit was merely keeping pace with the growing number of unemployed – the question was, who would foot the bill? The answer was obvious on both wings of the government coalition. The Social Democrats wanted contributions raised by 1 per cent, with the employers bearing half of the additional costs. On the other hand, the People's Party, as the 'party of industry', would not hear of such a division of costs – and here, too, a worried glance at the export markets offered some justification, or at least a plausible argument, for the defence of declining profits. The gap should be plugged, they argued, not by increasing income but by cutting benefits.

No agreement was reached in the spring. In August a compromise began to emerge which was passed by the Reichsrat in September, and by the Reichstag at the beginning of October – albeit by a very slender margin. The bill combined a series of cuts in benefits (of no very drastic nature, in fact) with a rise in contributions by a half of 1 per cent to $3^1/_2$ per cent. The trade unions had finally accepted this proposal from a panel of experts in social policy; the employers, on the other hand, had turned it down. The Social Democrats accordingly voted for the bill, while the People's Party were only just persuaded to abstain – thus saving not only the bill but also the coalition. His part in this compromise was the last service Gustav Stresemann was able to render the Republic before his death.

As it was by no means certain that the rise of half a per cent would salvage the scheme, then the solution arrived at clearly meant no more than a stay of execution. This was because even the compromise had cleared the parliamentary hurdle only after all the controversial points, especially the increase in contributions, had been removed and incorporated in a second bill which was valid only until the end of March 1931. Thus, if there was no major change in the situation on the labour market – and no one could seriously contemplate that there would be – the problem of unemployment insurance was certain to crop up again shortly one way or another.

Circumstances did not allow even this deadline to be reached. For now the drop in investment and the weakness of foreign markets following 'Black Thursday' (not Friday) on 24 October 1929 began to be increasingly marked from month to month, even on the American market. The crisis naturally had an immediate effect on the labour market. During the first quarter of 1930 there were never less than 3 million unemployed; the deficit in the insurance fund threatened to reach a new record level, so that there were ever-increasing demands on the cash reserves of the Reich, not to mention its inability to repay the old 'loans'.

Once more the two fronts within the coalition faced each other, even more unyielding than before on account of the worsening economic situation. Nevertheless, agreement was once again reached in the cabinet, and was also approved by the Reichsrat on 24 March 1930. Given a majority of votes by representatives of the employers and the work force, the governing board of the insurance institute was to raise contributions from the 'provisional $3\frac{1}{2}$ per cent' to the 4 per cent originally demanded by the Social Democrats. Four of the partners in the coalition agreed, but the People's Party categorically refused to accept this ruling.

What lay behind this undoubtedly urgent topical issue of social legislation was perfectly clear: the People's Party no longer wanted to be allied with the Social Democrats; industry did not want it either, nor did the Reichswehr, and the President had not wanted it, at least since March 1929 (in so far as he and the others had ever wanted it at all). They all felt it to be almost unnatural that they should be allied with socialists, while their friends in the Nationalist Party were in fruitless opposition. On the other side there were also powerful factions in the Social Democratic Party, especially almost the entire trade union camp, that were weary of the coalition.

The demonstrative resignation of the President of the Reichsbank, Schacht, helped to create an atmosphere of catastrophe, as it was meant to do. It is true that his deflationary policy had made the critical situation even worse (although Brüning was also to follow in his footsteps), but for the nation at large his resignation was bound to look as if the rats were leaving the sinking ship.

In the midst of this cabinet crisis a fresh compromise, suggested by the Centre and the Democrats in a motion by Brüning and Meyer, seemed to offer a way out: contributions were to be raised according to the same procedure, but only by $3\frac{3}{4}$ per cent. The loans to cover the deficit in each case, however, should be replaced by subsidies specified annually in the budget. Now it was the turn of the Social Democrat parliamentary group to reject the suggested compromise, under pressure from trade union representatives – over one-third of the parliamentary party. They were thus left holding the baby – which, it was implied, along with the newly forged link between the Centre Party and the People's Party, was the actual object of the whole Brüning exercise. Even when the last point was considerably modified, the parliamentary group of Social Democrats still stood by their verdict of 'unacceptable', in opposition to three of their four ministers.

Since the insurance reform was coupled with urgent finance bills in a 'bill in preparation for financial reform', with the Finance Minister refusing to separate them, Müller's cabinet raised the white flag that same evening. He decided to quit without seeking a confrontation with the Reichstag. His resignation took place on 27 March 1930 and it marked the end of the German democracy of Weimar.

9

Brüning's government

It was obvious that there could no longer be any parliamentary solution. To make matters worse, in that same month the Centre Party had publicly stated what it meant to propose 'if the Reichstag failed to cope': a dissolution, or else government by emergency decree under Article 48, 'or both'. Together with Stresemann, the Centre had hitherto been the indefatigable architect of successive governments. At the end of 1928 there had been a change in the party chairmanship: Wilhelm Marx was at the end of his tether and he was replaced by Prelate Ludwig Kaas, the candidate of the middle and the right wing of the party. The trend to the right of this sociologically mixed party had been apparent ever since 1925, and it became clearly obvious in 1929, when Kaas launched Brüning as the new parliamentary leader.

But the swing to the right was also evident elsewhere. In large sections of the middle classes people were sick of parties and parliament. They thought that the obvious solution was a 'sensible' authoritarian regime that would put an end to the endless squabbles of the parties in the Reichstag and their manifest inability to govern. Such a solution corresponded to a German need for authority, while the personified Tannenberg memorial in the presidency actually suggested a suitable background, at least for a regime of that sort.

Agitation from the right had of course encouraged this feeling of general dissatisfaction (and its influence had once again increased, thanks largely to Hugenberg's efforts), but agitation alone would not have been capable of creating this kind of mood from nothing. Unfamiliarity with the rules of the parliamentary game, both in the case of those who were expected to operate them, and − even more so − in the case of the general public, who were accustomed to authoritarian rule and who automatically associated the adjective 'feeble' with 'compromise', would have engendered that kind of disdainful aversion even without outside assistance. A third factor was the idea that people had even been cheated of the compensation they had hoped to get for accepting this rotten Republic – namely, that they would escape the most serious consequence of losing the war. This was a wound which was liable to re-open – or be re-opened – with every new settlement relating to the war, however much relief it might bring.

There were indeed enough people who were keen to keep the Republic's wounds open at all costs. Good taste and fairness had no part to play here. For instance, anyone who came from the old Prussian state that was famed for the integrity of its administration found it hard to accustom himself to corruption scandals in which open-handed politicians were seen hob-nobbing with shady profiteers and swindlers. All at once there were civil servants who were ready to make up in other ways for the loss in social prestige caused by the cuts the Republic had made in their salaries.

In September 1929 a new sore of this kind had just burst open. The three Sklarek brothers, who owned a clothing factory, had perpetrated frauds involving millions; in their pockets had been found not only membership cards of the Social Democratic Party, which had brought them lucrative contracts, but also the names of a whole series of local authority politicians who had been in their pay. Tended with loving care by the right-wing press, this scandal spread its vile stench through German political circles for months on end. A somewhat forced, but symptomatically plausible, comparison has been made between the fur coat given by the Sklareks to the wife of the Berlin Oberbürgermeister and Marie Antoinette's necklace. Particular cases of this kind lent colour and a dangerous appearance of credibility to suspicions involving politicians in the system or the system as a whole.

In spite of everything, matters might have carried on much the same as before, with an outcry now and then, had not the economic crisis held people in its grip, destroying or at least threatening their livelihood – or at any rate their social status. For increasingly large sections of the population it was no longer just a matter of denunciations that introduced a little excitement into their humdrum everyday lives, or indulgence in sentimental dreams of 'the good old days' that embellished their leisure hours; things were beginning to get under their skin.

The workers, wherever they might be, saw themselves threatened by 'cutbacks'. After getting rid of its debts during the inflation, agriculture had quickly plunged back into the red. Given the unprofitable operation, in comparison with the competition of the world market, of small farmers as well as the major estates east of the Elbe, the rural population had become desperate and increasingly radical in outlook, with the 'Country Folk' (*Landvolk*) movement in Schleswig-Holstein beginning to assume anarchistic features. Even more ominous was the mood among young people, especially students, who were having to study very much in the spirit of 'art for art's sake', with very little prospect of ultimately gaining any employment what-soever – much less jobs commensurate with their qualifications. And since the preceding year the old schemes for staging a *coup d'état* and setting up a directorate had been surreptitiously circulating in various quarters of the Reichswehr. In short, everything that the Republic had spent so long trying to escape from was back again.

After a brief period of deceptive recovery and illusory prosperity, the relapse, the worldwide scale of which could only encourage a sense of hope-lessness, had an even more devastating effect. It was now that the radicalism of left and right was able to gain the kind of ground it had held in the years of economic collapse and inflation that had destroyed the livelihood of so many. But the right had at its disposal the larger reservoir of support in the disintegrating centre. It was there that a positive yearning for a 'strong man' who would 'put everything to rights' grew out of discontent with the political parties.

The global extent of the depression helped to create a situation in which those fluctuating sections of the political – or, to be more precise, the *a-*political – centre who had hitherto supported the Republic without really finding a political home there, tended to make light of the threatening danger from the right. The choice was even more obvious than in 1923. If weakness or internal dissension made it advisable to ally oneself with one of the two extremes then, however *déclassé* and opposed to nationalism the middle-class citizen might be at heart, he would prefer to back a conglomeration of special interests that had in common *petit bourgeois* disappointments and grievances and that was combined into a party on the right which sported the purely decorative title of a 'workers' party'.

Real danger was actually seen as coming only from the left. Stalin and the Communists had recently dropped the policy of a 'proletarian common front' they had been following and taken up a left-wing line according to which everything beyond the limits of the Party – from genuine Fascism to the 'social fascism' of the Social Democrats – was to be opposed with equal ferocity as a 'Fascist common front'. Blood had been shed during riots in Berlin on 1 May 1929, when the police, commanded by the Social Democrat Zörgiebel, had been forced to open fire on Communist demonstrators – thus providing a new symbol and a new 'murderer of the workers', a new Noske. In the lee of the fear of world revolution Hitler was able to reap his harvest undisturbed.

By the time his advance had acquired the scale and the momentum of an avalanche, the Republic had in fact already given up the struggle. Until the resignation of Müller's government the National Socialists' success had been far from spectacular. After they had been embraced by Hugenberg in the Reich Committee, however, and again following the start of the economic crisis, they had gained rather more recmuits. Before then Landtag elections had taken place on 12 May 1929 in Saxony, and on 23 June in Mecklenburg-Schwerin Hitler's party had registered slight gains, rising to 4 and 5 per cent of the poll respectively. On the Sunday following Wall Street's 'Black Thursday' the National Socialists had won 7 per cent of the poll in Baden. In Thuringia on 8 December they succeeded for the first time in clearing the 10 per cent hurdle: with 11.3 per cent of the vote they not only became the third strongest party but, a month later, the second strongest party in a coalition of middle-class and agrarian representatives which took power from an opposition that had stretched from the Democrats to the Communists. A member of the Reichstag, Wilhelm Frick, took over the Thuringian Ministry of the Interior and Education as the first National Socialist to achieve such a rank. In that capacity he anticipated on a small scale everything that was to follow in terms of actual and potential legislation.

At the same time the National Socialists were able to put into practice their 'mandate to restore order' in the first of the German cities: in Coburg, a stronghold of nationalism, they gained for the first time an absolute majority on a local authority council, winning thirteen out of twenty-five seats. The Prussian local elections on 17 November 1929 also caused a sensation, with the Communists and the National Socialists gaining, largely at the expense of their Social Democratic and Nationalist neighbours. In Berlin, for instance, both radical parties won thirteen seats – the National Socialists had hitherto not had a single seat. In that same year elections for student representative councils turned out to be a positive triumph for the National Socialists. But even then the writing on the wall was not, it seems, sufficiently plain.

In the following year the dam finally burst. The government crisis in March 1930 had not lasted long. Only three days after Müller's government had resigned, a new cabinet was formed under Brüning, with the Reichswehr – and that now meant General von Schleicher – rendering sterling service at the birth of its 'Hindenburg cabinet'. People spoke – and this is a clue to the change of climate – of a 'cabinet of front-line soldiers', and in fact, apart from his Catholicism, it was his experiences at the front that had most clearly marked the personality of the new conservative and Catholic Chancellor. One result of this was his admiration for Hindenburg, which went far beyond even what was normal at that time, and his close links with the Reichswehr, to whose interests he felt obliged to give top priority. This he never denied, and it was to be borne out by his policy in the future.

Under Brüning most of the ministers from Müller's cabinet stayed at their posts – with the exception, of course, of the Social Democrats. In an extension of the cabinet to the right, representatives of the Economics Party, the Reichslandbund and that sector of the racial nationalist wing that had officially broken with Hugenberg were brought in. It was, however, the same old story over again: it was once more, but this time on the express instructions of the President of the Reich, a 'cabinet of personalities', lacking clear links with the parties in parliament. In fact a coalition would not have helped much: it would not have had a majority to back it in parliament – unless it proved possible to win over the divided Nationalist Party, which had been split ever since Hitler had foisted on it the 'imprisonment' clause of his 'Liberty Law', and which was also divided in its view of the 'Hindenburg cabinet'. It was on this possibility that Brüning was banking – in so far as he was banking on parliamentary support at all. Getting the Nationalists on to his side, however, would involve disposing of Hugenberg in favour of the populist opposition to him, which was partly within the party but partly already outside it.

At first there did seem to be some hope of doing just that. A vote of no confidence put by the Social Democrats in reply to Brüning's statement of government policy was survived with the Nationalists' aid. Hugenberg could not very well refuse to support his opponents in the parliamentary party, in spite of his objection in principle to Brüning. After all, the government had promised to rescue the 'Green Front', which was once more united in a common desperate plight. In particular, it had announced a programme of aid to the eastern provinces that had been asked for by the President of the Reich, who had been since 1927 – thanks to artfully placed donations from industry and farming interests – himself an East Prussian landowner and powerful agrarian lobbyist.

A far-reaching agrarian programme was in fact the next major bill introduced by the government. It was passed in the Reichstag with a bare majority on 12 April. This majority of eleven votes was made possible only by the fact that the Nationalists had split once more: only their agrarian wing had voted in favour. Hugenberg's faction had voted against it because of the government's covering financial proposals, which would entail tax increases and which were put forward in a package along with the agrarian programme. In itself, of course, approval of the agrarian programme implied a success for the Chancellor. In a wider context, however, following the split in the Nationalist Party he had had to bury any hopes he may have had of putting together the desired parliamentary basis for his cabinet that would have stretched from the Nationalists to the Democrats. What was to prove fatal was his present hope that new elections would strengthen the Nationalist dissidents and hence his parliamentary majority. But Hugenberg's successors were occupying different seats.

Nor had the financial crisis been eased by the success of the agrarian bill. As a consequence of all the old troubles – a decline in tax revenue, new deficits in unemployment insurance, the burden of reparations – the normal annual budget was sinking ever deeper into the red. The budget for 1930 had still not been passed; its first reading did not take place until the beginning of May. Already during the debate, unemployment insurance, that bottomless barrel, had appealed for a further bill to cover its losses. It was a question of scraping funds together from every quarter in order to plug a gap that grew larger every day. In the following month the Finance Minister fell because his programme to cover the deficit had been rejected. But the proposals his successor put to the Reichstag in July could not be realized either without raising taxes. It might be noted in passing, incidentally, that the unemployment insurance contribution that had brought down Müller's government was now to be raised to $4\,^1/_2$ per cent.

On the left, Brüning's financial policy was felt to be socially reactionary: it cut only social expenditure and spared business and industry (from which it was hoped recovery would come). On the right, its tendency to *dirigisme* and restraint on the economy was criticized. Brüning was convinced, however, that a course involving a deflationary policy and strict control of expenditure was correct, and he proposed to pursue it with all the bigotry of the expert – with or without parliamentary support. He appealed to the parties' sense of responsibility; otherwise, he threatened, he would 'use all the constitutional means' at his disposal. For the first time since 1923, Article 48 was once more on the cards.

Whether in fact security and public order were 'seriously disrupted or imperilled' was a moot point, and depended very much on one's political stance. The act which, according to Article 48, was to provide 'a more precise definition' had never been passed. But after all, a state cannot simply declare that it is bankrupt. The missing money ultimately has to come from somewhere. The Social Democrats might have been prepared to listen to reason if the government had been prepared to abandon, or at least modify, its new citizenship tax, which was denounced on the left as a socially unjust 'poll tax', because it was not graded. Brüning believed, however, with this one article of the constitution in his pocket and the President of the Reich in the background, he had no need to go in for old-fashioned 'horse-trading'.

The crunch came on 16 July. In a vote on the so-called 'aid for the Reich' clause included in the finance bill, a proposal to tax civil servants' earnings, the government found itself in a minority of 193 against 256. The Chancellor declared bluntly that he was not interested in continuing the discussion. Following these words, as the record states, there was a 'commotion'. That evening the finance bill was passed into law by emergency decree. The Social Democrats immediately moved the suspension of the decree. On 18 July their motion, which was linked with a vote of no confidence and supported by Communists, National Socialists and most of the Nationalists round Hugenberg, was passed by a bare majority. Immediately after the vote had been taken, the Chancellor rose and informed the House that the President of the Reich had ordered its dissolution.

That the Communists and National Socialists had wanted a dissolution and now applauded it was understandable and, as was shortly to appear, justified. And Hugenberg was a fool whose role in German politics consisted in destroying everything he claimed to represent. On the other hand, what prompted the Social Democratic hecklers to shout for dissolution is hard to understand. Perhaps with a kind of primitive death-wish, the representatives of the Social Democratic Party (although not all of them by any means) plunged into defeat, and doomed to destruction the state they themselves had founded. True, that state had changed – changed radically, in fact. It might already be predicted that what would succeed the Republic would not be an improvement in a socialist or democratic, and certainly not in a Social Democratic, sense.

Here and there in the Social Democratic Party there was rather more foresight, and it may be that a compromise might have been reached in those July days. But very probably this would merely have postponed the end of parliament and of parliamentary government as such until the next quarrel, or the one after that. The fate of Weimar democracy had been sealed once the representatives of the various social classes had retreated so precipitately from the attempt at collaboration that was essential if democracy was to survive in the given circumstances. If the attempt was not repeated, with rather more clear-sightedness than had been shown thus far, there was little hope for the patient, who was now virtually at death's door. But it was hardly to be expected that clear-sightedness would increase, given the continued deterioration in the economic situation.

On 14 September new elections were held against a background of economic hardship. The number of unemployed – which had fallen in July of the preceding year to 1.35 million – had stayed just under the 3 million mark throughout 1930, but had recently reached that level once again. All that the results did was to ratify the demise of the Republic that had already taken place in the spring. The clamorous agitation of the radical parties, who had gone hunting for votes among the hordes of unemployed, or those who feared unemployment and the bailiffs, had paid off magnificently.

The principal gainer was the National Socialist Party with its 6.4 million votes (18.3 per cent), won for the most part in Protestant rural areas. Instead of the little band of twelve members they had hitherto had, 107 uniformed(!) National Socialists filed into the Reichstag as the second strongest party – with the declared aim of abolishing that institution. On the opposite wing, the Communists gained 4.6 million votes and now had seventy-seven seats instead of fifty-four. It was not only young voters and non-voters who had brought about this increase in radical representation (there was justifiable talk of a 'Spartacus rising' of political blockheads). The blame was also shared by the adjacent parties: in future there would be only 143 Social Democrats in the Reichstag (in 1928 there were 152) and no more than forty-one Nationalists (in 1928 there had been seventy-eight). True, they were now all staunch supporters of Hugenberg, and this was, after all, nine more than had voted with Hugenberg following the latest split.

In the centre, the Catholic parties had been able to record slight gains: the Centre rose to sixty-eight seats (from sixty-one in 1928), the Bavarian People's Party to nineteen (seventeen in 1928). The People's Party, on the other hand, bereft of Stresemann, forfeited fifteen of the forty-five seats they had held in 1928, although they had merged with Artur Mahraun's 'Young German Order', which had been suddenly inspired with a sense of its civic respons-ibilities. The alliance was so unnatural, however, that it collapsed shortly afterwards, as did all the hasty attempts at mergers into which the Protestant middle-class centre had plunged under the Damocles sword of radicalism that loomed over them following the dissolution of the Reichstag. The united lobbyists of the Economics Party retained their twenty-three seats; a further forty-nine seats went to agrarian lists and other conservative groups, for the most part those racial nationalist splinter groups on which Brüning had been banking. He had to bury his hopes of a viable right-wing coalition, however.

Coalition arithmetic produced the following results: the old grand coalition with 280 seats had become so small that it could no longer form a majority, even if those involved had wanted to do so. At a pinch, the inclusion of the Economics Party or a number of conservative splinter groups or agrarian members might – on paper – have scraped a majority together (as was in fact done indirectly in voting down motions of no confidence with varying majorities). But even a new bourgeois bloc including the Nationalists – unthinkable in the Hugenberg era – could have mustered no more than 178 seats, or 201, if the Economics Party was included. Including all the agrarian and conservative splinter groups, it would have had only 250 seats out of 577. Even without Hugenberg, the radical opponents of the system were able to form a blocking minority because the 143 Social Democrats were unable to form a coalition with any parties further to the right than the People's Party. And it had been obvious enough in the final phase of Müller's government how that would turn out.

This election result, with its massive displacement of votes, had assumed the proportions of a landslide – a metaphor often used without such manifest justification. At that time, before opinion polls had become common, the outcome baffled even those who had carefully noted the results of preceding polls (the only one in 1930 had been the Saxon Landtag elections on 2 June, which had given Hitler 14.4 per cent of the vote). It baffled the Chancellor, who had been responsible for the lunatic decision to dissolve parliament. It had been lunatic, in fact, only in so far as it was based on a hope of restoring a parliamentary basis for government in this way (even if only for the passing of an enabling act). On the other hand, if Brüning had been toying with the idea of some kind of authoritarian regime under a 'strong man' in the President's shadow, or even – and this was more Brüning's style – a return to the kind of regime that had such a long tradition in Germany, with the Field-Marshal-cum-President as a kind of administrator, a 'Kaiser substitute', and a purely ornamental parliament, then he now seemed to have some justification. For it was now obvious that a Reichstag had expressed confidence in a German government for the last time on 14 December 1929. Hitherto the parliament had seemed reluctant to do its job: it was now obviously incapable of doing it.

And so, parliamentary government, democracy and the First German Republic were done for. Done for, at any rate, if it did not prove possible to halt the rise in the number of unemployed and to get at least a million of those desperate individuals off the streets. But the very opposite happened: in the following winter there were 5 million out of work, throughout 1931 never fewer than 4 million, and in the winter of 1931/32, the record figure of 6 million was reached and surpassed by a considerable margin. This level did not decline during the summer of 1932. Given this development, only one question remained undecided: who would be heir to all this? The answer could not be much in doubt bearing in mind who best knew how to harness the nation's despair, and who on the right, to which the trend was ever more clearly moving, cut the most dashing figure.

Of those years in Germany's political history that now followed it is commonly stated that this is when the 'dissolution' of the Weimar Republic took place. 'Liquidation' would probably be a more appropriate term, for Brüning's governments, or even those of Papen and Schleicher, have little more to do with the democratic First Republic than with Hitler's regime. This is not to say by any means that they should all be lumped together: the *totalitarian* state, or to be more precise non-state, was set up in a period, of course, which may be defined as lying between the 'decree for the protection of nation and state' and the 'law prohibiting the reconstitution of political parties', i.e. between 28 February 1933 and 14 July 1933. The anti-, or at any rate aparliamentary *authoritarian* state, on the other hand, had become a constitutional reality with the election on 14 September 1930, although Brüning's mode of governing might be euphemistically paraphrased as 'parliamentary rule with the aid of Article 48'.

Certainly, Brüning did not govern *against* the will of parliament – even when the illusion of a 'right capable of holding office', a viable centre–right parliamentary basis, had evaporated with the September election. He even found an 'emergency majority' in a half-right–centre–left constellation (with the half-right varying from case to case) to furnish him with a parliamentary alibi for his authoritarian policy. On the right wing of the Brüning parties, among the People's Party, racial nationalist and especially agrarian splinter groups, nervousness and a tendency to defect were growing, but Brüning's majority was made possible by the Social Democrats, who were once more following a policy usually termed 'toleration'.

This marriage of convenience, reluctantly entered into by both parties, gave birth to a special kind of toleration. It was different in principle from what had been granted to the 'minority cabinets', whose bills found their way on to the statute book by consent, or else by abstention. In the Brüning era, with few exceptions, only trifling legislation was passed in a normal procedure by the Reichstag, and in the period from 27 March 1931 until 11 May 1932 there was not even a single bill of that kind. Bills were replaced by presidential decrees under Article 48. In 1930 there were five decrees of this kind, in 1931 forty-three and in 1932 nineteen under Brüning out of a total of fifty-seven. 'Toleration' in this case was limited to helping to vote down motions of no confidence and motions calling for the suspension of Brüning's emergency decrees. It goes beyond the bounds of permissible simplification to claim, given this situation, that Brüning still commanded a majority in the Reichstag.

Among the Social Democrats at any rate, the heroic 'no' of March had quickly been followed by a reluctant climb-down. Ideological loyalty to the principles of the class struggle was replaced by a feeling that can be boiled down to the phrase: 'Anything except Hitler.' Brüning's policy was indeed embellished with a few flourishes favourable to the consumers, the workers and the trade unions that were included in return for this support by social-ists and the left wing of the Centre Party. With his economic policy set to follow a compass-bearing chosen to favour capital, he was now so far to the right of the common ground on which differences had been settled in March that he was practically out of sight. Still, compared with the looming danger of Fascism, he undoubtedly looked like the lesser of two evils.

This swing to the right on the part of the Social Democratic majority, which is certainly understandable in the context of the time, is nowadays, even with the benefit of hindsight, given credit for being a return to political common sense, an expression of responsible and constitutional thinking. On the other hand, however, the question might be asked – and it would apply to the whole Brüning era – whether it would not have been better perhaps to let the whole clumsy system disintegrate before Hitler ceased to be just a threat and became an overwhelming force. As far as that goes, Brüning personally not only laid himself open to the common charge that he did not exhaust the possibilities of forming a parliamentary majority and that he did not try to pass legislation constitutionally, even where that was feasible, but instead chose the easier path of Article 48, as a mere adjutant appointed by the President and dependent on the latter's confidence. Looked at from a historical point of view, Brüning's regime was more than that: by its very existence and by the time it allowed for Hitler to gather strength, it became the incubator in which National Socialism assumed gigantic proportions. Leaving ethical qualities and issues of statesmanship aside, it was not the minor civil servant Papen who officiated at the cradle of the Third Reich and hence at the coffin of the Republic, but Heinrich Brüning.

It is not only the circumstances of his appointment that assign Brüning his place in the evolution from parliamentary government to the Führer state, but also the circumstances of his departure. It was not the Reichstag that withdrew its confidence in him, but the President of the Reich; it was not that the legislative machinery failed him but that he was deprived of the emergency decree mechanism. It was not a majority in the Reichstag that demanded his resignation, but a combination of cliques and pressure groups who were accredited in the place where Germany's fate was henceforth to be decided: in the presidential palace.

Along with the leadership of the Reichswehr and the lobbyists from industry – and even more so, representatives of major landowners – the President's State Secretary and his son, who was not 'provided for in the constitution', had grown into institutions whose influence far overshadowed any form of legal authority. We may make fun of the fact that all other conceivable qualifications paled into insignificance before the term of service in the Third Regiment of Footguards, but the fact remains that the old man, who regarded himself as the guardian of the Reich in those emotional areas not covered by his oath of office, was the last barrier stemming the National Socialist flood.

For Brüning's recipe proved to be ineffective. Thrifty as any responsible head of a household, he rescued the Reich's finances from the calamities that in Müller's time had left the state's coffers empty virtually from one month's end to the next. Even if he did not manage to drag the budget out of deficit, he was able, in spite of aid for the eastern provinces and unemployment insurance, to match expenditure to a dwindling revenue, reducing the deficit by no less than 38 per cent, from 11,400 million marks in 1928 to 7,000 million in 1932 (incredible figures nowadays!). It was in fact this deflationary honesty that hastened the end, for its price entailed (as soon became apparent) a fateful blindness to the facts of domestic politics. The sovereign disregard for the nation's mood with which Brüning pursued his lonely path, his eye firmly fixed on a better future, bore bitter fruit. It turned out that he was running on the wrong track, so that his race against the growing crisis was lost. Even the possibility that his policy might have been viable in the long term offers no justification, because a longer term than Brüning's two years was hardly thinkable. Once this became apparent, his flank on the home front was effortlessly turned.

The economy had not responded to 'cranking up' by Brüning's methods – as the popular expression had it at the time. On the contrary, his economies had only rendered more acute the problems of unemployment and markets. Nor might any relief be expected from exports. It was inevitable that in order to increase the sale of German goods on the world market, prices had to be reduced. And a condition of lower prices was perhaps lower wages. However, because almost the entire world was ultimately suffering under the crisis, prices were going down everywhere, quite apart from the fact that – beginning with the USA – there was a growing tendency to protect home production by means of ever higher tariff barriers. And so it happened that measures taken by the Germans were perpetually one step behind those taken by the Americans, and were thus pointless.

What did have an effect, however, was the cutting of wages. For in so far as prices went down at all on the home market – in spite of the emergency decrees – the reductions were in no way proportionate to the fall in wages. In the case of essential commodities, tariff protection for the threatened agricultural sector left little room for manoeuvre. The employers, who were themselves up to their necks in trouble, naturally seized every opportunity to rid themselves of their obligations. And in this respect, almost anything was possible: after all, with 5 or 6 million unemployed people who could hardly wait to grab any job that was offered, the trade unions were as good as defenceless.

It was not only the growing army of unemployed, whose dole was cut to a bare minimum, that was liable to be subjected to drastic measures. Even those who were still earning a living, apart from the constant fear of losing their jobs, were struggling with incomes that steadily dwindled in real terms. They were bound to feel that their basic rights were being threatened by the thoroughly unpopular measures being taken by the government. Even that section of the population that supports any government (albeit to a very limited extent in the case of this state), the civil service, was bound to see how their employers were dipping into their pockets in order to recoup the premature and over-generous increases in civil service salaries they had granted in 1927. The same thing was true of pensions. And then there were increased taxes and new taxes on anything that could possibly be taxed.

And so dissatisfaction increased all round. Expert economists in fact doubt whether inflationary 'deficit spending' could have been used as a remedy by Brüning's government, even if it had not had to reckon with the German horror of inflation. Given the close integration of the world economy at that time, such a policy would scarcely have had a chance of succeeding without American leadership, unless it was coupled – which Germany could not yet afford – with the withdrawal from the world economy that was entailed in Hitler's policy of self-sufficiency.

Since 1930 at the latest Brüning had had another reason for rejecting 'deficit spending': he believed he could exploit the great crisis in order to shake off the burden of reparations, and was therefore not interested in overcoming it before that goal had been reached. In Brüning's view Germany must appear to be insolvent if her creditors were to be persuaded to renounce further reparations payments. In the interests of his reparations policy, which was meant – along with the reinforcement of the army – to regain the financial and political freedom of movement Germany needed to achieve a revision of Versailles, Brüning felt justified in asking the Germans to submit to a period of hardship. Foreign policy successes to which Brüning could point were not enough to remedy, or even to alleviate, the critical situation at home. With his policy in regard to reparations he was able in fact to achieve successes of monumental significance, which were nevertheless not enough to counteract the hate campaign at home. There was nothing for which his opponents on the right or left would give him credit. On the contrary, their policy was specifically aimed at accelerating the economic and financial catastrophe, so that the seeds of sedition might germinate. Wherever they could, they pursued this aim: what was more, their own policies were calculated to bring about the desired effect. A first clear proof of this had been provided by the Young campaign of the Reich Committee and the second Hague conference. A further confirmation was offered by the elections of September 1930: the National Socialist landslide brought about a drastic fall in the value of German stocks and shares on the Stock Exchanges as well as a withdrawal of gold, foreign currencies and domestic capital estimated at 1,000 million marks – half of the annual rate of reparations payments.

This flight of short-term foreign capital never came to a halt. At the same time an unprecedented incident took place. Following the failure of one of the largest German textile firms, one of the four major German banks, the Darmstadt and National Bank (Danat), was forced to close its doors on 13 July 1931. The general run on the banks set off by this financial collapse was met by a desperate expedient: a decree allowing the ordering of general 'bank holidays' provided a desperately needed breathing space, and the Stock Exchanges were also closed. The Reich had no choice but to come to the rescue with a supporting action and take-over guarantees. When, at the end of the month, the Dresdner Bank was also threatened with insolvency, the exchequer came to its aid, this time in the form of a capital investment. In the wake of these events came a perfect hailstorm of emergency decrees. Foreign exchange controls, mainly known as a feature of Hitler's Reich, were introduced, as well as a levy of 100 marks on foreign travel, although this was revoked at the end of August because of protests from abroad.

Germany was so shaken by these financial upheavals that she needed help from abroad more than ever. Developments over the preceding months had made international aid imperative, for growing lack of confidence had turned the flight of capital from Germany into an international disaster. At a hastily convened conference held in London from 20 to 23 July to deal with the German financial and economic crisis, the German delegation was able to arrive at a standstill arrangement with their foreign creditors by which the remaining foreign short-term capital in Germany was frozen. As far as possible it was to be converted into long-term loans. Moreover, a 100 million dollar international loan that the Reich had just received as emergency aid was extended.

The private capital thus tied up in Germany was to assist its 'host country' in future in a way that no one had thought of to begin with. For Germany's ability to pay, so it seemed at any rate, supposing it was ever restored, would doubtless be very limited. The private creditors would take second place behind the public reparations liabilities, so that there was practically no prospect of them seeing their money again in the foreseeable future. In this way, then, thanks to their common interest, foreign private capital, particularly American capital, became Germany's best ally in her struggle to shake off finally the burden of reparations.

True, in the bank crisis of the summer of 1931 there wasn't much left to shake off – at any rate not *de facto*. Preliminary hints by Brüning had fallen on deaf ears abroad. However, when Hindenburg signed the 'second decree securing the economy and finance' on 5 June, which put in the shade everything that had preceded it in terms of increased taxes and economies, it was submitted to the public with a government appeal, of which the tenor was: 'The limit to which we can submit our nation to privations has been reached!' The situation of the Reich, it went on, demanded imperatively that 'Germany be relieved of her intolerable obligations by way of reparations'. This appeal had the effect of a declaration of bankruptcy by Germany: as Brüning was assured from various sides, it destroyed German credit, chased considerable amounts of foreign capital from the Reich once again, and contributed materially and psychologically to the banking crisis that broke out a few weeks later. But it was this very consequence that created a situation in which Brüning was able to reopen the reparations issue.

Even before the government of the Reich was forced to take any action, the realization that the situation was indeed serious had gained ground in the United States. On 20 June President Hoover proposed a postponement of all war debt and reparations payments for one year with effect from 1 July. So it was America that made the sacrifice, and Germany that reaped the benefit. But the intermediate links in the chain of payments could only be satisfied with this solution, for a German moratorium was in the offing anyway.

Only France expressed misgivings – justifiably so, as it later transpired. The fear in Paris was that if Germany once stopped paying reparations she was hardly likely ever to start again. A compromise was found in a technical banking transaction: the Reich would continue to pay France's share of the unsecured annuity to the Bank for International Settlements, but the money would at once return as a loan (albeit a commercial one) to the railways of the Reich. On 6 July Hoover was able to proclaim the deferment of payment: the 'Hoover holiday' year.

Hardship was rendered even more acute by the winter, and on 8 December a 'fourth decree securing the economy and finance' imposed new burdens and economies on the German people. A 'Reich Commissioner for Price

Supervision', Goerdeler, was appointed, and the subsequently notorious tax on leaving the Reich was devised. Pointing out the drastic measures taken by his government, Brüning prepared for the final assault on reparations. On 20 November he applied for a meeting of the special committee provided for under the Young agreement. The committee met early in December and submitted its report before the end of the year. It described the Young Plan as having been overtaken by the crisis and recommended the suspension of all international payments, even after the expiry of the Hoover year. The governments concerned now wished for an international conference. It was to meet in Lausanne and begin on 18 January 1932.

For once, everyone in Germany, from the Chancellor down to the last National Socialist, was agreed: the result of the conference must and would be the end of all reparations. In January 1932 Brüning had said so in so many words to the British ambassador: neither now nor in the future would the Reich be in a position to pay reparations. The crisis and the sense of catastrophe in the Reich gave Brüning so much support in his policy abroad that he was in a position to decline a mere extension of the Hoover moratorium, even as an interim solution. How things had changed since Stresemann's day!

Brüning's government, however, was not destined to reap the benefit. Abroad, especially in France, there was understandably a certain amount of resistance, to which the propaganda of the right in Germany contributed: 'Lend as much as you like – *we* shan't pay it back!' The Chancellor's premature candour also played its part. The Lausanne conference was postponed, and when it finally did begin on 16 June Brüning was no longer in office. We may anticipate the outcome of the agreement that was signed on 9 July: the German government was to hand over to the Bank for International Settlements as trustee promissory notes drawn on the Reich to a value of 3,000 million marks; these could then be placed on the market after an interval of three years. The reparations would then – a total of 12,700 million marks having been paid to date* – be regarded as settled once and for all.

The Lausanne agreements were never ratified because the United States, as creditor nation, was unable to come to an understanding with its war debtors.† Moreover, in 1935, under Hitler's government, there was no mention, even of the 3,000 million marks. In comparison with the 112,000 million of the Young Plan, this sum seemed like nothing more than a

---

*There were, apart from occupation costs, deliveries in kind which the two sides estimated differently, so that the overall amount varied between 53,000 and 20,000 million marks.

†Apart from Finland, the debtor nations stopped paying interest in 1932/33 and thus solved their problem, in spite of American protests.

gratuity! What a triumph! So one might think. There is no reason to mourn Brüning's fate, in that he fell in those celebrated 'last hundred metres short of the winning-post'. As the subsequent response of the German public showed, they were frightened by the spectre of crisis and whipped into a frenzy by unbridled right-wing propaganda, so that Brüning would not have profited from his success. For *any* success was taken for granted, or even used as a propaganda weapon against the defunct Republic.

To be fair, however, this cannot be blamed exclusively on the rabble-rousing campaign conducted by Hitler and Hugenberg. Appearances were against the system, with which the 'emergency decree Chancellor' was, albeit unjustly, associated. For what did it all boil down to, in fact? All that was necessary, as the right-wing parties had claimed from the very beginning, was to thump the table and say 'no' with sufficient determination, and all the fuss about Versailles (or a large part of it, at any rate) would vanish into thin air. In what sort of light was Rathenau's and Stresemann's conciliatory policy bound to appear now, even in the eyes of those who were in principle well-disposed? Every triumph of this kind was bound to cast a dubious light on the policy of fulfilment of the past years: nothing was to blame, then, for Germany's plight but the feebleness of her democracy.

Anyone who looked more closely, however, could hardly fail to see that this was not true – at least for the most part. Where thumping the table had led when it was last tried had been seen in 1923. It was only in the meantime that things had changed to the point where that method was likely to prove effective. And every logical argument suggested that it was the worldwide economic crisis and the devastation it caused that had upgraded Germany's position. That was what had secured her the reputation of being a dangerously incalculable entity that had to be handled with kid gloves – and had also put the fear of God into the victors of 1919.

Brüning's foreign policy was also successful in another area that was allegedly even dearer to the hearts of his nationalistic hecklers: the question of unilateral German disarmament. In the preamble to the military fifth section of the Versailles Treaty German disarmament had been justified as 'making possible the beginning of a limitation of the armaments of all nations'. Although the German delegation had constantly returned to the topic in the meantime, the preparations for a general disarmament conference had dragged on for years: enthusiasm on the part of the former hostile powers was not exactly excessive in various quarters. This International Disarmament Conference finally met in Geneva in February 1932.

Germany's wish for parity, which the Chancellor expressed at the opening of the conference, was in fact sympathetically received by the Anglo-Americans and also by the Italians. So were his proposals to allow the Reich a further 100,000 men under arms, to shorten the term of service with the Reichswehr and to replace the restrictions in the fifth section of the

Versailles Treaty by fresh agreements. France on the other hand, as Germany's next-door neighbour and thus potentially on the receiving end, found it hard to come to terms with any such proposal to punch holes in the Treaty of Versailles. When the statesmen reassembled in April to continue the conference, the French prime minister, Tardieu, was prevented from travelling to Geneva by a throat infection.

The final solution to the problem had to be adjourned and Brüning was unable to throw the all-important consent of France into the scales of his home policy. Here, too, his successors would profit from the 'activation' of German foreign policy he had initiated. After the German delegation had once more thumped the table at the Geneva Conference by leaving it on 14 September, the other participants, including France, in a formal declaration on 11 December, conceded German parity in a future 'security system for all nations'. This was to entail preparations for a disarmament conference that was augmented (albeit not for long) by the inclusion of Germany. Adolf Hitler then solved the disarmament problem in his own fashion, but as far as Brüning was concerned, what has been said above applied once more: even with this declaration of military parity in his pocket, he need not have expected that the response to him at home – or his personal fate – would be altered one iota.

On the other hand, he was given full credit for foreign policy failures. The gravest of these put an end to the plan for a German–Austrian customs union that had been announced in Berlin and Vienna on 23 March 1931. There were sufficient economic reasons to suggest the idea of such a fusion, especially in the case of the Alpine rump-state. It was just as obvious at home and abroad, however, that behind this plan lurked the *Anschluss* that had been frustrated by the Entente powers in 1919. The fact that its authors had thought it either risky, or at least unnecessary, to take soundings in foreign capitals increased the impression that this was some kind of *coup*. France took countermeasures.

When an expert opinion from the International Court in The Hague stated on 5 September 1931 that the customs union was inconsistent with the obligations Austria had assumed in 1922 when she had received a League of Nations loan, the die had already been cast elsewhere. The cancellation of credits – particularly French credits – in May had plunged Austria's largest bank, the Bodencreditanstalt, into such difficulties that it had to be supported by the government. That was not possible without aid from abroad, which the Reich, itself staggering on the brink of a financial precipice, was too weak to provide. On the way to Canossa, i.e. Geneva, for another loan, the plan for a customs union had to be finally buried.

This experiment had consequences, however, not only for Austria, but also for Germany. Following an increased withdrawal of capital, by which countries abroad expressed their dissatisfaction, and which played an essential part in the financial disaster of those summer months, the Foreign Minister, Curtius, resigned. As a party colleague and successor to Stresemann, he had felt obliged to continue Stresemann's foreign policy and had consequently long been under fire from the right. Brüning used this opportunity to make a concession to his superior and supporter in the presidential palace and to the leadership of the Reichswehr, who had been urging him for months to encourage more support from the right. On the right wing of the 'emergency majority', too, there was growing irritation with the voting pact with the Social Democrats. These nationalists felt they were compromised, and it was now a question of forestalling the imminent defection of the last groups to the right of the Centre Party. Hindenburg had demanded the heads of three ministers as an unavoidable concession to the 'nationalist opposition' during the summer, and now they fell.

However, all those who hoped to purchase at this price a modicum of toleration by the right were disappointed: on the right wing the mood was anything but tolerant. Hindenburg, Schleicher – and Brüning as well – would have been prepared even to let Hitler's party share the responsibility of government. But that was by no means to the latter's taste. There could be no talk of sharing; his slogan was 'All or nothing'. Thus, the Centre minister, von Guérard, was dropped along with his left-wing colleague, Wirth, who had been as much a target of right-wing propaganda at the Ministry of the Interior as Curtius had been at the Foreign Office. Racial nationalists like Treviranus and Schlange-Schöningen were brought into the government, but not even the People's Party were included, so that the desired 'shift to the right', as far as the 'nationalist opposition' were concerned, did not actually come about. Circumstances prevented any change in the 'emergency majority'. The most remarkable feature of Brüning's new cabinet, which was appointed on 9 October, was his pair of 'double eagles': Brüning now occupied not only the Chancellery, but also the Foreign Office; Groener was not only Minister of Defence, but also Minister of the Interior. The latter arrangement was again the patent remedy suggested by the 'adopted son', Schleicher, once the original idea had fallen through.

In the course of negotiations over this cabinet reshuffle, the President of the Reich had received the National Socialist leader, Adolf Hitler, who had given him a detailed account of the political aims of his 'movement'. This, too, had been arranged by the indefatigable Schleicher. Those aims were not such, admittedly, as would recommend themselves to the Prussian Field-Marshal, but the following day, when the 'nationalist opposition' held a grand parade in Bad Harzburg, a local authority in Brunswick that was under Nationalist control, the leader of the brown *sansculottes*, having been 'received at court' and basking in the glory of this consecration, was in a position to join all the bourgeois right-wing politicians, industrial magnates, princes, generals and leaders of the Stahlhelm. And he could even afford to slight his friends of the red, white and black faction who had now made him respectable in the eyes of the middle-class public. When his Storm Troopers had passed the platform with its eminent guests and was followed by the Stahlhelm, he ostentatiously left the scene. And during the following weeks his publications attacked his comrades of the 'Harzburg front' as fiercely as ever. It was Hugenberg who had set the Harzburg event on its feet, but the beneficiary of this grand nationalistic show was, as soon became evident, Adolf Hitler.

In fact the Nazis had been for some time now people of whose acquaintance no respectable middle-class nationalist need be ashamed. This had begun with the Reich Committee on the Young Plan, and in the following year, on 25 September 1930, Hitler had sworn his famous 'legality oath' before the fourth criminal bench of the Leipzig Central Court. Three lieutenants of an artillery detachment in Ulm had formed a National Socialist cell and had been charged with treason. The defence had called the leader of the National Socialist Party as a witness. And Hitler had seized this chance and assured the eager public on oath that his NSDAP was pursuing its aims exclusively by legal means and that there was no intention of overthrowing the constitution by force; the interlude of 1923 had been finally expunged.

The opposing witness for the government did not play his cards very astutely, the political shortsightedness of the court did the rest – and Hitler gained significant ground. His opponents might sneer at 'Adolphe Légalité', but anyone who had been hesitating about the idea of going over to the National Socialists now had a further argument at his disposal and could take the step with a clear conscience. This Hitler who had been so decried together with his associates was in fact not some revolutionary intent on subverting the bourgeois order, like the wicked Bolsheviks. He could certainly be 'tamed', and of course it was more than likely that his motley National Socialist conglomeration would in any case fall apart in the foreseeable future. There had already been signs of that in the crises that had been brought about in 1930/31 by renegade party officials like Otto Strasser, or dissatisfied SA leaders like Walter Stennes.

Admittedly, the detailed plans for a take-over of power 'following the abrogation of the current supreme authorities' that had been worked out by the NSDAP leadership in Hessen and handed to the police by a defector at the end of November 1931 were not entirely consistent with the notion of legaliity. The Chief Public Prosecutor and government departments made light of these so-called Boxheim Documents, however, and they had no adverse consequences, judicially or otherwise, for the NSDAP. Two months later, for instance, on 27 January 1932, Hitler was given an enthusiastic reception by West German industrialists – never mind Boxheim! – who had invited him to speak at the exclusive Industry Club in Düsseldorf. This is where he got his big break with the captains of industry, who were on the point of turning their backs on Brüning. For this man Hitler was promising not only to guarantee the perpetuation of the existing social order and property rights, he had also undertaken to wreck the trade unions!

A blind eye was turned to the excesses of the Nazis on the principle that you can't make an omelette without breaking eggs. There were incidents enough and they grew more and more common and increasingly violent. Street clashes between National Socialists and Communists were soon ending in almost daily bloodshed. Most of the victims were adherents of these two factions, occasionally members of the Reichsbanner (who were now proceeding, for better or for worse, to undergo 'special battle training' in newly formed 'self-defence squads', just like their opponents). Now and then the victims were policemen, sometimes just innocent passers-by. Fights between rival demonstrations were more or less an everyday occurrence in the streets. Sometimes, especially at the weekends that were now generally feared, they turned into full-scale pitched battles. Almost worse were the treacherous political murders.

The aggressive behaviour, especially of Hitler's Storm Troopers, led to bans – on demonstrations and on the wearing of uniforms and insignia. They were in part enacted by Brüning's government through emergency decrees, but mostly it was the states that took the initiative, because it was in their hands as a rule that the police authority lay. Such bans did indeed mainly affect the NSDAP, at which they were primarily aimed, but they were still comprehensive. When, however, in March 1932, Severing's Prussian police were able to unearth further compromising material during house-searches on NSDAP premises, the state governments intensified the pressure they had begun to exert in November for a direct and specific ban on Hitler's civil war army, the SA.

They managed to convince Groener of the need for such a step, although he also subscribed to the 'taming' theory of his 'adoptive son', and wanted to 'contain the Nazis'. Threats by the Prussian and Bavarian governments to go it alone if necessary finally made Brüning toe the line, although he was anything but keen. On 13 April, 'under the pressure of arguments urged strongly in person by the Minister of the Reichswehr and the Interior and of the Chancellor of the Reich', and in spite of opposition from his associates, Hindenburg signed an emergency decree 'to secure the authority of the state', banning the SA and the SS.

The 'old gentleman' felt that he had been put under duress, and the nationalist friends of those affected mounted violent attacks on the decree. (Amongst others, the former Crown Prince felt obliged to protest to Groener against the disbanding of 'this magnificent body of men'.) This was obvious from a letter in which, two days later, Hindenburg expressly demanded that the Minister of the Interior should ban 'organizations of a similar type' – a suggestion that had been mentioned in previous discussions. He had just been 'informed through the submission of documentary proof' that such organizations existed in other political parties. By 'other parties', in fact, only one was meant: the Social Democrats, and by 'organizations' the Reichs-banner, which had moved ever closer to the Social Democrats after its members from the Democrats and the Centre Party had defected. Since 1931 it had formed an 'Iron Front' in common with workers' sports clubs and other left-wing republican associations. The office that had submitted 'document-ary proof' (press cuttings from right-wing publications) was none other than the Ministry of the Reichswehr, which thus disowned its own Minister. Severing's revelations about the NSDAP's 'military betrayal' in the eastern provinces (when the SA had hung back on the occasion of an incursion by the Poles) had led to the approval of the Minister's action in the short term, but in the final analysis it ran counter to Schleicher's idea of 'taming' Hitler and letting him share power. The worst feature of the affair was, however, that Hindenburg, that same day, handed his letter to the press.

Of course, they read the 'old gentleman' the riot act as usual. There was one argument with which it had always been possible hitherto to awaken doubts and misgivings in him: that, with this or that signature, he would 'let down those who had once voted for him'. This argument no longer worked, however, for Hindenburg's voters had changed. In April 1932 the 84-year-old President's term of office had expired, but before then a curious situation had arisen: all those who had voted in 1925 for the Democratic opposition candidate, Marx, were now moving heaven and earth to keep Kaiser Wilhelm's Field-Marshal on his presidential throne.

Look where one might, democracy was out for the count and had no candidate of its own who might be put up against the 'nationalist opposition' with even the faintest chance of success. Brüning had no one either, and in any case he had fared no worse with his President than the Republic had before him. Even Hindenburg's opponents were forced to admit that he had loyally kept his oath on the constitution, and where he had acted against its spirit it had not been his fault. Indeed, this leopard had changed his spots and had overcome his antecedents, tradition and his inner convictions in a manner for which not even the greatest optimist in the democratic camp would have given their victorious opponent credit in 1925.

In order to avoid the political turmoil of an election, Brüning tried first of all to have Hindenburg's term of office extended by parliamentary means. But the attempt to achieve the two-thirds majority necessary for a bill amending the constitution failed because the 'nationalist opposition' said 'no' (with Hugenberg proving to be more recalcitrant than Hitler). Thus, a new election was inevitable. Hindenburg, who did not conceal his disappointment over the Nationalists' negative response, was not easily persuaded to stand for election. He was, indeed, fond of his patriarchal office, and his sense of duty tended to make him forget all the squabbles that ought actually to have made this office a source of torment in the recent past. But he wanted a convincing proof of confidence, and above all he did not want to face his own flesh and blood as the candidate of the 'Sozis' and the Catholics.

When not only Hugenberg but even the leadership of the Stahlhelm could not be persuaded to vote in favour of Hindenburg, the President agreed on 16 February that he would stand for election – at the request of 'independent' Hindenburg Committees. These had collected 3 million signatures for the 'old gentleman', for the most part 'creditworthy', i.e. conservative, names. On 22 February Goebbels announced that Hitler would stand as a rival candidate. His Harzburg friends had been unable to agree on a joint candidate (the Crown Prince had been prevented from standing by a paternal prohibition issued in Doorn). On the following day the black, white and red faction presented the deputy national leader of the Stahlhelm, Duesterberg, as their candidate. Inevitably, Thälmann was standing once again for the Communists; a certain Herr Winter, who was promising to restore the value of the red printed 1,000 mark notes from the Empire, was also standing, thus ensuring that the tragedy did not lack an element of satire.

It was clear from the outset that only Hindenburg and Hitler would make the running. It was equally clear who would be in the right-hand lane, and who would perforce be on the left. It is true that Hindenburg explicitly stated that he had been offered the candidature by the parties between the Centre and the Nationalists. However, this scanty black, white and red fig-leaf (extending barely as far as the Kyffhäuserbund), with which he sought to cover his nakedness, could not conceal the fact that he was indeed primarily the candidate of the 'Sozis' and the Catholics. Along with them, as a kind of appendage, there was the half-right remainder of Brüning's 'emergency majority', which did not extend even to the outskirts of the Harzburg camp. In a confidential memorandum the President attempted to justify this unhappy turn of events to any Nationalist friends he might still have left. One can imagine how he felt when he saw the Social Democrats' appeal to 'Vote for Hindenburg!' Even Brüning could hardly have seemed to him like an ideal election agent in the given circumstances.

Polling day was 13 March. With 18.65 million votes, Hindenburg gained a clear victory over Hitler, who had 11.34 million. Thälmann finished well down the field with barely 5 million. Duesterberg was even further behind, with 2.5 million, which confirmed that Hugenberg now counted for very little in the 'nationalist opposition' camp. The young cuckoo from the Young era was getting ready to oust his elders from the nest. In percentage terms the result meant that the victor, with 49.6 per cent of the votes, had fallen short by a hair's breadth of the necessary absolute majority on the first ballot. A second ballot was thus required. The black, white and red parties withdrew Duesterberg from the race and left their voters a free choice. On 10 April 700,000 of them opted for Hindenburg, who was thus able to embark on a second term of office. A majority of those who had previously voted for Duesterberg, plus over a million former supporters of Thälmann, voted for Hitler, who now, with 13.4 million votes, had almost 37 per cent of the German electorate behind him.

This was the Hitler whom Groener, at the insistence of the state governments, dared to challenge with a ban on the SA only three days after the second ballot. The situation was particularly awkward in that the round of elections was by no means completed by the two presidential ballots. The radicals were liable to score a whole series of successes, each more re-sounding than the one before and each a propaganda boost for its successor. On the next Sunday but one, parliaments in five of the states were due to be re-elected, including those of Prussia, Bavaria and Württemberg.

The Prussian election in particular was of enormous significance. In the largest of the states the Weimar coalition still ruled, and the Social Democrat Severing still controlled the executive on two-thirds of the territory of the Reich. Already in the spring of 1931 the 'nationalist opposition', at that time on the initiative of the Stahlhelm, had tried to force a premature dissolution of the Prussian Landtag by means of a plebiscite. On 9 August the plebiscite failed, but its sponsors had been able nevertheless to win 9.8 million votes, 37 per cent of the Prussian electorate.

Now, on 24 April 1932, a Landtag was elected which bore practically no resemblance to the old Landtag elected in 1928. The great victor was of course once again the NSDAP, which had 162 seats instead of nine and furnished by far the most powerful parliamentary group. Otherwise only the Communists could boast of (albeit much smaller) success, adding nine seats to the forty-eight they had previously held. The Centre Party only just managed to hold its own (sixty-seven instead of seventy-one members), while all the other parties were virtually decimated: the Social Democrats went down from 137 to ninety-four, the State Party from twenty-two to two, the People's Party from forty to seven and the Nationalists from seventy-one to thirty-one seats.

Overwhelming as Hitler's triumph was, there was still not a 'national' majority. Of 423 seats the parties of the right, including the People's Party, controlled 200, the old coalition 163. The third bloc – on no account ready to join a coalition – was formed by the Communists. That meant that there was no less of a stalemate in the Prussian Landtag than in the Reichstag. The Braun–Severing cabinet resigned but stayed on as caretaker, because there was no government majority and because the old Landtag had at the last minute incorporated into standing orders something resembling a construct-ive vote of confidence.

The results of the other elections were similar. Only in Bavaria was the situation marginally more favourable: the Bavarian People's Party had been able to hold its own, although it was now closely followed by the Nazis. In any case Held's government had only been acting as caretaker there ever since 1930. This now tended to become the rule: the elections in Hessen in the previous autumn had already led to similar results. Hardly anything was left except caretaker administrations, which naturally impaired the functioning of the states as the last strongholds of the democratic Republic. The only alternative was formed by right-wing governments in the smaller states: besides Brunswick there was Anhalt which had recently, on 21 May, appointed its first NSDAP Prime Minister. The same was true in both Mecklenburgs and in Oldenburg, where the first absolute NSDAP majority was elected to a German assembly on 29 May, the very day on which Hindenburg brought down the Chancellor, Brüning.

Traditionally the Chancellor was dismissed by a vote of no confidence in the Reichstag. This was now replaced by a vote of no confidence from the President of the Reich. Traditionally the Chancellor had to go if the Reichstag was no longer prepared to pass his legislation. Now he had to resign because the President declared that he would not sign any more emergency decrees. For the Reichstag now barely existed.

In the recent past the Reichstag's mode of operation had generally looked something like this: parliament would assemble; the right or the left, or sometimes both together, would start a brawl; their vote of no confidence or their motion for the cancellation of an emergency decree would not command a majority, whereupon they would ostentatiously leave the chamber, declaring that they would no longer collaborate with the other parties. The rump parliament would then, in the ensuing lull, pass – or fail to pass – a few not very important bills, and adjourn for a matter of weeks or even more, well aware of its own impotence. The legislative function was transferred to administrative channels as the only viable option. In June 1931, following the second emergency decree on finance and the economy, the two radical wings had tried to have the adjourned Reichstag recalled, but in vain. The Reichstag was no longer of any account, and it was of little help to Brüning that he managed to have two bills passed and the customary vote of no confidence defeated in the chamber on 12 May, following a fist-fight that had, of course, been started by the National Socialists. The only institutions that mattered now were the presidency and the high command of the Reichswehr.

Schleicher, who had not failed to note that Brüning's star was sinking in the presidential palace, had been saying for some time that 'good old Heinrich' would not last much longer. After the ban on the SA, the largest of the 'defence associations', he had ceased to confide in Brüning and had openly sought to bring the Chancellor down. He had already accounted for his own minister: Groener had declared his resignation as Reichswehr Minister, having been practically forced to do so by Schleicher. Clinging on to his post in the Ministry of the Interior (which he occupied merely as a deputy) was a hopeless gesture on his part. But Groener's departure was merely the prelude.

The Landtag elections had suggested more clearly than ever that there had been an organized shift to the right. To carry out this manoeuvre with Brüning at the helm, as had been planned in 1930 and 1931, had turned out to be impossible, however. The parties of the right, where the palace contingent and the leadership of the Reichswehr had taken soundings, left no doubt about that. Moreover, conditions were being stipulated for the toleration of a fresh cabinet appointed by the President: they included, apart from the lifting of the ban on the SA, which was generally taken for granted, new elections to the Reichstag. Having learned from his experience in 1930, Brüning would not hear of this. He had even refused to ban the Reichsbanner (a refusal was justified because of its cautious policy and the voluntary disbanding of its 'self-defence squads'), and had merely added the Communist free-thinkers and atheists to his list of prohibited organizations. Indeed, for psychological reasons, it was hard to imagine that even the ban on the SA would be lifted as long as Brüning was in charge.

Brüning was in the way, then. There was a further factor: it was not of prime importance, but it acted as a trigger in that it made Brüning utterly *persona non grata* with Hindenburg. As was well known, an aid programme for the eastern provinces was a feature of his government's policy. Class interests as well as the nation's political interests (no experiments in the imperilled east!) meant that the plan was primarily a matter of baling out debt-ridden landlords. There were, however, any number of bankrupt estates which could not be salvaged. The government's plan was to acquire such properties, if necessary by compulsory purchase, and settle tenants there, thus reducing, to some extent at any rate, the armies of unemployed workers in the major cities. The landowners, however, were anything but overjoyed at the prospect of acquiring proletarian small-holders as neighbours who would threaten their political preserves east of the Elbe. At that moment Hindenburg was spending the Whitsun vacation on his estate at Neudeck and was constantly urged by the agricultural lobby to prevent this kind of 'agrarian Bolshevism'. As the Director of the East Prussian Agricultural Society put it in a letter of protest, the very thought was enough to rack the tender souls of those who had 'hitherto been the bearers of the national will to resist Poland by force of arms'.

The 'old gentleman' was presumably horrified. Bolshevism was bad enough, but *agrarian* Bolshevism – and in his own bailiwick to boot! When he returned to Berlin on 28 May, the die had been cast. Hindenburg has often been accused of ingratitude in this connection, but that is justified only up to a point. Certainly, his re-election had been promoted to a significant degree by Brüning, and certainly the President must have felt distinctly uneasy when he recalled with whose unwelcome assistance he had been kept in office as a 'pillar of the establishment'. And perhaps he really did take it amiss that Brüning had prevented him from standing as the candidate of the 'nationalist opposition', or at least had not promoted his candidature with sufficient zest. But it is not true that he was trying in some way to take revenge on his election agent, or that, with a Prussian sergeant-major's sense of fair play, following the election of 1932, which he had won principally with democratic votes, he had suddenly veered to the right – the exact opposite of what had happened after the 1925 election.

The fact was that Hindenburg's dissatisfaction with Brüning dated back to 1931. In September, it is true, the leaders of the Reichswehr had persuaded him, at the cost of sacrificing Curtius, Wirth and Guérard, to keep Brüning on, but only for the forthcoming winter. In the presidential palace it had been crystal clear following the Prussian elections that a change was due. This could be effected only in the form of an impeccable presidential cabinet; if possible tolerated by the right but under no circumstances with support in the democratic, and certainly not in the Marxist, camp.

Thus, with Brüning's fall and what was to follow, there was no question of Hindenburg cheating his new voters. If there could be any talk of betrayal, then it was a betrayal by those who, in March and April, presented to their supporters a Hindenburg who was quite obviously lurching to the right.

10

Via Papen and Schleicher to Hitler

Brüning's cabinet resigned on 30 May 1932. The new Chancellor was sworn in two days later. He was called Franz von Papen, and only those who were well versed in politics had ever heard this name before. Until the last election, when he had not been adopted as a candidate, Papen had been a Centre Party member of the Prussian Landtag and had attracted disapproving attention in his parliamentary group on account of his nationalistic vagaries. This had only been within his own party, however: he had not had the chance hitherto to play even a minor part on the national political stage.

But he had played a major part in the feudal and reactionary 'Gentlemen's Club', he was (thanks to his marriage) wealthy, and had for some time been the majority shareholder in the Centre Party's official publication, *Germania*. Moreover, he was a retired cavalry major, a friend of Schleicher, who had been a classmate in his General Staff course. Indeed he was, as people said with justifiable malice, in general 'Schleicher's creature'. 'Fränzchen' was to serve as a man of straw, an amenable 'spokesminister' for the Reichswehr General Staff. His cabinet – or rather, the cabinet assembled by Schleicher – consisted of 'officers of the reserve', 'barons', 'experts' or 'gentlemen' and was not marred by a single member of the middle class, and certainly not by any representative of the working classes. One might have thought, it was mockingly said, that the German people 'consisted of landowners, industrialists and eggheads'. It was an almost completely new team, with eight Nationalists – among them five who were able to keep their posts under Hitler, some of them to the bitter end. *One* minister, it is true, fell victim to Hitler, and that was the Reichswehr minister, Schleicher the kingmaker himself.

If Hindenburg had explained to the departing Brüning that a right-wing cabinet was necessary because he hoped the time for emergency decrees was past, then this hope turned out to be illusory: the time for emergency decrees was not past, it was only just beginning. For in spite of the lurch to the right, in spite of all the offers and all the prior concessions, Hitler could not be persuaded to tolerate Papen and his gentlemen, nor could he be 'tamed' in the sense that the black, white and red faction had in mind.

In spite of great efforts the leader of the National Socialists could not be persuaded to give a written guarantee that he would not oppose Papen's cabinet; he would certainly not support it in the event of fresh elections. However, 'Hindenburg's cabinet' did have his promise and, relying on Hitler's word, it began to govern in a dashing manner. The dissolution of the Reichstag took place on 4 June, with the results of the latest Landtag elections being given as the reason. On 16 June the ban on the SA was lifted – disguised as an interim ruling in the final sentence of a 'decree against political excesses'. Hitler's party, however, took good care that this capitulation did not go unnoticed. It gave a clear signal for new activity, for after all, if the new regulations were rightly interpreted, the threatened penalties applied only to 'instigation to murder by the Reds and provocative acts by the Centre Party'.

In the preceding days, while Papen's government was trying to cope with the misgivings of the south German states in particular, the National Socialists had already grown restive because of the delayed resurrection of the SA. Papen had not been entirely successful, for a number of state governments enacted prohibitions on the wearing of uniform or the holding of meetings, or else kept existing bans in force. There could be no objection to this, since they were in charge of the local police, but it was bound to have a detrimental effect nevertheless on Papen's prestige and his policy alike. When a conference of Ministers of the Interior in Berlin failed to change the situation, he abrogated the regulations of the individual states by a presidential decree issued on 28 June. The government of the Reich was determined at any price not to provoke the National Socialists, on whose assistance they were banking.

When the states tried to protest, one state that had hitherto proved to be a tower of strength against any threat from the right remained unusually restrained: Prussia. For the sword of Damocles was already hanging over Prussia in the form of the Reich Commissioner. Papen had let it be known that the plans for a reform of the Reich that had simply lain on the table for years without being implemented were a particular concern of his. As was well known, the crucial problem was Prussia, the state that occupied two-thirds of the Reich; it was a curiosity that had become even more of an obvious anomaly now that the political trends of the two governments in Berlin were drifting ever further apart. Braun and Severing, along with Brüning, had earlier been arguing for a far-reaching union between the institutions of Prussia and those of the Reich that would be tantamount to the incorporation of the one into the other. This suggestion favoured

Papen's shrewd timing of his plans for reform. In fact, the Chancellor had quite different motives. Above all he had in mind a unified, authoritarian, conservative and aristocratic corporate state, which he had derived from the ideas of the young 'conservative revolution', and which would have room neither for Prussia nor for the 'Marxists'. Second, the demolition of the Prussian bastion was planned as a further prior concession designed to gain Hitler's goodwill. Third, Papen saw this as a good chance to manufacture ammunition for his own use in the forthcoming election campaign.

The Prussian government under Braun had resigned on 19 May and Braun himself had gone on holiday shortly afterwards, worn out by strife and leaving little doubt that he had no intention of returning to his post. The Landtag was certainly capable of despatching a totally senseless vote of no confidence in the wake of the departing cabinet (which had already resigned), but it was incapable of setting up a new government – although Papen had asked the National Socialist chairman of the Landtag to do just that, over the heads of Braun's administration and in defiance of all protocol. A coalition of National Socialists, Nationalists and the Centre, which was here mooted for the first time and which the Chancellor tried to bring about, fell through because the National Socialists demanded the leadership of the government plus four ministerial posts, or even support for a National Socialist Prime Minister with full powers to appoint his own cabinet. So Braun's cabinet remained in office as caretaker under the Deputy Prime Minister, Hirtsiefer, of the Centre Party, anxiously concerned to avert by its exemplary conduct the appointment of a Reich Commissioner which was currently being debated.

The government of the Reich, however, stung by National Socialist derision of their reactionary and spineless attitude, had already drafted the text of the relevant decrees which were intended to put a stop to the 'Communist peril' that was allegedly being tolerated by the Prussian government. On 12 July the day and hour were fixed when Prussia would be 'pounced on': the campaign would start at 10 a.m. on 20 July. But then Severing ordered the strictest measures to be taken against demonstrations and the possession of arms. This did not fit in very well with the reasons the authorities of the Reich proposed to adduce for their action; they seemed to have missed the right psychological moment. Nevertheless, two days later Papen went to Neudeck to collect blank emergency decrees for the Reich Commissioner and – to forestall any possible resistance – decrees imposing a state of siege in Berlin and Brandenburg: the date he would fill in when it seemed appropriate. Hindenburg's readiness to co-operate was no doubt prompted by the discussions that Dr Abegg, the Social Democrat Secretary of State in the Prussian Ministry of the Interior, had been having with Communist members of the Reichstag about the possibility of forming a common front against the National Socialists and, if necessary, Papen's government. These discussions had taken place more than a month previously and had in fact led nowhere, but they were now skilfully exploited.

On 17 July incidents took place in Altona (which was still Prussian at that time); these enabled Papen's government to keep to its original Prussian schedule. The National Socialists organized a provocative march through Communist districts, the Communists fired from the rooftops, and the result of the ensuing street battles was fifteen dead. Three days later, punctually at 10 a.m. as planned, the decree appointing Papen as Commissioner of the Reich in Prussia, issued on 14 July and now dated 20 July, was read to Hirtsiefer and Severing in the Chancellery. The new Commissioner then declared that Braun and Severing had been dismissed.

The commander of the Reichswehr in the Third Military District, who was responsible for enforcing the decree, did not have much to do. Only Severing and three officials responsible to him – the Chief Commissioner of the Berlin police, his deputy and the commander of the local police force – required the use of 'force', to which they then yielded. The 'force' consisted of the entrance of a police officer or a Reichswehr patrol, for the Prussian ministers had already agreed during the preceding days that active resistance was bound to be pointless, given the balance of forces on the two sides. After Braun's administration had failed to attend a meeting of Papen's cabinet, the remaining Prussian ministers were also dismissed. Instead of force the deposed Prussian government chose to take legal steps through the State Court in Leipzig. In the meantime Papen set about purging the Prussian senior civil service, not only of Social Democrats but, as far as he could, of republicans; 105 senior officials were either pensioned off or sent on compulsory leave.

The first setback to Prussia's case in Leipzig took place on 25 July, when the interim injunction that had been sought was refused – on the grounds that it would prejudice the verdict! Judgement was given exactly three months later, on 25 October, and was indeed a notable triumph of legal ingenuity. So as not to compromise the President of the Reich and his authority, the court refrained from testing the legality of the action taken on 20 July. All that was left of the case was then disposed of by means of an absurd legal compromise: authority in Prussia was simply divided. Papen was permitted to carry on as he pleased, and it was thus certified that what he had done so far was right and proper. However, neither he nor his representatives were authorized to represent Prussia in the Reichsrat, the Reichstag or anywhere else vis-à-vis the Reich or the other states: that function was retained by the old Prussian government (until Hitler spared them the trouble of discharging it). The case of Prussia was thus finally filed away. The south German states who had made legal representations in Berlin, or even (Bavaria and Baden) supported Prussia's appeal in Leipzig, had long since been plausibly assured by Papen that his coup d'état was not intended to serve as a model for similar actions in other states.

Not a hand was raised, then, to defend the strongest surviving stronghold of the Republic. The victims of 20 July 1932 have consequently been accused of cowardice in that they did not resist on this final occasion but resigned almost without protest and did not appeal to the masses, did not even at least call for a general strike, as had been done at the time of the Kapp putsch. However, the situation was a good deal different from what it had been in 1920. It has already been pointed out that a general strike would not have been very effective with a few million unemployed queueing at the labour exchanges and the welfare offices, and with the working population practically split into three camps who were literally at daggers drawn with each other. And there was also the fact that the civil service would pretty certainly have been in an opposing camp this time, while the Reichswehr would most definitely not have stood by waiting to see what happened. And besides, what kind of mandate did this Prussian government actually have? It was a mere caretaker administration and worn out by weeks of tacking backwards and forwards between a Landtag that detested it and a Reichstag that was forever seeking a quarrel with it. It could be argued that it still had more of a mandate than Papen's cabinet, but in Hindenburg he had at least a semblance of legality, and in the Reichswehr he had power behind him; besides, he had no need to appeal to anyone for anything.

Severing, on the other hand, told himself that he had no right to be courageous at the expense of his police officers. In July 1932, therefore, nothing more would have been possible than an ineffectual revolt by the Social Democratic Party, the Reichsbanner and the dispirited trade unions. Even the Communist Party would very probably have tried to run a side-show of its own. Whether resistance would have signified valour or folly, whether a realistic assessment of the balance of forces should be regarded as discretion or cowardice, depends on the onlooker's point of view. The 20 July had made at least one thing clear: not much effort would be needed to take over a state that was only formally propped up by its constitution. That Hitler was not aware of this, but still clung to his policy of 'legality' which had all but robbed him of victory, indicated gaps in his political intuition that were later to cost the German people dear.

The National Socialists, then, had every reason to celebrate. And the Reichstag elections on 31 July also turned out to be a triumph for them. Once more the voters went to the polls against the background of the mass unemployment that apparently nothing could halt – the background, indeed, to all the events of those final years before Hitler made his entry into the Chancellery. In July 1932 there were 5.4 million unemployed, as compared with 4 million in the corresponding month of the previous year. With this avalanche at his back Papen's position looked grim. The toleration promised him by the National Socialists had very soon vanished into thin air. This had become patently obvious when the Chancellor returned from Lausanne on

9 July, having obtained the long-awaited decision to abolish the Young Plan and to cancel the entire burden of reparations, except for a residual payment of 3,000 million marks which had been postponed to the indefinite future. Instead of praise, all he heard from the associates on the extreme right whom he had courted so assiduously was vilification and scorn over his feeble stance – and calls for a man with stronger nerves. And this was the keynote of the election campaign conducted by Hitler's stalwarts.

On 31 July 13.7 million people voted for Hitler. His 110 seats became 230 – by far the strongest parliamentary party then, or ever before. This time the gains were not due to new voters but were mainly at the expense of the bourgeois centre, which, apart from the Centre Party (seventy-five seats instead of sixty-nine) and the Bavarian People's Party (twenty-two instead of nineteen) suffered losses on a catastrophic scale. The People's Party, the Rural Party, the Economics Party, the State Party and the Christian Social Union were reduced from about a score of members apiece to insignificant splinter groups (from twenty-seven to seven, eighteen to one, twenty-one to two, sixteen to four and twenty-one to three, respectively). Altogether, the liberal and moderately conservative parties retained only twenty-two of their previous 122 seats. Even the Nationalists had to relinquish five of their forty-two seats. On the left, on the other hand, there were no major changes, although the pattern was typical: the Social Democrats lost three of their 136 seats, the Communists added eleven to their seventy-eight seats. Thus, the two totalitarian parties, as had been the case in the Prussian Landtag, now also held in the Reichstag an absolute majority (319 out of a total of 608 seats) but it was a negative majority, calculated ultimately to paralyse the parliament.

If we take into account the fact that the Chancellor had nothing behind him but the Nationalists and a handful of conservative splinter groups, it might be supposed that, having been rudely wakened from his illusions, he would be in despair. But among the features that distinguished Franz von Papen was an invincible and indestructible optimism. And so he now gave every sign of this – without very much justification, as it soon turned out. Because, after this triumph, there could be even less talk of 'support' from Hitler. What the latter was now demanding for his party was the leadership of the government and the Ministry of the Interior in the Reich as well as in Prussia, and a handful of other ministerial posts into the bargain. At the end of May, after Papen had been dropped by his party (he resigned soon afterwards), he had been virtually forced to take the Chancellor's chair by Hindenburg's appeal to his patriotic sense of duty and traditional Prussian discipline. Now, however, he showed little inclination to vacate it. He was prepared to let Hitler participate as Vice-Chancellor and to hand him a number of ministerial posts, but nothing more. His strong man, the Minister of Defence, Schleicher, took quite a different view: he had been so impressed by Hitler's victory that he was willing to accept him as Chancellor and was doing his best to convert the 'old gentleman' in Neudeck to this view.

Hitler had two irons in the fire: on the one hand, over the heads of the Nationalists who stood by Papen, he was discussing a coalition with the Centre Party and the Bavarian People's Party. If the three parties joined forces with their 327 out of a total of 608 seats this would at last have provided the Reich with a government firmly based on a parliamentary majority, although it might not have proved a very durable administration. Hitler's motive was obvious: for his leap into the saddle he needed stirrup-holders, whom he sought and found elsewhere in the following year. The motives of the Catholic parties for an alliance with the Devil are less obvious, if we discount their ardent desire to get their own back on the defector Papen, who had not hesitated to take the place of Brüning, whom they had treacherously removed. In the meantime authoritarian trends and the rejection of democracy had gone to such lengths in these quarters that their vision was fatally impaired on the right-hand side. And, after all, Kaas and his friends were not the only ones to misjudge Hitler and his aspirations to power, although he had certainly proclaimed and demonstrated them plainly enough. At that time their negotiations had proceeded fairly far – for instance a candidate for Chancellor of this odd coalition had already been discussed: Schleicher, in fact. In the end there were too many irreconcilable factors to be brought together, and resistance in the ranks of both partners was too fierce.

Hitler's other aim, however, was a presidential cabinet of the Papen type, bestowed by the hands of the President himself. In the meantime, Hindenberg had taken a great liking to Papen. He had no intention of dropping him and exchanging him for this disagreeable fanatic who did not keep his word, and who, moreover – so he had been informed – came from Bohemia. And even Schleicher could not make him change his mind. On 13 August, while his units were getting ready to seize the power that seemed to be within their reach, Hitler was doing the presidential rounds in Berlin: first he called on Schleicher, then Papen, and finally, in the afternoon, Hindenburg. He refused once again to co-operate with the present government, either as Vice-Chancellor, or in any other way: he would co-operate only if he and his party were allowed to lead. This the President refused him: he could not accept that responsibility, he said, before God, his conscience and the Fatherland. A very clear and stringently worded communiqué issued by the palace made sure that Hitler's fruitless attempt to grasp power was widely publicized. Hitler's response was to oppose Papen even more ferociously: this was intended in fact to keep his disappointed followers together, and above all to keep in check the SA, who were constantly straining at the leash.

Papen was now mainly concerned to frustrate the threatened coalition between the NSDAP and the Centre Party, which could have unseated him effortlessly via the Reichstag. He was helped by the fact that Hindenburg had reached the point where he thought it an impertinence that parliament was trying to dictate his government to him. Thus, on 30 August Papen was able to obtain another blank cheque in Neudeck authorizing him to dissolve the newly elected Reichstag, which had not yet even met. The President and the Chancellor were agreed that new elections should be delayed as long as possible (if necessary, infringing the two-month limit stipulated in the constitution). In the meantime they would try to bring together in a kind of presidential party those forces that were well disposed to a regime operating by emergency decree.

That Papen had in his possession a dissolution order could not, and was not meant to, remain a secret. The National Socialists and the Centre Party protested, pointing out that a 'nationalist majority' was on the point of being formed and was claimed to be already viable. Hindenburg, on the other hand, declared that he would stand by his favourite, Papen, even if a vote of no confidence went against the latter. The Reichstag was convened by its new Speaker, Hermann Goering, on 12 September. The fraternal bonds of the new would-be coalition partners were already so close that, in a business session on 30 August, it had been possible, without any sort of friction, to elect a team of Speakers for the Reichstag, led by a National Socialist, with Deputy Speakers from the Nationalists, the Centre Party and the Bavarian People's Party.

In the preceding month four members of the SA had attacked a Communist worker in the Upper Silesian town of Potempa and had brutally kicked him to death before his mother's eyes. Sentenced to death by a special court in Beuthen two weeks later, under the terms of a newly issued emergency decree against terrorism, the killers and their ringleader had now been pardoned – after their party leader had praised them in public and hurled furious challenges at the government. This in no way detracted from Hitler's respectability. Such was the background of violence in front of which the new Reichstag now assembled.

The intention of the black and brown coalition architects was indeed to teach Papen a lesson, but nevertheless to keep this congenial Reichstag alive. This aim was frustrated at the very beginning of the session through a vote of no confidence moved by the Communists. During a recess the Centre Party tried to persuade their friends in the NSDAP to join them in opposing it, but in vain. Although he shrank from the prospect of new elections following his unhappy experiences of the previous weeks, Hitler gave the signal for battle. After the session had been resumed Goering studiously ignored both Papen's attempt to speak and the decree dissolving parliament that had been laid on the desk in front of him. And so it came about that the dissolved Reichstag was given the chance to fire a parting shot in the form of an overwhelming vote of no confidence carried by 512 votes against a mere forty-two. In the days that followed there were mutual accusations of breaches of the constitution, with Goering fancying himself in the role of guardian of the constitution, in which he had been cast by his party – now that the Weimar basic law suited their purposes. Here, however, the government naturally had the better of the legal argument.

The 'Papen party' that it was now proposed to organize never in fact saw the light of day. All that Papen gained was a few months in which to govern – something he had not had a chance to do before. His cabinet was now once again tinkering with plans to reform the Reich, with the only result that they once more had the south German states on their backs. A union of Prussia with the Reich was an essential feature of any such reform, but a restoration of Prussia in any shape or form was now being flatly rejected in the circles round Hindenburg. An economic programme was put into force by emergency decree on 4 September, and was designed to put $1^3/_4$ million jobless back to work. The employers at least gave every sign of satisfaction at this chance to undercut wages in return for creating new jobs. Tax vouchers for the same purpose, which could be issued by employers from 1934 on in lieu of cash, and the powers granted to the government 'to simplify the social services and cut costs' were also the object of approving interest in the same camp. The employees, it is true, were less keen. Nevertheless, Papen's basic idea can be seen in a positive light: it was a departure at last from Brüning's dire policy of financial cuts, and a transition to a policy of boosting industry by creating jobs – a 'limitless' project which promptly elicited protests from the employers. This was when, amongst other things, the Voluntary Labour Service was started.

New elections were held on 6 November – the latest permissible date under the constitution. The National Socialists in fact suffered a not inconsiderable setback, but this was due only in small measure to Papen's economic policy. It was more a reaction to Hitler's futile attempt to seize power. Many of his supporters who had been driven to him by adversity could not readily understand why he appeared to be condemned to barren opposition, wavering between claims to legitimacy and revolutionary slogans, between socialistic promises and conservative contacts, manifestly with no clear idea of where he was heading. Doubts began to stir as to whether the man of 'all or nothing' was really in a position to take any positive steps – or whether he even had the will to do so.

Besides, the uninterrupted series of elections had depleted the NSDAP's coffers, which had previously been well endowed, thanks to donations from business circles. Their election campaign was consequently less mettlesome than it had been in the summer. Of the 230 NSDAP seats thirty-four were lost, because only 11.7 million (instead of 13.7 million) Germans voted for them. The percentage poll, it is true, was only 80.6 as compared with 84 per cent. There was jubilation at the time over this incipient decline in the ranks of the brown-shirts. Later analysts have often concluded that Hitler's fall would have been inevitable at this point, and that it was merely a question of holding out a little longer. This is doubtful, however. Certainly, a setback of this kind was a severe handicap to a 'movement' accustomed to the glamour of constant victory, and certainly the local elections which followed (in Saxony on 13 November and, especially, in Thuringia on 4 December) confirmed the loss of votes to the NSDAP. Nevertheless, none of this justifies the apodictic claim that the trend was bound to continue, especially as Hitler succeeded in weathering the crisis rapidly and without dividing the party.

And what was more, the losses that the National Socialists had suffered were more than made good, as far as they were concerned, by the gains made by the Communists who, with an additional eleven seats, were able to send 100 members to the Reichstag. There were those in the bourgeois camp who had been inclined to gloat over Hitler's setback, but their elation was damped by the manifest rise of a 'Bolshevik peril'. This helped to drive into the arms of Hitler – even after his setback – all those who believed they could 'tame' him or 'canalize' the forces he represented. The other victors on 6 November were the Papen parties, of which the Nationalists rose from fourteen to fifty-one seats and the People's Party from four to eleven seats. The other parties declined, although that was partly due to the reduction in the size of the Reichstag by twenty-four seats. The Centre Party was reduced to seventy, and the Bavarian People's Party to eleven seats, while the State Party was cut by half to no more than two seats. The Social Democrats, who had lost almost exactly what the Communists had gained, had 121 seats and were now only slightly stronger than their extremist rivals.

Papen could boast of no more that a minor triumph, but he had gained *one* advantage: his nightmare, the 'emergency coalition' of National Socialists, Centre and Bavarian People's Party had not come about, although the Catholic parties were still calling for the National Socialists to be included in the responsibility of government, even if it meant nominating Hitler as Chancellor. Papen therefore began by stating his unwavering determination to continue the policy he had pursued hitherto, denying that he had any intention of resigning. On 17 November he nevertheless did resign at the request of Schleicher. Now it was once more up to Hindenburg to find a new 'cabinet of national concentration'.

When it came to the point, the President had no desire to do any such thing. He had indeed accepted Papen's resignation, but he assured the departing Chancellor of his continued confidence, prompting him to form a new government – not that Papen needed much persuading. Hindenburg had even promised his easy-going, agreeable and pleasantly aristocratic retainer that he would dissolve the Reichstag once more. Of course, the President would have to take soundings from the political parties (to the right of the Social Democrats, naturally), although the true purpose of these soundings would be to influence Hitler, and persuade him to support Papen.

Hindenberg's discussions had the following result: Hugenberg would prefer to leave everything as it was. That would also suit Dingeldey of the People's Party, although, on the other hand, he, like the Centre Party and the Bavarian People's Party, was ready to join a majority government with the NSDAP, even with Hitler as Chancellor and in the form of a presidential cabinet. The Catholic parties had long been advocating a solution of this kind, which, however, did not prevent Kaas emphasizing the need to depart from parliamentary government of the old type: a 'loyalty pact' of three or four 'courageous party leaders' was what he had in mind to put in its place.

The only significant negotiations in the end, those with Hitler, had grotesque features. What the two participants basically wanted, was clear: Hindenburg wanted the status quo with Papen, and Hitler wanted precisely what he put into practice a year later. What he most wanted was the plenary powers of a presidential cabinet, with the help of which he proposed to extort an enabling bill from the Reichstag as soon as possible, so that he would then be independent – not only of parliament, but also of the goodwill of the President. Various ruses and tricks in the course of the negotiations were intended, especially on Hindenburg's part, to disguise the true purpose of the discussions. For instance, he began by demanding from Hitler something which in fact he never wished to see again – the formation of a majority government, albeit in a very brief period of time and in the full awareness that his demand could not be met. And in the end he burdened the presidential cabinet that Hitler wanted with a reservation allowing the President unrestricted use of Article 48 and power to make his own appointments to the Reichswehr Ministry and the Foreign Office. The negotiations then duly broke down and, as had been planned, the only remaining possibility was to allow Papen to 'carry on'. However, at the end of November a real alternative emerged: responsibility could be passed on to Schleicher, who had so far acted only as a kind of scene-shifter.

The two men's paths had parted after 'Fränzchen' had become increasingly recalcitrant. Politically speaking, the Papen and Schleicher alternatives were these. Papen felt that he had been so cheated and provoked by Hitler that he was now of a mind to hit back. The path he proposed to follow entailed a breach of the constitution, which had in any case long since become a mere illusion as far as the intentions of its progenitors were concerned, and which had merely served Hitler as a crutch on his way to power. Papen's path led straight to a presidential dictatorship, out of the twentieth century and back into a system which was nevertheless called the 'New State', without parties and trade unions, but with an authoritarian leadership, a bicameral administration (a resurrected Prussian 'Herrenhaus') and a pluralistic franchise.

Schleicher, on the other hand, wished to exploit to the full the possibilities of negotiation with the National Socialists. He saw – and a tactical exercise mounted by his officers provided him with the confirmation he wanted –

that his Reichswehr, which had been largely infiltrated by National Socialists, had not the slightest chance of imposing Papen's will on the radicals of the right *and* the left – not to mention 'nine-tenths of the nation' – and suppressing a rising of all the extremists. The two extremes were quite capable of making common cause; that this was no mere theory had been proved by a public transport strike in Berlin in the days just before the election. The deadly enemies who were normally out to cut each other's throats had cheerfully sat cheek by jowl in the strike committees. But now Hitler had turned Schleicher down as well, announcing in fact that he would oppose him fiercely, and forbidding his followers, who already had their eye on government jobs, to take any part in a Schleicher administration. Thus, Schleicher's plan had failed, even before he was in a position to take over from Papen in the Chancellery.

It is often said that Schleicher was now pursuing the idea of winning over Gregor Strasser and creating a split between 'constructive' National Socialists and the NSDAP. The government would then rest on a 'trade union axis' extending from the Social Democratic General Trade Union Congress (ADGB) via the Christian unions to precisely those National Socialists who were dissatisfied with their leader's obstructive policy and were prepared to collaborate to the exclusion of Hitler. In all probability, at least in that precise form, this is mere legend. Alleged minutes of negotiations between, first Papen and then Schleicher on the one hand, and trade union leaders and Strasser on the other, have turned out to be forgeries fabricated at the time. Certainly, in those months that were rife with speculation, such an idea must have passed through the heads of a number of individuals, both in Schleicher's entourage and in circles round Gregor Strasser, as well as in various other political circles in Berlin. All that can be proved is that Hans Schäffer, Secretary of State in the Ministry of Finance under Brüning (and later managing director of the Ullstein publishing house) and Erwin Planck, Secretary of State in the Chancellor's private office, had tried to make both Papen and Schleicher see that it would be useful to form better contacts with trade union leaders and 'sensible' National Socialists like Strasser. They had also tried to influence the trade unions in the same direction. The contact that was made between the government and the unions, thanks to these efforts, apparently never went beyond noncommital talks devoid of any political substance which were then presumably discontinued. In the discussions between Schleicher and Strasser, which were arranged through other channels, and in which the trade union representatives did not participate, it was a matter, in Schleicher's view, of 'taming' the National Socialist movement by assimilating it, without immediately getting rid of Hitler. Since the general was not unaware that Gregor Strasser, unlike Hitler, was not insisting on being given the post of Chancellor, but would be content with ministerial appointments for the NSDAP and the Vice-Chancellorship for himself, he no doubt thought from time to time of outflanking Hitler and doing a deal with Strasser. But Schleicher apparently soon realized that Strasser was not the right partner for that sort of manoeuvre, and Strasser's inability to mount any serious opposition to Hitler quickly became obvious to the general public. When Papen's period as Chancellor was approaching its end, and Schleicher could see the day approaching when he would take over that office, both men had long since given up the proposal for a government on a trade union basis as an unwelcome and unrealistic idea – if ever the general, as the less reactionary of the two leaders, had seriously considered such fanciful notions as may have been circulating among his closer or more distant associates. Besides, Schleicher had most probably also discarded the plan of splitting the National Socialist Party.

Schleicher, whose whole mentality disinclined him from stepping from the wings into the limelight, had wished to await the results of his wooing of the NSDAP before declaring his readiness to take over the post of Chancellor. Hindenburg was becoming impatient, however, and demanded a decision. He summoned the two candidates on 1 December. It was Franz von Papen who left the palace as victor – with the assurance that all the presidential powers would be at his disposal in the battle he expected to fight against the Reichstag, which he meant to dissolve at once, i.e. before it had even met. He proposed to have it re-elected only after a lapse of six months, which was a breach of the constitution.

However, when the victor appeared before his cabinet the following day, his ministers left him in the lurch. With a single exception they preferred the 'Schleicher solution'. The latter was even given an opportunity to have one of his officers report on the tactical exercise which had recently been mounted and which demonstrated the Reichswehr's uncertain prospect of coping with unrest on a major scale. Papen went forthwith to Hindenburg, reported what had happened and tried to have a new Minister for the Reichswehr appointed. But the President, who had stubbornly stood by his Chancellor in the face of every kind of opposition, now dropped him, albeit with a heavy heart: 'Then, in God's name, we must let Herr von Schleicher try his luck.' But the failure rankled with Hindenburg, and he more or less invited Papen to join his camarilla, which invitation Papen put to good use against the man who had replaced him as the Field-Marshal's right-hand man. Chancellors who succeeded to office at the eleventh hour had a hard time indeed coping with their predecessors. The tangle of intrigues during those months offered splendid scope for vengeance of every kind.

Events leading up to the change of government seemed to suggest that the most natural thing would be for Schleicher to take over Papen's old team, and this is what he did – with only two exceptions. The only sign of an original plan was the appointment of a Reich Commissioner for Employment. The government got off to a not unpromising start. Neither the parties nor the public seemed to be positively hostile – outside the socialist camp, at any rate. Indeed, the Reichstag, which met on 6 December, even showed signs of a hesitant rebirth of parliamentary rule: it passed an amnesty bill, mustered a majority to repeal the cuts in social legislation that Papen had imposed by emergency decree on 4 September and passed a law specifying a deputy for the extremely elderly President. This last measure, it is true, was indirectly aimed at Schleicher, since the constitution stipulated that the Chancellor would 'in the first place' take over from a President who was unable to act. A return to Brüning's policy of a balance tolerated by a majority in the Reichstag seemed to be on the cards. The reason for this, however, was simply that the parties were worn out and dreaded a fresh dissolution. This is why the National Socialists joined the other parties in voting for an indefinite adjournment.

There was, it is true, a special reason for the NSDAP's docility. The party was in fact caught up in a crisis. Now that power, or at least a modicum of power, was within their grasp, large sections of the NSDAP and the SA wished to see every chance of a share in government exploited, even if it were on less advantageous terms than Hitler had in mind. The fact that Strasser acted at some point as spokesman of this internal opposition group threatened, or at least seemed to threaten, the cohesion of the National Socialist movement, since Hitler was still insisting on a policy of 'all or nothing'. Strasser's attitude, at any rate in Hitler's eyes, seemed to suggest the possibility of a deal between Schleicher and Strasser that would exclude the Führer. The situation turned out to be not much more than a temporary embarrassment.

Since the end of November Strasser's party leadership had excluded him from the power struggle. On 8 December he left the field, resigned from all his party offices and his seat in the Reichstag and set off for the sunny south to recuperate. Hitler, only fleetingly disconcerted, was able unopposed to reassert his apparently unsettled ascendancy in the leadership and among the rank and file of the NSDAP: the party did not split. How perilous the situation had been in Hitler's view, however, was indicated a year and a half later on 30 June 1934, when the two potential coalition partners, Schleicher and Strasser, fell victim to the bullets of their erstwhile adversary.

The truce concluded during the Christmas season at least secured the Chancellor a breathing-space in which to sketch the outlines of the policy he proposed to follow: the creation of jobs, a programme to alleviate the rigours of the winter, an emergency youth project and a Voluntary Labour Service, or even a year's 'military service' (the equality in armament agreed in Geneva on 10 December had opened the way for this measure). The resettlement policy prepared during the final weeks of Brüning's government was revived. Schleicher regarded this as a just return for the aid which major landowners in the eastern provinces had received and he meant to implement it even more rigorously than his last predecessor but one had done in the spring. At that time this had been the reason for the *coup de grâce* administered by the agrarian lobby to Brüning, who was already stumbling to his fall. But they had not administered it in order to swap Brüning's plan for an even more drastic form of 'agrarian Bolshevism'. Schleicher, then, did not fare much better in those critical January days when the infuriated leaders of the Reichslandbund made their way to the palace and beset their honorary agrarian colleague with loud lamentations. Schleicher, they complained, had connived in an impoverishment of agriculture 'such as would hardly have been thought possible even under a purely Marxist government'.

This prompt social and political reaction was not matched by similar agility on the part of the leading man who had played his part behind the political scenes for so many years. It became increasingly questionable how far he really still enjoyed the President's confidence. And it consequently also became doubtful whether he really still had at his disposal the weapon that restrained his opponents, the instrument that, during those curious months, was virtually included among the German Chancellor's insignia of office: the power to dissolve the Reichstag. It was clear to Schleicher that he had to try again with the National Socialists – if necessary, without Strasser. After all, without them it would not be possible to achieve the 'national concentration' around which basically all the presidential cabinets of the previous years had revolved. He thought he could now afford to let Hitler make his entry.

But Hitler did *not* make his entry, for already the net was being contrived in which Schleicher was to become enmeshed. In the middle of December Papen had contacted Hitler, initially on his own initiative. He had found it hard to take leave of his illustrious office, and revenge on Schleicher as well as an attempt to make himself indispensable to Hindenburg, and hence pave the way for a return to the limelight, were among his essential motives. Papen's lust for power had been a key factor in political events ever since the summer of 1932: as long as he sat in the Wilhelmstrasse he had blocked Hitler's path; once he had been removed, however, he hoped to return with Hitler's help. The seemingly bewildering changes of position during these final months may be reduced to a very simple common denominator: whoever was out in the cold invariably made overtures to Hitler.

On 4 January 1933, thanks to mediation by business circles friendly to the National Socialists (and such circles were growing ever wider), Papen and Hitler met again in the home of the Cologne banker von Schröder. Once the Strasser wing had been eliminated, Hitler was able to come to understandings with bankers and leaders of industry openly and without risk. The results, admittedly, were at first not all that impressive, for Papen was not prepared to consider anything other than a duumvirate. Still, the National Socialists were now inclined to see the schemer Schleicher rather than the suave Papen as the man who had actually pulled the strings on that 13 August which had constituted a nightmare for Hitler; Papen's share of the blame was in a way balanced against the Potempa affair. On his return to Berlin Papen reported to the 'old gentleman', who agreed that Papen should keep the line open. For Hindenburg this was a new way of arriving at an agreement with the 'nationalist forces'. For Hitler, on the other hand, it opened up the prospect of getting back into the political game and making his way into the Chancellery after all.

First of all, however, following his electoral setbacks at the end of the previous year, he wished to strengthen his claim, for the benefit of his negotiating partners as well as his supporters. The Landtag election in Lippe on 15 January was ideal for the purpose, for Hitler's depleted resources were just enough to meet the cost of a campaign in this minute state. He and his party strained themselves to the limit and pulled out all the stops. In July Hitler had gained over 42,000 votes here, but in November it had been only 33,000. Now his efforts were rewarded with a respectable total of 39,000 ballot forms. And so it had been proved that the NSDAP was making a comeback, and that had been the object of the exercise. That other parties, the Social Democrats as well as the recently decimated liberal parties, had made the same sort of gains is generally overlooked: the test case of the NSDAP was given that much prominence.

With these fresh laurels and an increased aversion to empty compromises, and with his party's ranks unmistakably 'firmly closed', Hitler was in a position to devote himself to the Berlin intrigues with fresh energy. On 4 January the Council of Elders had decided that the Reichstag would meet on 24 January. A vote of no confidence had already been tabled, and Schleicher knew that this would put an end to his short-lived rule unless he was able to obtain from the President a dissolution of parliament and – if it was not to be a mere stay of execution – an unconstitutional postponement of fresh elections. This was precisely what Papen had asked for a month and a half earlier, and what he had been refused at Schleicher's instigation.

The Chancellor, however, was beginning to have misgivings, – at any rate ever since the Papen–Hitler flirtation in Cologne, which had not remained a secret (and which had been followed a week later by another meeting in Berlin after Hindenburg had become involved). He began groping uncertainly, not only to his right, but also to his left. It is typical that first the Social Democrats rejected *his* approach, and then *he* rejected an approach from Otto Braun, who offered him joint parliamentary opposition to the NSDAP in the Reich and in Prussia; many in the Social Democratic Party were now prepared to go that far. Hindenburg, however, with his horror of blatantly unconstitutional measures, would certainly not care for a constellation of that kind, as Schleicher no doubt very well knew. Besides, he believed he still had time on his side – and the dissolution decree as a final argument. But the ranks of his adversaries were now closing round him.

Papen was basically in agreement with Hitler, although he was obliged to confess that his influence in the palace was not at the moment sufficiently powerful to secure Hitler's appointment as Chancellor. However, the President was beginning to take a new interest in the leader of the NSDAP. On 13 January the Centre Party put a motion to the Budgetary Committee of the Reichstag calling for the allocation of aid to the eastern provinces, and in particular for certain well-endowed rehabilitation schemes, to be looked into more closely. There was actually talk of a parliamentary committee of investigation, and it was even appointed on 25 January, with the joint assistance of the Social Democrats and the National Socialists. It is true that Hindenburg had not personally benefited from the improvement scheme; after all, the President had only recently been given his estate. All the same, for reasons of economy and in order to evade death duties, Neudeck had been immediately made over to Oskar, and Hindenburg hardly wanted this fact shouted from the rooftops. And besides, there were his friends and neighbours to think of.

At any rate, at a meeting of the conspirators on 22 January they gained a new ally: Oskar von Hindenburg, the President's son and adjutant, who had been appointed as a further go-between. Hitler made a 'concession' which much impressed Hindenburg's associates: he would not be diverted from his claim to the Chancellorship, but he deigned to offer the concession of a 'generous proportion of ministers from the middle-class parties'. And they would be found. In the meantime the Stahlhelm, or at least one wing of that organization under Seldte, had come to terms with Hitler. If the Nationalists could now be won over, then the 'national concentration' would be complete and Hindenburg would no longer resist.

In the middle of the month Hugenberg was in fact still negotiating with Schleicher. He did not find sufficient response, however, to his favourite ambition to become minister of a combined department of economics, food and agriculture, which would have given him virtually dictatorial powers over the country's economy. Schleicher's economic, social and political ideas diverged too far from those of Hugenberg for him to countenance such sweeping powers. Since then, therefore, Hugenberg and the government party that had participated in the presidential cabinets had been free to consider other possible combinations. Efforts to revive the Harzburg Front might now begin.

For it had become clear in the meantime that the only way to eliminate the 'old gentleman's' aversion to Hitler was to put the Führer in a 'frame' of respectable individuals – to use the metaphor for this latest illusion. Hindenburg would not be persuaded to grant Hitler a presidential cabinet. At the moment, in fact, he could not be moved to do anything at all. When

Papen reported to him on the day following his latest conversation with the National Socialist leaders, Hindenburg brushed him aside, as he had done previously: no Chancellor Hitler, if you please! He said the same thing to the generals of the Reichswehr Ministry when they tried to intervene on Schleicher's behalf: they surely would not expect him to make this Austrian corporal Chancellor of the Reich! The President had been most ungracious; he no doubt resented generals who dabbled in politics (at least after 1920).

In the meantime, Schleicher was, politically speaking, practically defunct. The Council of Elders had now postponed the meeting of the Reichstag to 31 January as the irrevocable final date (those who were active behind the scenes wished to wait and see the results of their efforts). Hindenburg had not actually refused Schleicher's request for a dissolution of the Reichstag, naturally reminding Schleicher of the latter's attitude at the beginning of December: he wished to think about it. What he probably *had* refused was the postponement of fresh elections under a kind of national emergency – and for the Chancellor this was inextricably bound up with a dissolution of the Reichstag. Indeed, Hindenburg, no doubt encouraged by Papen, now cared so little for the incumbent Chancellor that he did not even want to leave him with the Wehrmacht Ministry. This aversion made it easier for Hitler to enforce his party line, although we may assume that he would have outplayed the exhausted Schleicher in any case, without any great effort.

As 31 January approached, Schleicher's need for a clear decision grew. Without the dissolution edict there was no point in even showing his face in the Reichstag. On 28 January, therefore, he waited on Hindenburg once again, and when the latter bluntly refused to give him the authority to dismiss parliament, Schleicher handed in his resignation. No Chancellor was now in a position to govern without a dissolution decree in his pocket. In the mistaken conviction that he was nevertheless indispensable in the Reichswehr Ministry, Schleicher began to promote Hitler's plans, trying to play him off against Papen *vis-à-vis* Hindenburg. The fact was that Papen had two variants in mind: first, the combination Hitler–Papen–Hugenberg and second (supposing the first variant was frustrated by the President's stubbornness), a presidential cabinet under Papen and Hugenberg. And it was this second plan, which looked even more like a triumph for Papen, that the retiring Chancellor was determined to deny his foe. Unclear about Papen's order of priorities, he was in fact merely playing the latter's game and helping Hitler to seize power.

Commissioned by a Hindenburg who was relieved once again to see the danger of a blatant breach of the constitution fading away, Papen set about 'clarifying the political situation within the framework of the constitution and in agreement with the Reichstag', i.e. taking soundings regarding the formation of a government. The list of ministers he concocted and the promises he received were so contrived that they would be valid for both contingencies. Should the 'constitutional' Hitler plan fall through for any reason, then he would simply switch to the 'unconstitutional' Papen 'battle cabinet'.

The most awkward obstacle to Hitler's chancellorship was removed, however, on 28 January: only two days after he had rebuffed the generals, Hindenburg was prepared to make the Austrian corporal Chancellor. Manipulation by the presidential camarilla, which had been won over by Hitler, and intervention by landowners horrified by Schleicher's resettlement scheme, as well as by industrial magnates similarly worried by the Chancellor's economic policy, had finally had an effect. Besides, the old man, who was ultimately almost totally isolated, was drawn to the pseudo-legal path that seemed to be opening up. It was a path that might even lead to a restoration of the monarchy, for Hitler had left all possibilities open.

And what great risk was there? Hindenburg had been persuaded that, with so many good conservatives in the cabinet, this Hitler fellow scarcely posed a threat. For his demands were indeed modest: apart from the post of Chancellor, he was claiming no more for himself than the Ministry of the Interior and the Commissioner for Prussia – otherwise there was only an Air Ministry that would have to be created some time in the future for Goering, who was keen on that sort of thing. True, Hitler did not much care for the coalition cabinet with the Nationalists that Papen was busy fashioning and which was the only arrangement to which Hindenburg had consented. What he still had in mind was a presidential cabinet with all the powers 'that had become customary'.

The *homo regius*, Papen, succeeded during that eventful weekend of 28 and 29 January in removing the last of the remaining obstacles. He managed to persuade Hitler to collaborate with the Nationalists and even talked him into giving up the post of Reich Commissioner for Prussia, which position he had reserved for himself (Vice-Chancellor alone was a somewhat colourless title) and which Hindenburg wished to see in the trusty hands of his faithful Papen. Admittedly, the National Socialist leader had demanded instead the post of Commissioner in the Prussian Ministry of the Interior for Goering, i.e. control of the Prussian police, which was what really mattered to him. And he also asked for fresh elections to the Reichstag that would help him to get his enabling bill. That was a point which the 'honest broker' left pretty much in the dark for the present and which he played down in discussion with Hitler's future partners. The main thing was that he had obtained Hitler's consent. Hugenberg, on the other hand, concerned that he might miss the 'national concentration' bus, was persuaded to join by being assured of the approval of his combined economic 'crisis ministry', which it was hoped would prove popular with the public.

On the afternoon of 29 January everything had been settled, apart from Hindenburg's final assent and some faint but not invincible misgivings on Hugenberg's part concerning new elections to the Reichstag. The final decision, due on the following day, was eased considerably by – false – rumours of an alleged putsch by the leadership of the Reichswehr. Fear of Schleicher's intrigues gave the cabinet-makers an uneasy night haunted by visions of the Potsdam garrison on the march. The solution that was about to be put into practice was the lesser of two evils, as far as the generals were concerned. What they were actually trying to prevent was the alternative of a Papen 'battle cabinet' and their deployment against 'nine-tenths of the nation', which they had feared in November. What Schleicher had in mind, then, was merely to outmanoeuvre Papen *vis-à-vis* Hitler and Hindenburg at the very last minute: a final intrigue, but not a *coup d'état*.

In the meantime, General von Blomberg, the former commander of the Wehrmacht in East Prussia and Reichswehr Minister designate, the urgently required 'General against Schleicher', was already on his way to Berlin. He had been recommended on account of his close contacts with the National Socialists, and had to be summoned by telegram from Geneva, where he was taking part in disarmament talks. When he arrived at the Anhalter station on the morning of 30 January he was met by Oskar von Hindenburg, who conducted him past Schleicher's waiting emissary into the palace. There he was at once sworn in – a few hours before his Chancellor, but what did that matter?

In the further course of the morning the new government assembled at Papen's house and crept through ministerial gardens to the Chancellery to be sworn in, keeping a wary eye open for field-grey uniforms. Suddenly a new obstacle appeared. Hugenberg had turned stubborn overnight: no, he said, there could be no question of new elections. The head of the Ufa film corporation could not bear to imagine what the ultimate result of these new elections might be. His misgivings were that his party, which had just suffered a crushing defeat once again in Lippe, could expect no good from election as the junior partners to the victor.

No amount of encouraging talk by his colleagues made any difference. This scene, with the lone Hugenberg surrounded by his colleagues wringing their hands and pleading with him to give way, should have convinced Hitler's potential partners, had they not been totally blind, that they were providing him with a very dubious 'frame'. But when the swearing-in ceremony was already a quarter of an hour late, and Hindenburg's Secretary of State appeared, watch in hand, with a reproachful look on his face, Hugenberg realized that the President could not be kept waiting any longer for the sake of such a trifling matter. He finally consented: Hitler should be permitted to seek a dissolution decree.

So now the deed had been done. Now Papen (not Hitler) was able to introduce his new ministers to the 'old gentleman' Hindenburg. Amongst the ministers there were some who were setting eyes on their Chancellor for the first time. 'And now, gentleman', Kaiser Wilhelm's Field-Marshal concluded his speech at the coffin of the infant Republic, after he had sworn in its totalitarian heirs, 'let us go forward with God!' Hitler needed no encouragement to 'go forward', but God had precious little to do with what followed.

Neither did what followed have much to do with the ideas of those who had provided him with his 'frame'. Hitler very quickly proved that he had picked his positions well, and all the 'safeguards' by which his black, white and red partners had planned to curb his energy and lust for power turned out to be mere toys. The Reichstag elections of 5 March in fact secured the NSDAP, in spite of all the fuss, in spite of state propaganda and – in northern Germany at least – the support of the police, no more than 43.9 per cent of the vote. Still, together with their Nationalist friends, they commanded an absolute majority. Eighty-one Communist members had been elected, but were then not allowed to take their seats; in the circumstances a superfluous precaution. To say, as is regularly done in accounts of this period, that 56 per cent of Germans had voted against Hitler on that 5 March is, of course, nonsense. That 56 per cent did not vote *against* Hitler, they voted *for* this or that other alternative. What might not be called in question if this argument were followed to its logical conclusion?

A week before the election the Reichstag fire had given Hitler's government a welcome pretext to issue an emergency decree 'for the protection of the nation and the state' which allowed basic rights to be swept away and gave the government an instrument to use against recalcitrant governments in the states. When the new Reichstag met for its first session on 23 March, all the states had been brought into line in the meantime. This first session was also the last: thanks to the obliging attitude of the middle-class parties – hardly surprising after their behaviour during the previous six months – Hitler obtained a two-thirds majority for his enabling bill, with the Social Democrats alone voting against it. And the Reichstag could then take its leave.

In the following month, on 7 April, the states were placed under governors appointed by the Reich and the civil service underwent a purge. The traditional May holiday was an appropriate occasion for the abolition of the last surviving trade unions (the 'Red' unions had, of course, long since vanished). At the end of June and the beginning of July the political parties, which had become utterly superfluous, disbanded 'voluntarily' following the banning of the Social Democratic Party. Hugenberg, part of Hitler's respectable 'frame', now left the cabinet, and that other illusionist, Franz von Papen, made his exit a year later to become Ambassador in Vienna. This happened in the aftermath of 30 June 1934, when Hitler finally bound the totally subservient Reichswehr leadership to him as his criminal accomplices in the removal of his disgruntled SA henchmen. When the President, after months of total lethargy, finally closed his eyes forever on 2 August, there was nothing left to remind people of the Weimar state except the constitution.

Admittedly, it had long since ceased to have any substance, but it remained in force *pro forma* until the 'thousand years' had passed: Hitler did not think it worth the trouble of repealing it, much less replacing it with a new constitution.

And so the end had come – ingloriously, but by no means painlessly. Something that had not been fought for on the barricades, or at least with a fervent will, presumably could not be better defended. It had been a petty age, mainly for small men. But the 'great' age that now dawned, with its 'great' men cost the nation so dear that the Weimar state, even decades after its demise, still has many more friends than it ever had during its lifetime.

Suggestions for further reading

Compiled by Celia Applegate, University of Rochester

General histories and essay collections

Bessel, Richard and E. J. Feuchtwanger (eds), *Social Change and Political Development in Weimar Germany*, London, 1981.

Eych, Erich, *A History of the Weimar Republic*, 2 vols, Cambridge, Mass., 1962–64.

Halperin, S. William, *Germany Tried Democracy: a Political History of the Reich from 1918 to 1933*, New York, 1965.

Holborn, Hajo (ed.), *Republic to Reich: the Making of the Nazi Revolution*, New York, 1927.

Kolb, Eberhard, *The Weimar Republic*, English translation, London, 1988.

Nicholls, A. J., *Weimar and the Rise of Hitler*, rev. edn, New York, 1979.

Nicholls, A. J. and Erich Matthias (eds), *German Democracy and the Triumph of Hitler*, London, 1971.

Stachura, Peter (ed.), *The Nazi Machtergreifung*, London, 1983.

The German revolution

Angress, Werner, *Stillborn Revolution: the Communist Bid for Power in Germany, 1921–1923*, Princeton, NJ, 1963.

Carsten, Francis, *Revolution in Central Europe, 1918–1919*, London, 1972.

Haffner, Sebastian, *Failure of a Revolution: Germany 1918–1919*, Chicago, 1986.

Mitchell, Allan, *Revolution in Bavaria, 1918–1919: the Eisner Regime and the Soviet Republic*, Princeton, NJ, 1965.

Morgan, David W., *The Socialist Left and the German Revolution: a History of the German Independent Social Democratic Party, 1917–1922*, Ithaca, NY, 1975.

Rürup, Reinhard, 'Problems of the German Revolution, 1918–1919', *Journal of Contemporary History*, vol. 3, no. 4 (October 1968), pp. 101–35.

Waldman, Eric, *The Spartakist Uprising of 1919*, Milwaukee, 1958.

Politics, personalities, and political parties

Breitman, Richard, *German Socialism and Weimar Democracy*, Chapel Hill, NC, 1981.

Caplan, Jane, *Government without Administration: State and Civil Service in Weimar and Nazi Germany*, Oxford, 1988.

Dorpalen, Andreas, *Hindenburg and the Weimar Republic*, Princeton, NJ, 1964.

Epstein, Klaus, *Matthias Erzberger and the Dilemma of German Democracy*, Princeton, NJ, 1959.

Fritzsche, Peter, *Rehearsals for Fascism: Populism and Political Mobilization in Weimar Germany*, New York, 1990.

Frye, Bruce B., *Liberal Democrats in the Weimar Republic: the History of the German Democratic Party and the German State Party*, Carbondale, Ill., 1985.

Hunt, Richard N., *German Social Democracy, 1918–1933*, New Haven, Conn., 1964.

Jones, Larry Eugene, *German Liberalism and the Dissolution of the Weimar Party System, 1919–1933*, Chapel Hill, NC, 1988.

Rosenhaft, Eve, *Beating the Fascists? The German Communists and Political Violence, 1929–1933*, Cambridge, 1983.

Turner, Henry Ashby, *Gustav Stresemann and the Politics of the Weimar Republic*, Princeton, NJ, 1972.

Military and foreign policy

Bennett, Edward W., *Germany and the Diplomacy of the Financial Crisis*, Cambridge, Mass., 1962.

Bennett, Edward W., *German Rearmament and the West, 1932–3*, Princeton, NJ, 1979.

Bretton, W. L., *Stresemann and the Revision of Versailles*, Stanford, Cal., 1953.

Carsten, F. L., *The Reichswehr and German Politics 1918–1933*, New York, 1966.

Craig, Gordon A., *The Politics of the Prussian Army, 1640–1945*, Oxford, 1955.

Deist, W., *The Wehrmacht and German Rearmament*, London, 1981.

Diehl, James, *Paramilitary Politics in Weimar Germany*, Bloomington, Ind., 1977.

Gordon, Harold, *The Reichswehr and the German Republic 1919–1926*, Princeton, NJ, 1957.

Gratwohl, Robert P., *Stresemann and the DNVP: Reconciliation or Revenge in German Foreign Policy, 1924–1928*, Lawrence, 1980.

Jacobsen, John, *Locarno Diplomacy, Germany and the West, 1925–1929*, Princeton, NJ, 1972.

McDougall, Walter, *France's Rhineland Diplomacy, 1914–1924: the Last Bid for a Balance of Power in Europe*, Princeton, NJ, 1978.

O'Neill, R. J., *The German Army and the Nazi Party*, London, 1964.

Post, Jr., Gaines, *The Civil–Military Fabric of Weimar Foreign Policy*, Princeton, NJ, 1973.

The Weimar economy

Feldman, Gerald, *Iron and Steel in the German Inflation, 1916–1923*, Princeton, NJ, 1977.

Feldman, Gerald, Carl-Ludwig Holtfrerich, Gerhard A. Ritter and Peter-Christian Witt (eds), *Die Deutsche Inflation: Eine Zwischenbilanz/ The German Inflation Reconsidered: a Preliminary Balance*, Berlin and New York, 1982.

Gatzke, H. W., *Stresemann and the Rearmament of Germany*, Baltimore, Md., 1954.

Hardach, K., *The Political Economy of Germany in the Twentieth Century*, Berkeley, Cal., 1980.

Hughes, Michael, *Paying for the German Inflation*, Chapel Hill, NC, 1988.

James, Harold, *The German Slump: Politics and Economics, 1924–1936*, Oxford, 1986.

Kent, B., *The Spoils of War: the Politics, Economics and Diplomacy of Reparations, 1918–1932*, Oxford, 1989.

Maier, Charles, *Recasting Bourgeois Europe: Stabilization in France, Germany, and Italy in the Decade after World War I*, Princeton, NJ, 1985.

Ringer, Fritz (ed.), *The German Inflation of 1923*, New York, 1969.

Stachura, Peter (ed.), *Unemployment and the Great Depression in Weimar Germany*, London, 1986.

Culture and society

Barnouw, Dagmar, *Weimar Intellectuals and the Threat of Modernity*, Bloomington, Ind., 1988.

Deak, Istvan, *Weimar's Left-Wing Intellectuals*, Berkeley, Cal., 1968.

Diephouse, David, *Pastors and Pluralism in Wurttemberg, 1918–1933*, Princeton, NJ, 1987.

Eksteins, Modris, *The Limits of Reason: the German Democratic Press and the Collapse of Weimar Democracy*, Oxford, 1975.

Franciscono, Marcel, *Walter Gropius and the Creation of the Bauhaus at Weimar*, Bloomington, Ind., 1971.

Gay, Peter, *Weimar Culture: the Outsider as Insider*, New York, 1968.

Herf, Jeffrey, *Reactionary Modernism: Technology, Culture, and Politics in Weimar and the Third Reich*, Cambridge, 1984.

Klemperer, Klemens von, *Germany's New Conservatism: its History and Dilemma in the Twentieth Century*, Princeton, NJ, 1957.

Koonz, Claudia, *Mothers in the Fatherland: Women, the Family, and Nazi Politics*, New York, 1987.

Lacquer, Walter, *Weimar: a Cultural History*, New York, 1974.

Lane, B. M. and L. J. Rupp (eds), *Nazi Ideology before 1933*, Austin, Tex., 1978.

Lebovics, Hermann, *Social Conservatism and the Middle Classes in Germany*, Princeton, NJ, 1969.

Lewis, Beth Irwin, *George Grosz: Art and Politics in the Weimar Republic*, Madison, 1971.

Mosse, George, *The Crisis of German Ideology: Intellectual Origins of the Third Reich*, New York, 1981.

Niewyk, Donald L., *The Jews in Weimar Germany*, London, 1980.

Ringer, Fritz, *The Decline of the German Mandarins: the German Academic Community, 1890–1933*.

Struve, Walter, *Elites Against Democracy: Leadership Ideals in Bourgeois Political Thought in Germany, 1890–1933*, Princeton, NJ, 1973.

Willett, John, *Art and Politics in the Weimar Period: the New Sobriety 1917–1933*, London, 1978.

Wingler, H. M., *The Bauhaus*, English translation, Cambridge, Mass., 1969.

Wright, J. R. C., *'Above Parties': the Political Attitudes of the German Protestant Church Leadership, 1918–1933*, Oxford, 1974.

Adolf Hitler, the rise of Nazism, and the end of Weimar

Abel, Theodore, *Why Hitler Came into Power*, reprint, Cambridge, Mass., 1986.

Abraham, David, *The Collapse of the Weimar Republic: Political Economy and Crisis*, Princeton, NJ, 1981.

Allen, W. S., *The Nazi Seizure of Power: the Experience of a Single German Town*, rev. edn, New York, 1984.

Bessel, Richard, *Political Violence and the Rise of Nazism: the Storm Troopers in Eastern Germany, 1925–1934*, New Haven, Conn., 1984.

Broszat, Martin, *Hitler and the Collapse of Weimar Germany*, Leamington Spa, 1989.

Bullock, Alan, *Hitler: a Study in Tyranny*, New York, 1964.

Childers, Thomas, *The Nazi Voter*, Chapel Hill, NC, 1984.

Fest, Joachim, *Hitler*, trans. Richard and Clara Winston, New York, 1974.

Gordon, Harold, *Hitler and the Beer Hall Putsch*, Princeton, NJ, 1972.

Grill, Johnpeter Horst, *The Nazi Movement in Baden, 1920–1945*, Chapel Hill, NC, 1983.

Kater, Michael, *The Nazi Party: a Social Profile of Members and Leaders, 1919–1945*, Cambridge, Mass., 1983.

Kele, Max, *Nazis and Workers: National Socialist Appeals to German Labor, 1919–1933*, Chapel Hill, NC, 1972.

Koshar, Rudy, *Social Life, Local Politics, and Nazism: Marburg, 1880–1935*, Chapel Hill, NC, 1986.

Maier, Charles, Stanley Hoffmann and Andrew Gould (eds), *The Rise of the Nazi Regime: Historical Reassessments*, Boulder, Colo., 1985.

Merkl, Peter, *Political Violence Under the Swastika: 581 Early Nazis*, Princeton, NJ, 1975.

Noakes, Jeremy, *The Nazi Party in Lower Saxony, 1921–1933*, London, 1971.

Orlow, Dietrich, *The History of the Nazi Party*, 2 vols, Pittsburgh, Pa., 1969–1973.

Pridham, Geoffrey, *Hitler's Rise to Power: the Nazi Movement in Bavaria, 1923–1933*, London, 1973.

Stachura, Peter, *Gregor Strasser and the Rise of Nazism*, London, 1983.

Turner, Henry Ashby, *Big Business and the Rise of Hitler*, New York, 1985.

Waite, R. G. L., *Vanguard of Nazism: the Free Corps Movement in Postwar Germany, 1918–1923*, Cambridge, Mass., 1952.

Index